Graduate Studies in Second Language Writing

SECOND LANGUAGE WRITING
Series Editor: Paul Kei Matsuda

Second language writing emerged in the late twentieth century as an interdisciplinary field of inquiry, and an increasing number of researchers from various related fields—including applied linguistics, communication, composition studies, and education—have come to identify themselves as second language writing specialists. The Second Language Writing series aims to facilitate the advancement of knowledge in the field of second language writing by publishing scholarly and research-based monographs and edited collections that provide significant new insights into central topics and issues in the field.

BOOKS IN THE SERIES

The Politics of Second Language Writing: In Search of the Promised Land, edited by Paul Kei Matsuda, Christina Ortmeier-Hooper, and Xiaoye You (2006)
Building Genre Knowledge by Christine M. Tardy (2009)
Practicing Theory in Second Language Writing, edited by Tony Silva and Paul Kei Matsuda (2010)
Foreign Language Writing Instruction: Principles and Practices, edited by Tony Cimasko and Melinda Reichelt (2011)
Scientific Writing in a Second Language by David Ian Hanauer and Karen Englander (2013)
Graduate Studies in Second Language Writing, edited by Kyle McIntosh, Carolina Pelaez-Morales, and Tony Silva (2015)

GRADUATE STUDIES IN SECOND LANGUAGE WRITING

Edited by

Kyle McIntosh, Carolina Pelaez-Morales, and Tony Silva

Parlor Press
Anderson, South Carolina
www.parlorpress.com

Parlor Press LLC, Anderson, South Carolina, USA

© 2016 by Parlor Press
All rights reserved.
Printed in the United States of America

SAN: 254-8879

Library of Congress Cataloging-in-Publication Data

Graduate studies in second language writing / Edited by Kyle McIntosh, Carolina Pelaez-Morales, and Tony Silva.
   pages cm. -- (Second Language Writing)
 Includes bibliographical references and index.
   ISBN 978-1-60235-713-6 (pbk. : alk. paper) -- ISBN 978-1-60235-714-3 (hardcover : alk. paper)
  1. Language and languages--Study and teaching (Higher)--Research. 2. Rhetoric--Study and teaching (Higher)--Research. 3. Academic writing--Study and teaching (Higher)--Research. 4. Report writing--Study and teaching (Higher)--Research. 5. Second language acquisition--Research. I. McIntosh, Kyle, 1972- editor. II. Pelaez-Morales, Carolina, 1982- editor. III. Silva, Tony J. editor.
  P53.27.G73 2015
  418.0071--dc23
                                    2015034197

2 3 4 5

Second Language Writing
Series Editor: Paul Kei Matsuda

Cover design by Paul Kei Matsuda and David Blakesley
Printed on acid-free paper.

Parlor Press, LLC is an independent publisher of scholarly and trade titles in print and multimedia formats. This book is available in paper, cloth and eBook formats from Parlor Press on the World Wide Web at http://www.parlorpress.com or through online and brick-and-mortar bookstores. For submission information or to find out about Parlor Press publications, write to Parlor Press, 3015 Brackenberry Drive, Anderson, South Carolina, 29621, or email editor@parlorpress.com.

Contents

Acknowledgments vii

1 Introduction 1
    Kyle McIntosh, Carolina Pelaez-Morales, and Tony Silva

2 Second Language Writing Dissertations at Doctoral Level
    Universities: The Case of Indiana University of Pennsylvania.......... 7
    Dan J. Tannacito

3 On My Initiation into the Field of Second Language Writing........ 33
    Karen A. Power

4 Doctoring Yourself: Seven Steps 57
    Alister Cumming

5 Doctoring Myself: Observation, Interaction, and Action 71
    Luxin Yang

6 The Will to Build: Mentoring Doctoral Students in Second
    Language Writing 93
    Paul Kei Matsuda

7 Choices in Identity Building as an L2 Writing Specialist: Investment
    and Perseverance 111
    Tanita Saenkhum

8 From Doctoral Education to the Tenure Track: Lessons and
    Observations from the Journey.. 126
    Christina Ortmeier-Hooper

9 The PhD Process as Activity 145
    Wei Zhu

10 The PhD Process as Growing in a Community..........................158
   Iona Sarieva

11 Knowledge Consumer to Knowledge Producer: Preliminary Exams
   and the Prospectus (A Dialogue) 170
   Tony Cimasko and Tony Silva

Contributors 191

About the Editors 195

Index..197

Acknowledgments

We would like to acknowledge the guidance and support of Paul Kei Matsuda, editor of the Second Language Writing Series at Parlor Press, and David Blakesley, founder and publisher of Parlor Press, in producing this collection. We are also immensely grateful to the authors of the chapters included within for their contributions and cooperation throughout the publication process, as well as the anonymous reviewer whose insightful feedback benefitted us all. Last but not least, we would like to thank our spouses, Carol Chun Zheng, Robert O'Melveny, and Margie Berns, for their continued love and encouragement.

1 Introduction

Kyle McIntosh, Carolina Pelaez-Morales, and Tony Silva

Research into second language (L2) writing has increased significantly in recent years (see Leki, Cumming & Silva, 2008). This growth has been reflected in the number of students enrolling in academic programs that place an emphasis on L2 writing and in the number of dissertations submitted that address L2 writing-related topics and issues. This collection advances scholarship on graduate study and professionalization in the field of second language studies (e.g., Casanave & Li, 2008; Kubota & Sun, 2012) by addressing the ways in which an array of processes and personal interactions shape the experiences of those who are entering the field, as well as those who provide them with guidance and support, focusing specifically on the experiences of scholars in second language writing contexts.

To bring greater attention to graduate study in L2 writing, the organizers of the 2012 *Symposium on Second Language Writing* paired up several noted scholars with their former mentees, now established scholars in their own right, to discuss the professional development process in the context of their mentor-mentee relationships. This collection takes select insights gained from that conversation and makes them available to a wider audience, including current graduate students in L2 writing and those looking to enter the field, as well as faculty advisors and university administrators involved in such programs.

The chapters included in this collection explore intersections between the personal, professional, and institutional demands of graduate study in L2 writing, highlighting the constant negotiation that occurs at different stages in one's academic career. In doing so, they often evoke, explicitly and implicitly, the concepts of *discourse commu-*

nity (Bazerman, 1979; Swales, 1990) and *community of practice* (Lave & Wenger, 1991). Although these two concepts overlap somewhat with respect to the ways in which newcomers gain membership in communities formed around common goals by learning their approved modes of speech and behavior, there are key differences: a discourse community revolves around the production of knowledge and information via relatively conventionalized communicative events (i.e., genres), while a community of practice focuses on the social interactions in which people are engaged, the different ways they negotiate meaning, the identities they form, and how those identities shape their actions as they move from the periphery toward the center of a given community.

Nevertheless, in academic fields like L2 writing, these concepts often enter into a complementary relationship so that, as graduate students learn to become members of a discourse community by reading published work and writing their own course papers and theses, they simultaneously enter a community of practice through their relationships with advisors, mentors, and other experts. The contributors to this collection graciously offer up their own experiences with graduate study in L2 writing and recommendations for navigating its sweeping landscape to help current and future students find their way to becoming part of the larger disciplinary community.

Overview

To capture the reciprocal nature of doctoral study in L2 writing, this book is divided into five exchanges between graduate advisors and their former students.

In the opening exchange, Dan Tannacito tracks an increase in the number of dissertations on L2 writing and presents this as evidence that the field is expanding and exercising its influence beyond a mere handful of schools. He then turns to his own involvement in the development of the graduate program in L2 writing at Indiana University of Pennsylvania (IUP). Based on his experiences as an advisor, Tannacito makes several suggestions for the continued expansion of the field. Specifically, he advocates strengthening the disciplinary identity of L2 writing by fostering greater cooperation between students and advisors, allowing for more flexibility and innovation within graduate programs, and promoting collaboration across disciplines. He also examines the power dynamics involved in the advisor/advisee relationship and warns against some of the pitfalls that may cause students to become trapped at the dissertation stage.

As Tannacito's former student and a product of the L2 writing program at IUP, Karen Power traces her own "rite of passage" from novice learner to professional researcher. First, she conveys all the excitement and confusion that arose from her initiation into the L2 writing discourse community, the difficulties of comprehending ongoing debates in the field, and the challenges of finding a suitable direction for her own research. She then recounts her interactions with a number of established L2 writing scholars, including her advisor, that formed the basis of her dissertation project: a social history of L2 writing. Throughout the chapter, Power uses these accounts to highlight the importance of establishing strong socio-academic relationships, of seeking advice from various mentors to gain different perspectives, and of remaining connected to one's own history in the quest to form a professional identity.

In the next exchange, Alister Cumming draws on his years of experience as a graduate advisor in L2 writing to distill the journey toward a doctoral degree down to seven basic steps that he believes will greatly increase one's chances of success. Of course, following these steps still requires a great deal of time and commitment on the part of graduate students, as well as on the part of advisors and program administrators, who must provide adequate incentive and support for conducting research and writing the dissertation. Creating such a receptive academic community requires a lot of planning and effort but, as Cumming points out, the reward is a more diverse and vibrant future for the field of L2 writing.

Through a series of vignettes and email exchanges chronicling her journey from college English teacher in China to international graduate student in Canada, Luxin Yang explores her interactions with her advisor, Cumming, and other members of her new academic community. Her eventual socialization into the North American L2 writing scene is followed by the shock of returning to her native China as an English writing researcher where she again found herself unfamiliar, at least initially, with the conventions and expectations of another new academic community. Fortunately for those readers facing similar dilemmas, Yang also conveys the means by which she learned to shuttle successfully between these two worlds.

Paul Kei Matsuda begins the third exchange by documenting his own journey toward becoming an internationally recognized L2 writing professional as a way of providing guidance to the next generation of scholars. In discussing his personal experiences and approach to mentorship, he emphasizes the need to expose his students to the often unspoken assumptions and practices of academia and to set a good example for them through his spirited approach to life and work. Matsuda manages to engage his students on multiple levels, from helping them to plan and revise their projects to involving them in his own research and other professional pursuits. He even exposes them to some of the setbacks he has faced so that they may see how to overcome similar challenges in their own careers.

As one of Matsuda's former students, Tanita Saenkhum maps out the unique career path that has led her from working as a journalist in Thailand through attending graduate school in the US, and ultimately, to securing a tenure-track position as an L2 writing specialist at a renowned research university. She explains how, along the way, she was able to construct a new professional identity through her involvement in professional conferences like TESOL and CCCC, her collaborations with her advisor, and administrative apprenticeships in the writing program.

Another of Matsuda's students, Christina Ortmeier-Hooper, employs personal narrative to provide a chronological account of her initiation into the community of L2 writing professionals, reflecting on the different selves that emerged at various stages in the process. As she goes from being a secondary school teacher to a graduate student, and later, to a faculty member at her alma mater, Ortmeier-Hooper shares the lessons she learned along the way, including, among other things, the overlap between personal and professional identities, the importance of staying connected with family and peers, the need for transparency in the academic workplace (which Matsuda provided), and the will to persevere in the face of uncertainty.

The fourth exchange begins with Wei Zhu looking at the PhD process through the lens of activity theory, focusing on interactions with one of her former students, Iona Sarieva, to reveal the transformation that occurred as Sarieva moved from being a novice scholar, through the dissertation stage, to becoming an L2 writing professional. Zhu also notes the transformation that she experienced in her role as advisor. Throughout the chapter, she reflects upon the different, yet interconnected, cycles of activity and the mediating tools, individuals, and communities involved in the process. In particular, Zhu centers her discussion on three key constructs: motive, activity system, and the resolution of contradictions.

Using a discourse community framework, Iona Sarieva describes the different adjustments she made, beginning with her first year as a PhD student, as she went from seeking out a professional community to figuring out how to become a member. In doing so, she stresses the value of listening to experts, as well as learning to live within the limitations imposed by programs, advisors, and the limits of her own knowledge. While acknowledging the many challenges that graduate students face—such as balancing a research agenda with teaching and family—Sarieva encourages them to find support and strength, as she did, in the multiple communities, both professional and personal, to which they belong.

The fifth and final exchange is presented as a dramatic dialogue between advisee, Tony Cimasko, and his advisor, Tony Silva. Together, they discuss the transition that doctoral students make between becoming familiar with an area of study and making original contributions to that field. Cimasko describes his transformation from a novice (or knowledge consumer) to an expert (knowledge producer) in the field of L2 writing and the lessons he learned along the way. Silva, on the other hand, focuses on the institutional transformations that the PhD program at Purdue has undergone over the years, recalling his own experiences as PhD student in the same institution and emphasizing how those experiences spurred the institutional changes that he helped to implement as a faculty member.

By presenting these accounts from both mentors and their former mentees, we believe this collection makes a unique contribution to research on the professionalization of L2 writing. These pairings provide complementary perspectives of different individuals' entry into local and international academic communities and, consequently, enhance our understanding of both the individual and social dimensions of this complex, interdisciplinary field of study.

REFERENCES

Bazerman, C. (1979). Written language communities. Paper presented at the Convention of College Composition and Communication. Minneapolis, MN.

Casanave, C. P. & Li, X. (Eds.). (2008). *Learning the literacy practices of graduate school: Insiders' reflections on academic enculturation*. Ann Arbor: University of Michigan Press.

Kubota, R., & Sun, Y. (Eds.). (2012). *Demystifying career paths after graduate school: A guide for second language professionals in higher education*. Charlotte, NC: Information Age Publishing.

Lave, J., & Wenger, E. (1991). *Situated learning: Legitimate peripheral participation*. Cambridge: Cambridge University Press.

Leki, I., Cumming, A., & Silva, T. (2008). *A synthesis of research on second language writing in English*. New York: Routledge.

Swales, J. M. (1990). *Genre analysis: English in academic and research settings*. Cambridge: Cambridge University Press.

2 Second Language Writing Dissertations at Doctoral Level Universities: The Case of Indiana University of Pennsylvania

Dan J. Tannacito

To research and write a doctoral dissertation is the culminating experience and, perhaps, the ultimate achievement in doctoral education in North America. Doctoral dissertations in second language writing (SLW) have been produced at different types of universities in the US. Most of my experience has been at Indiana University of Pennsylvania (IUP), classified by the Carnegie Foundation for the Advancement of Teaching (CFAT) as a Doctoral Research University (DRU) where graduate programs are predominantly focused on multi-disciplinary professional preparation. This IUP doctoral program is relatively unique in its design among leading programs nationwide in applied linguistics and rhetoric/composition, in offering the study of SLW, and it is highly productive as well.

Over the last 35 years, I have directed more than 60 dissertations—33 of which focused on SLW between 1977-2012. As Boud and Lee (2009) remind us, "At the heart of the doctorate, there are a set of practices that produce both objects (knowledges, artefacts, institutions) and subjects (persons with skills, capabilities and attributes)" (p. 3), none more deeply invested in research than the dissertation. But dissertations, perhaps more than any other element of graduate education, are set in the context of particular graduate programs. In this

7

chapter, I consider the local factors that contribute to this conjuncture of practices. Strain (2000) presents a similar viewpoint on two doctoral programs in rhetoric and composition. By viewing the dissertation practices at one university against the tapestry of how dissertation growth in SLW has developed nationwide, I hope to shed light on both the historical and the ongoing process of graduate education in second language writing.

Research and pedagogical interests in second language writing have grown historically out of two distinct disciplinary research traditions: Applied Linguistics and Composition Studies, as Paul Kei Matsuda (1998, 1999, 2003), Leki and Silva (2004), and more recently, Karen Power (2012) have shown. Yet research and reflection on doctoral education from the perspective of the practitioners in these fields have been largely undocumented. What is the design model for a doctoral program in SLW when a new program is considered or the review of an existing program takes place? Is it sufficient for faculty advisors to reproduce the way in which they themselves were inducted into the discipline or should they consider alternative ways of advising dissertations? Without better information, how do we know what are the best practices in advising doctoral students in SLW?

In this chapter, I discuss local factors that have shaped the dissertation practice (objects) and the writers (subjects) at one university that has contributed significantly to the national growth of dissertation research in SLW. By comparing these practices, other programs, supervisors, colleagues, and students as well as those who exercise stewardship of relevant disciplines are better positioned to meet the needs of students and faculty interested in second language writing as a field.

THE NATIONAL CONTEXT: HOW MANY OF US ARE WE?

Doctoral dissertations in the field of second language writing have been regularly identified in a series of annotated bibliographies to date (see Tannacito, 1995; Silva, Brice & Reichelt, 1999, and the subsequent serial bibliographies by Silva & associates published in the *Journal of Second Language Writing* (*JSLW*)). Despite the fact that it is useful to know how many SLW dissertations have been written, no complete listing yet exists. To estimate the number of dissertations produced in the field, I compiled a list of 667 dissertation titles on SLW written between 1967-2012 from a search of *Dissertations Abstracts International* (DAI). Most of these dissertations are limited to universities in North America and a few additional countries that submit dissertations to UMI.

Since the turn of the century, according to my calculations, slightly more than 100 institutions contributed 359 research doctorates in SLW, or an annual average of 28.25 dissertations each year during this 12-year period. This level of production contrasts favorably with the preceding period (1967-1999) when 309 dissertations were produced, or an annual average of about 9.6. This seems to me to be a substantial increase in dissertation production, bearing out the judgment of distinguished leaders who have called SLW an "explosively growing field" (Leki, Cumming, & Silva, 2008, p. ix). This fact makes it all the more curious that SLW has yet to receive recognition as a field *per se* by such organizations as the National Science Foundation (NSF). For example, the Survey of Earned Doctorates (SED) conducted by NSF collects data on the number and characteristics of dissertations in research doctoral degrees (excluding non-research doctoral institutions and recently reclassified Education doctorates) from all accredited US institutions. But because SLW dissertations are an unidentified component of the "English language and literature" category of the SED, no statistics are published by SED about SLW.*

Nonetheless, based on my DAI survey (n=359), the clear trend in dissertation production in SLW at the national level between 2000-2011 has been one of significant increase, more than tripling the num-

---

* NSF counts as a field only those research doctorate degrees bearing a specific verbatim field name as reported by institutions and meeting the SED 10-3-3 rule, i.e. ten doctorate recipients from three different universities in three consecutive years. To consider an "emerging field" or to distinguish a "subfield specialization from a true field," according to Mark Fiegener, project manager, SED periodically assigns contractors to evaluate whether there are a sufficient number and an adequate distribution of dissertations with the verbatim field name in the publicity for the research doctorate from an institution (personal communication, July 17, 2012). A glance at Table 1 suggests that while SLW may meet the 10-3-3 rule, the multiplicity of degree programs that do not explicitly name SLW as a "field" represents a challenge to this qualification. If institutions were to more prominently identify SLW as a named dissertation research field, it might earn its own SED code under the Aggregate category "Letters" or as its own "fine" field designation (similar to creative writing and folklore in the present scheme).

ber of dissertations annually from the beginning of the period (n=19) to the end (n=62), as shown in Figure 1.

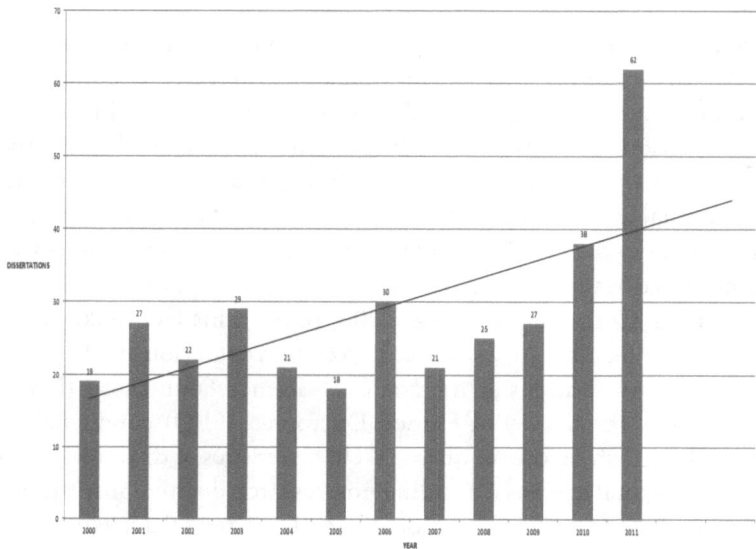

Figure 1. National Growth in SLW Dissertation Production, 2000-2011

This figure also shows that early in the period there was some year-to-year fluctuation in the number of dissertations, with a steady increase in the second half and a recent burst in production. In general, we can say there has been steady growth over this period that forecasts continued growth.

As shown in Table 1, IUP tops the list of leading universities producing SLW dissertations. The majority of these universities are classified by the Carnegie Foundation for the Advancement of Teaching (CFAT) as having comprehensive doctoral graduate programs (meaning across most disciplines) at high and very high activity research universities. Dissertations contributed by the leading universities ranged from at least 10 dissertations during this period to as many as 80. This result indicates that institutions across all of the CFAT classifications: Research Universities (very high activity), Research Universities (high activity), and Doctoral/Research Universities (Professional Dominant) support writing dissertations in SLW, a notable validation of the field's existence.

Table 1. SLW Dissertations: Carnegie University Ranks, 2000-2011 (range 10-80)*

University	Carnegie Basic	Graduate Instruction
Indiana University of Pennsylvania	DRU	Doc/Prof
University of Toronto	(not included in CFAT database)	
Purdue University	RU/VH	CompDoc/MedVet
University of Illinois (UIUC)	RU/VH	CompDoc/MedVet
University of Arizona	RU/VH	CompDoc/MedVet
Teacher's College, Columbia University	RU/H	Doc/Prof
Southern Illinois University	RU/H	CompDoc/MedVet
Michigan State University	RU/VH	CompDoc/MedVet
Harvard University	RU/VH	CompDoc/MedVet
Northern Arizona University	RU/H	CompDoc/MedVet
Arizona State University	RU/VH	CompDoc/MedVet
University of Texas at Austin	RU/VH	CompDoc/MedVet

RU/VH= Research University/Very High Activity
RU/H= Research University/High Activity
DRU= Doctoral Research University
CompDoc/MedVet= Comprehensive Doctoral/Medicine-Veterinary
Doc/Prof= Doctoral Professional Dominant

    This growth in SLW dissertations is quite likely attributable to the multiplication of graduate programs with doctorates that address SLW since the 1970s. Behind this growth is the increase in the number and diversity of NNES writers, including international sojourners from a wide range of cultural contexts, diverse populations of bilingual minorities in North American schools and universities, and marginalized "basic" second dialect and second language writers such as those Mina Shaughnessy (1977) first discussed. All these subgroups have challenged us to define our field (Silva, Leki, & Carson, 1997) and to meet their instructional needs (Leki, 2007). Moreover, the teaching of writing to NNESs has spread widely in international EFL circles. Doctoral dissertation research on SLW is a national response to pressure from outside and below. As a consequence, the growth of doctoral research in SLW during this same period has created a cadre of highly qualified faculty distributed at universities in North America and throughout the world where the pedagogical and curricular needs of second language writers are beginning to be noticed and addressed.

* For additional information, see http://classifications.carnegiefoundation.org/descriptions/grad_program.php

A Brief History of the PhD at Indiana University of Pennsylvania (IUP)

IUP became the leading producer of dissertations in SLW over the course of its thirty–year history as a single doctoral program thrice-revised. In 1976, alongside the previously established literature and criticism concentration, IUP developed a distinct track of its PhD in English, then known as English Education. Composition/Education scholar Marilyn Sternglass and applied linguist Frank Como designed the program primarily for employed two-and four-year college English teachers who wanted a program flexible enough to accommodate taking courses mainly during the summer periods. The program did not initially offer opportunities for international students nor did it have any curriculum devoted explicitly to second language studies until it was completely revised as Rhetoric and Linguistics by compositionist Patrick Hartwell, myself, and others in 1983.

The program and its successor during this phase anticipated the teacher-scholar model, made famous by Boyer's report (1990), as most suitable to the faculty resources, institutional mission, and student clientele. The faculty load at IUP is twenty–four credits per year with supplementary contracts for summer courses, and a reduction of six to nine credits per year for graduate teaching. The student clientele is largely employed college language and writing teachers from around the country and the world. To undergird the stability of the doctoral program local institutional constraints were developed at IUP, such as the creation of a labor-management agreement to permit graduate students to teach undergraduate classes (otherwise illegal at state-owned universities in Pennsylvania) but needed to release faculty to teach graduate courses, as well as the establishment of a set of qualifications to teach graduate courses that identifies the IUP faculty qualified to teach and advise doctoral students.

In 1996, after the addition of a number of faculty and more full-year students, the curriculum was revised to feature courses focused on the second language field as well as the addition of an equal number of new courses in composition studies. Thus, Second Language Literacy, Second Language Acquisition, and Second Language Teaching as well as other TESOL courses prepared candidates to understand writing broadly in Applied Linguistics and Composition. Indeed, during this phase of the program's development, the most distinctive feature of the program was probably its interdisciplinary nature (between first language (L1) and second language (L2) literacy). The suitability of this alliance was borne out theoretically on the second language side by several factors, including the then current SLA theory (Krashen, 1985) in which L2 acquisition was regarded as highly similar to L1 acquisition, by the unique characteristics of ESL writers (Silva, 1993), as well as by the common interest of L1 and L2 writing pedagogy in the dominant process paradigm of the day (Power, 2012).

SECOND LANGUAGE WRITING DISSERTATIONS PRODUCED AT IUP

Several important facts arise from a glance at second-language writing dissertations produced at IUP, which, as noted earlier, ranked as the leading institution in SLW dissertation production. First, the total number of dissertations produced at IUP on SLW between 1977 and mid-year 2012 was 86.[*] This represents about 13% of all SLW dissertations written between 1967-2012 (n=667). Second, 66% of the IUP total since 1977 were authored by international students holding F-1 visas at the time of completion. Third, 45 of the 86 in my count (or 52.3%) were written by women and 47.7% by men compared to the SED rates (2009) in "English Language and Literature" of 65.7% women and 34.3% men. Finally, these IUP SLW dissertations were directed by as many as 16 different faculty members but only a few advised the majority (Tannacito, 38%; Aghbar, 11.6%; Gebhard, 9.3%; Heny/Fontaine, 6.9%).

One of the clearest trends among the SLW dissertations written at IUP from 1977-2012 is a shift in methodological concerns in this period. Using the categories employed by *JSLW* for comparability (cf. Silva, Brice, & Reichelt, 1999), the following distribution obtains:

Table 2. Distribution of IUP SLW Dissertations: Methodology (n=86)

Quantitative	4	.047	1985-2006
Qualitative	50	.582	1982-2012
Quan+Qual	13	.151	1985-2011
Interpretive	9	.105	1991-2012
Interpet+Qual	10	.116	1981-2010

---

[*] I am grateful to Ms. Divya Singh for her library research on IUP dissertations. All errors are my own, of course.

Except for a few studies, interest in qualitative methods and combinations replaced quantitative methodology, especially in the 21st century. While the bulk of SLW dissertations at IUP (73%) favored qualitative methods in whole or in part, interpretive studies (22%)—including critical, narrative and historical ones—gained steadily among IUP's more recent dissertation writers. This expansion of research methodologies used in SLW seems to reflect the same trend as in the published literature in the field.

Another notable trend among IUP SLW dissertations is the distribution of dissertations according to the contexts studied. Table 2 shows the distribution of SLW dissertations at IUP in terms of five categories derived from Leki, Cumming, and Silva (2008) whose first section comprehensively treats the scholarship of SLW in various contexts. Table 3 collapses several of their categories in order to highlight the patterns in the IUP data.

Table 3. Distribution of IUP SLW Dissertations: Contexts (n=86)

ESL: School	(3.5%)
ESL: Undergraduate/Graduate	(47.8%)
EFL	(38.4%)
Workplace, Scholarly, Community	(5.7%)
History, Ideology, Politics	(4.6%)

Thus, the majority (47.8%) of IUP SLW dissertations between 1977-2012 were written, unsurprisingly, about undergraduate and graduate ESL writers. More notably perhaps, a significant percentage (38.4%) have been about two EFL contexts: the Middle East and Asia, where the teaching of English is in-demand and affordable.

Finally, a look at the primary topics of the SLW dissertations at IUP shows approximately 47 distinct topics among the 86 dissertations, ranging from academic writing to writing science. Table 4 shows the distribution of these topics according to a framework (modified) employed by Leki, Cumming, and Silva (2008) in their comprehensive review of SLW scholarship.* Unsurprisingly, the majority of the

---

* Table 4 expands the Leki-Cumming-Silva taxonomy to separate my category "Teacher Education in Writing" from their "Instruction and Assessment," in order to acknowledge the importance of research on the former area. See Hirvela & Belcher (2007) and the special issue of 2007 *JSLW* edited by Hirvela and Belcher, as well as the prominence of teacher preparation as an

IUP dissertations during what has been designated the process period (Power, 2012) were devoted to the composing process as well as instruction and assessment with about equal emphasis on author and text.

Table 4. Distribution of IUP SLW Dissertations: Topics (n=47)

Instruction and Assessment	26.7%
Writer Characteristics	18.6%
Composing Processes	27.9%
Written Text: Grammar & Discourse	19.8%
Teacher Education in Writing	7.0%

SHAPING CHARACTERISTICS OF THE DOCTORAL PROGRAM

To better understand the production of SLW dissertations at IUP, we should examine some of the design characteristics of the doctoral program itself that shaped their development. According to the participants, what accounts for IUP's success among leading universities in producing SLW dissertations? Primarily, five broad features of the thrice-revised doctoral program at IUP, I would argue, account for much of the success of the program, and are especially influential on dissertations on second language writing. These five design features are: (1) the teacher-scholar model that stimulated IUP early on with a new vision for doctoral study, (2) the creation of a nexus of practices related to writing at IUP that provides diverse opportunities for tutoring, teaching, and research in close association with the doctoral program faculty who organized them, (3) the inter-disciplinary expertise and scholarship of the faculty and the curriculum they developed, (4) internationalism and cultural interaction among students and faculty, and (5) the unique residency option that brings students not only from around the country and the world to IUP, but also allows commuters from around our three-state area to complete their doctoral study while retaining their full employment as college language and writing teachers and administrators. In a sense, these design features cut across three different levels of doctoral education: (a) the ideological (teacher-scholar model; interdisciplinarity), (b) the political (nexus of

---

issue in CCCC *Statement on Second Language Writing and Writers*, 2009 for more detailed justification.

practices; internationalism), and (c) the organizational (nexus of practices; residency).

The Relevance of the Teacher-Scholar Model

For many doctoral programs in English and related disciplines where second language writing dissertations have been written, "the PhD is assumed to be a research degree, and its primary purpose is teaching junior scholars to conduct sound, rigorous research" (Golde & Dore, 2001, p. 3). Older traditions of doctoral work focus more on research than education and see the practices of supervisors and program coordinators at university and department level implicitly reproducing the ways in which they themselves were inducted into their discipline.

In the early nineties, however, an alternative vision emerged with the introduction of Boyer's teacher-scholar model supported by CFAT. This model became attractive to recently established programs, especially at doctoral-granting but not research-extensive universities, where faculty undergraduate loads are greater than at traditional research universities. Boyer contrasted the traditional view of scholarship found at research universities (currently labeled RU/VH, RU/H by CFAT) with a more dynamic view of scholarship, saying for example:

> What we have now is a more restricted view of scholarship, one that limits it to a hierarchy of functions. Basic research has come to be viewed as the first and most essential form of scholarly activity, with other functions flowing from it. Scholars are academics who conduct research, publish, and then perhaps convey their knowledge to students or apply what they have learned. The latter functions grow *out of* scholarship, they are not to be considered a part of it. But knowledge is not necessarily developed in such a linear manner. The arrow of causality can, and frequently does, point in *both* directions. Theory surely leads to practice. But practice also leads to theory. And, teaching, at its best, shapes both research and practice. Viewed from this perspective, a more comprehensive, more dynamic understanding of scholarship can be considered, one in which the rigid categories of teaching, research, and service are broadened and more flexibly defined (pp. 15-16).

The IUP doctoral program since the 1980s led the way in doctoral education design at IUP by embracing this model as the most appropriate for the mission of its faculty, graduate programs, and students. This expanded foundation legitimized the concern with teaching practice—at the foundation of the IUP program—as a value, important for faculty and students alike, not in itself but in relationship to both research and service.

A consequence of Boyer's broadened view of scholarship adopted by IUP along with a number of universities is a new look at the connection between practice as broadly conceived and theory as broadly articulated. This new relationship between theory and practice in second language writing, interestingly, was recently debated (Silva & Matsuda, 2010). Overall, the dominant concern in this debate seems to have been with theory, aptly embodied in the title: *Practicing Theory in Second Language Writing*. However, at least three contributors to this conversation—Atkinson's practice with a big P or "what teachers do . . . Teachers consciously mediate what they know" (p. 14), Goldstein's "finding theory in the particular" (p. 72), and Zhu's articulation of theory and practice as "bi-directional, interdependent, dynamic, and mediated" (p. 214)—all seem similar to or compatible with Boyer's vision underlying IUP's doctoral program.

The Relevance of Practice for Dissertation Writers

Recently I surveyed IUP dissertation writers about their experiences in the doctoral program and how it has impacted their careers and professional development. My questionnaire was distributed to 21 of the 86 (25%) SLW dissertation authors at IUP (up to 2012), of whom 18 or 86% responded (21% of the total population). The results of this sample showed several unequivocal responses.

Nearly all of the respondents, for example, recognized the relevance of practice to all phases of graduate education at IUP including the dissertation process. From admission policy to classroom dynamics, various kinds of experiences teaching writing are viewed as central to the program. As Wendy Bishop, former chair of CCCC and an IUP doctoral recipient, once said—the program tends to enroll "active writing teachers wanting/needing to complete terminal degrees but with classroom experiences they could share and use to test new theories" (Bishop, 1998).

Survey respondents revealed one unexpected role of prior practice. While IUP students are strongly encouraged to find and relate their dissertation research to a niche in the field (Swales, 2004), their home institutions often play a major role in that decision. Frequently, dissertation authors indicate that they selected their topic because of the community where they practice—whether due to issues raised by their own students or teaching, their colleagues or other actors in their workplaces. One doctoral student, for example, was asked to teach "writing for scientific publication" in English at a Mexican research institute, which alerted her to a whole new area of possible study and research with practical application to her EFL work. Another, an instructor and coordinator of First Year Composition (FYC) at a Historically Black College and University (HBCU) felt that his African-American students who were to varying degrees bi-dialectical were the "dominant influence that attracted me to my topic." Still others cited different experiences working at post-graduate, English-medium institutions in Europe and elsewhere as their motivating force. In general, IUP dissertation researchers were focused on connections between theory they were exposed to in IUP classrooms and those practices and knowledge from various contexts they brought to the graduate program.

Sites of Writing Practice

Not all dissertation authors surveyed had the prior experience from which to develop their dissertation research. Some—typically graduate students who pursue the doctoral degree immediately following an undergraduate and master's degree—found their role as teacher-scholars at IUP in sites of practice directly associated with the doctoral program. These sites offered students a nexus of writing practices that were relevant to their doctoral classroom experiences. During the early 1980s, I created an intensive English program (the American Language Institute) with multiple levels of writing instruction that prepared international students for undergraduate and graduate work. It was also a frequent site for SLW dissertation research and teaching practice and mentorship (see Tannacito, 2013). Colleagues also developed a Writing Center for native English-speaking students, as well as a writing assessment program that included ESL in the training of teacher raters and a Teaching Associate Program that mentored graduate students who were teaching freshman composition for the first time.

Students in my survey felt that opportunities to do hands-on work with first and second language writers was highly significant in their dissertation experience. And, conversely, the presence of doctoral students with interests in second language writing expanded the Writing Center's purview as that program developed to include L2 writers (Rafoth, 2013). For some students who lacked teaching positions when they started their graduate program, IUP's sites of engagement in writing practices provided diverse opportunities to discover their dissertation topics where they had not expected upon entering the program. As was pointed out by one student on the program's website, the integration of teaching, research, and service after her graduation, was a key to her subsequent career: "the comprehensive curriculum of the program provides students with sound theory as well as knowledge of effective pedagogical practices. Shortly after graduation from the program, I was hired to develop an intensive Academic ESL program in a community college" (IUP C&T website).

Interdisciplinarity

In his pioneering studies of the history of second language writing, Matsuda (1998, 1999, 2006) shows how "this academic specialty [second language writing] has been shaped by the interdisciplinary relationship between composition studies and second language studies" (p. 14). While there is not yet a widespread consensus on the meaning of *interdisciplinary*, it is generally assumed to mean a minimal relation between distinct conceptual frameworks or design/methodologies and different perspectives/skills from at least two disciplines (Aboelela, Laren, Bakken, Carasquillo, Formicola, Gied, Haas & Gebbie, 2007). This union of disciplines in the IUP doctoral program brought together rhetoric and composition studies as well as applied linguistics and education in the professional preparation of its faculty as well as in the course work offered within an English department.

Many of the SLW dissertation writers from IUP whom I surveyed placed interdisciplinarity high among the features of the IUP doctoral program. For example, some students point to how the program expanded their exposure to disciplines with which they had no prior contact. Others point out how exposure to other disciplines affected the focus of their dissertation in one discipline because they could incorporate research and methodological frameworks from both disciplinary fields in the dissertation to address the transitions from home, primary discourses to academic, secondary discourses. In a few cases, this interdisciplinary impulse led students to integrate research from unique areas, e.g. international relations and political studies, into their dissertation research. And, it also affected the choice of advisor and committee members to guide the process, according to many survey respondents.

Internationalism

IUP dissertation authors also emphasized that the internationalism of the IUP program affected their work from beginning to end. By internationalism I mean the participation of students as well as faculty in the contexts and concerns of EFL students and their teachers. A significant percentage of the doctoral faculty had some international experience during the period being discussed due to exchanges, Fulbright awards, conferences abroad, birth and education as well as invited lectures and workshops. Several of the faculty (both Nonnative English Speaking Teachers (NNESTs) and Native English Speaking Teachers (NESTs)) had significant international experiences prior to joining the program as well. This type of experience often provides insight into the practice and conditions faced by writing teachers worldwide.

On the other hand, many doctoral students embodied the internationalism of the program. Of the thirty to 35 students (summer and AY cohorts) admitted to the IUP Composition and TESOL doctoral program each year between 2000-2012, approximately half were international students. Two-thirds of the students who finished SLW dissertations from 1977-2012 were F-1 visa holders at the time of completion and 38% of the SLW dissertations examined writing in EFL contexts. The presence of doctoral students from other countries, as IUP intended, is viewed by many as an indicator of the high quality of the American system of doctoral education (see NSF, 2010).

Flexible Residency

The last major design feature to influence dissertations at IUP is the "flexible" residency options. This innovation in graduate education involves three options for students—either (a) take course work for three consecutive summers, or (b) for three contiguous semesters in an academic year, or (c) for an academic year with two contiguous summers—to accomplish the 36 credit minimum post master's course credit requirement (excluding dissertation credits). Following this course work, students are not required to be in residency for their dissertation but must continuously register with an advisor for the duration of the degree within the seven year time limit. These options are considered "flexible" because they offer alternative paths of study within the same curriculum and requirements to fit the residential life worlds of the students.

The first option seems to suit mainly ex-pats and other mid-career, and thus experienced and employed, writing teachers who are motivated to seek position, promotion, and/or permanency at their current institutions or at new ones. The summer schedule—taking courses up to six hours daily for ten continuous weeks in three contiguous summers—is intense. But it does allow students to teach and research at home during the intervening academic year. For many students, this also made available their dissertation research site, which assisted them in staying on track for the remainder of the degree.

The academic year option, on the other hand, usually viewed as the more traditional approach, attracts younger, novice teachers who need the longer residency for mentoring in teaching and the development of professional experience. However, experienced professionals and school teachers who were employed in nearby states also found this path vital to their contact with their dissertation advisor and committee. Thus, the flexible residency option overcame several stumbling blocks for many highly qualified teachers and enriched the IUP doctoral program through the diversity of contexts whence writing teachers brought their experience and conducted their dissertation research. This feature was, therefore, quickly imitated in doctoral programs across campus, such as in Psychology and Education doctoral programs during the 1980s.

Other Contributing Conditions

Finally, those students specializing in SLW as a field of research discussed two additional factors that influenced their doctoral work importantly—(a) personal experience with writing and the teaching of writing, and (b) the inspiration of scholars from the broader SLW community of scholars.

Some of those surveyed at IUP expressed their own struggles with writing as motivation for their selection of SLW as a topic. Some even discovered the challenge of writing whether English was learned as a native language, nativized language or mostly as a second language during their graduate work. Their own positionality opened topics and avenues of research to many second language dissertation writers at IUP.

Still others wanted to intervene in ways that could be of assistance to their own students who are required to master English. Teaching, tutoring, and testing make up the ecology of writing where IUP students conducted research. Many of those with ESL/EFL teaching experience used their investment to shape their dissertations—either in terms of the formation of their research questions, the selection of a population to study, or their focus on a specific program as a research site. In many cases, original research at many home and nearby institutions linked the IUP program to a network of other collaborating individuals and institutions.

Interestingly, contact with the expertise of individuals in the field of SLW is also reported by a number of IUP SLW dissertation writers as significant in shaping their identity and inspiring the development of their work. One writer recalled a talk on the literacy learning of Anglo-Indian women by Alister Cumming at IUP in 1986 as the inspiration for her dissertation interest in literacy (Cumming, 1991). Another cites attending the first Symposium on Second Language Writing in 1998 as formative in his development. Several nonnative English speaking dissertation writers noted the importance of contact with scholars with identity and perspective similar to their own through visiting lectures with scholars such as Matsuda and Canagarajah. The influence of the broader community of SLW scholars on IUP dissertation writers, mediated by scholarly books, articles, journals, and conferences clearly was a significant influence contributing to the development of IUP SLW dissertations and their authors.

The Doctoral Advisor-Advisee Relationship

Directing 33 dissertations on SLW at IUP has given me the privilege of working with many unique teacher-scholars, such as my mentee, Karen Power. Her background in teaching, at first as a junior high school ESL/Spanish language teacher and later for many more years as a college composition instructor at colleges and universities in Ohio, made her perfectly suited for admission to this practice-grounded program. Not only did Karen have the requisite amount of practice in teaching English to succeed in our program, but also she had academic preparation specifically in the two disciplines most relevant to our doctorate and to the field of SLW. Further, the summers-only residency pattern made it feasible for her to hold down a full-time college job, finish her course work toward the degree, and still have a home life. Her coursework with me over a one-year period following her residency (including two independent seminars on the history of second language writing in 2007-08) were our mutual introduction.

Karen's dissertation topic on the history of the SLW field originated with several people in several contexts. Although, as she says, "she never thought of herself as a writer," she did produce the seed of her eventual dissertation in her MA paper: "The Role of L1 in L2 Composing Process"—with Chris Hall at Wright State University. When she came to IUP, she re-prepared this paper for her Research Methodology course as a more theoretically grounded treatment of the process-product debate. As we discussed her work during her independent studies, our conversation turned toward recognizing the uniqueness of the L2 side of the disciplinary convergence, an important focus for the field provided by Silva (1993) at the time. While I had long wanted to undertake a history project myself, I encouraged Karen to use the skills she was learning in conducting oral interviews for a history while most of the principals were still alive.

From papers Karen submitted during her independent studies on history as a research methodology and the history of second language writing, I recognized that Karen would have no fear of writing metaphors and stories. But whether she could "map' the past as a grand narrative—imposing a sensible grid or grids on it, stifling certain particularities and privileging others in the interest of a legible history—was a question unanswered until she wrote her chapters. As it turns out, her sense of story enabled her to find several fitting organizational schemes for the information she gathered including, for example, notions of academic tribes and scholarly geography.

To write while the principal characters in a story are still alive takes a certain amount of *chutzpah* that, no doubt, Karen had. But to gather their recollections through live experience interviews was even bolder, perhaps foolishly courageous on Karen's part. Nonetheless, she maintained respect for the "immediate experience" imparted by her historical participants, although lured on more than one occasion into side lines by siren songs of self-aggrandizement or unfulfilling silence that guarded self-disclosure.

When Karen was in the process of researching her 35 subjects for her dissertation, she used me as a sounding board for the numerous anecdotes she collected on a number of occasions. Actually, this began to trouble me midway through the process because of the bad reputation of anecdote in traditional methodology. I was relieved, therefore, that her verbal tellings led me to Max van Manen's *Researching Lived Experience: Human Science for an Action Sensitive Pedagogy* (1990), which for me justified anecdote as a methodological device in phenomenological writing (115-124). Not for the last time in our mutual experience, the advisor learned from the advisee.

Dialogue between an advisor and an advisee is often crucial to the development of dissertation work. I recall numerous "sidewalk snatches," as Karen calls them, reacting to statements made about the work of specific pioneer authors as well as lengthier sit-down conferences where directions in reading were advised, from the historical precedents of the process approach in SLW in the dialogue journal research sponsored by the Center for Applied Linguistics to the then recent historicizing of the field by Paul Kei Matsuda (1999, 2003).

Taking seven years (the limit) to finish the doctorate when only two consecutive summers of course work were required leaves a considerable amount of time for written interaction between an advisor and an advisee when both are teaching full-time. My comments generally averaged about four single-spaced pages per chapter plus lots of low-level page editing in each dissertation chapter draft. Commentary at all stages of the manuscript development: from pre-proposal to archival copy tends to expedite the process of completion.

Comments always included praise for research and writing done especially well as well as specific points to improve. My comments seem to differ from those I would typically offer in an anonymous review of a manuscript submitted for publication or presentation in that they are aimed beyond mere criticism. Sometimes, there were lacuna to fill: "Be sure to include discussion of the internationalization of the field (inside-out: activities of scholars in supranational organizations and outside-in: movement of international students and teachers into the US to study with L2 writing scholars ..." (Tannacito comments on K. Power, August 13, 2010). At other times, there are reminders: "Use a little more methodology self-consciously as you open your chapters. For example, discuss the biographic interview method ..." On several occasions, I recall using rhetorical devices in responding to Karen's written work, such as the focusing device "Say This" to help the author anchor points about her topics in clearer statements or bring ideas into more prominent focus ("perhaps you should entitle this chapter ... 'The Matrix of Second Language Writing as a Field'"). The uptake by dissertation authors of comments is highly individual, and dependent on the advisor-advisee relationship, even within academic and disciplinary genres, such as the dissertation. Advisors do well to remember that there is usually a balance to achieve between acculturation into a discipline and how any given individual progresses. Fortunately, as Parry (1998) found, many writing norms and conventions of a discipline are tacitly learned at the level of the doctoral dissertation.

SOME FURTHER OBSERVATIONS ON DISSERTATION ADVISING

Most graduate programs place a premium on matching the research interests of the dissertation student and the faculty advisor. This is necessary if the student is to succeed in conducting quality research and publishing in a particular community of scholars. Yet, as Belcher (1994) reminds us quite frankly, even distinguished and experienced faculty members may have neither the awareness nor the skills to cognitively and socially mentor their students. Likewise, younger faculty members may not have had models of quality advising to fall back on, as studies continue to reveal (Buckingham, 2008). Thus, it may be useful to add to the facts and voices we have examined the perspective of the dissertation advisor.

According to Zhu (this volume), the doctoral advisor is a "mediator" and the student the "subject" in the PhD process conceived as activity. Doctoral dissertation advising is, in a manner of speaking, the keystone of a quality doctoral education experience. Departmental/program environments are enhanced, students are more successfully socialized into the discipline, and degrees are completed in a more timely way when we get dissertation advising right. ABDism—the tendency for doctoral students to drop their programs at the dissertation stage—may very well result from an unsatisfactory advising relationship. In addition, students can suffer what is sometimes called "dissertation anomie" when they are left isolated at the most unstructured and pressurized stage of doctoral work (Ali & Kohun, 2007). Taking on too many advisees or not anticipating the significant amount of time required to mentor a dissertation student through the process are common enough errors made by experienced and novice advisors alike.

Since publication ranks higher as a career-promoting activity in most professional contexts than does dissertation advising, advisors, especially younger faculty, are potentially in a double bind. As Johns and Swales (2002), among others, have pointed out, English dissertation writing imposes additional burdens on faculty and students. Nonnative English speaking students (NNESs) and their supervisors are required to spend additional time revising and correcting drafts (e.g., language, rhetoric, mechanics, organization) in addition to dealing with problems shared with native English speaking students (NESs), such as formulating the research question or hypothesis, finding a research space, designing a study, and interpreting results.

Issues of power that intertwine the relations of students and faculty in doctoral advising should be consciously recognized if an effective relationship is to develop. Regarding power, students and faculty are rarely equal, and not all faculty are equal. As Bourdieu (1984) contends: "Direction of doctoral theses is doubtless also one of the most powerful and reliable indicators of academic power" (p. 237). Further, he argues that professors in higher education possess two distinguishable sorts of power, roughly corresponding, on the one hand, to the global, research/theory pole of the academic continuum and, on the other hand, to the local, teaching/practice pole. Whether faculty members are closer to one pole or the other, they need to consider how their type of power impacts their students. This interesting continuum of power is usually present when students choose an advisor, if the program permits them to choose, as it does at IUP. That choice has a particular set of consequences that the dissertation student should consider when choosing one advisor over another.

Whichever type of a director a student chooses or is assigned, the advisor needs to exercise skill in mediating a student's committee work. Likewise, a student needs to take on the responsibility for her own work, neither seeking to ride the advisor's coattails nor exercising obstinacy or lack of self-awareness in the face of criticism (e.g., Don't piss off the IRB!). As is noted wherever a close working relationship in an organization is needed—in business and politics, as well as the academy—trust is the essential property that needs to be co-created (Dirks & Ferrin, 2002).

Trust is essential to caring in the self's trajectory to becoming a second language writing researcher. In my opinion, successful advising requires that the advisor ensures the conditions for mutual trust, fulfilling reasonable requests to meet on dates promised or to respond promptly and fully with feedback on ideas and drafts. On the advisee's part, sorting out what advice is really needed from the supervisor and what should be figured out for oneself or outsourced to a support network is the way toward autonomy in the apprenticeship model that dominates dissertation advising.

Of course, a power differential always exists between a student and an advisor, a reality that must be taken into account for a successful outcome by both partners. Usually, the development from powerlessness to relative power evolves over the course of a relationship with an advisor, maybe through coursework, conferences, teacher supervision, grant work, joint research, etc. For one thing, there is the question of how much control an advisor should have over the direction of the dissertation from topic selection through interpretation of results and conclusions. What is needed assistance and what is co-optation that creates dependency is a delicate dynamic at every level and stage of advising, varying with both the individual and the progress a student makes.

Additionally, the issue of power is implicated in the composition and conversation with other committee members as well. To what extent must a student frame the hypothesis or research question in the way every committee member would themselves conduct the inquiry? To what extent is the student or the advisor allowed to choose the best method for the study? To what extent do committee members permit advisors the final review of recommended revisions before final submission? Many of these questions regarding the degree of control permeate the dissertation process. Much depends on the compatibility of the advisor and student, and they with the committee as a whole. Whether a student chooses an advisor because of her scholarly/scientific authority or because of his academic/institutional power that allows that person access, a student should seriously consider the match between her own interaction style and that of the advisor. Grover and Malhotra (2004) suggest that doctoral students become aware of different coping mechanisms needed for interactional styles with different advisor personality types.

This discussion of advising perhaps points to the need for dissertation advisors to be more aware of the advising process, to exercise more leadership in maintaining trust and a balance of power, as well as to act ethically throughout the advising relationship. Expertise in the content or research method related to a dissertation topic is surely a sufficient condition for serving as an advisor. But having the skill and ethics to mentor a student in conducting research and writing for professional purposes, to manage a committee, and to navigate departmental and institutional procedures (including the IRB) is a necessary condition if a successful outcome is to be enjoyed.

Programs also need to take greater responsibility for the dissertation process than has traditionally been the case by supplying more context to support the advisee and advisor. Two suggestions seem particularly efficacious. First, departments can minimize the social isolation that leads to ABDism and writer anomie by establishing or expanding various dissertation support mechanisms, such as chapter workshops, colloquia, reading groups, etc. that build up writer/researcher autonomy.

Second, the dissertation process should be more open to innovation. One such innovation that seems to be catching on in some doctoral programs is the replacement of the monograph/book format with the multiple, publishable article genre as the dissertation project (Johns & Swales, 2002), although as Tony Silva has pointed out, this places an increased burden on journal editors if publication becomes a requirement. Alister Cumming describes how the University of Toronto where he serves as graduate director has crafted a workable formulation of this alternative, as does Tony Silva, director at Purdue University, where the "papers" option is offered (see their respective chapters in this volume).

Another innovative practice that IUP has had success with is the institution of an additional stage of formal evaluation—the three-chapter review defense—between the proposal and the final defense of the dissertation and before data collection is authorized. Of course, this innovation involves more faculty time, but I think it is partly responsible for higher completion rates and lowered social isolation during the dissertation stage at IUP than was the case prior to this revision of the program. Certainly, faculty satisfaction with this approach has increased. Reversals of what was accepted at the proposal stage but rejected at the final defense have been diminished. Greater opportunity for faculty intervention on medium to high levels of planning and committee advice about the use of specific research techniques have become available. Even a higher quality of "finish" is evident with the introduction of the three-chapter review.

I have suggested that students need to choose advisors carefully where they have a choice. Further, they need to engage their advisors appropriately and with trust. They also need to adopt coping mechanisms to deal with different advising personalities. Dissertation students should actively enter the wider disciplinary community and recognize resources outside of the advisor who are often more effectively and efficiently recruited for specific tasks they need to accomplish.

Conclusion

I began by showing that the national trend in SLW dissertations has been one of steady growth probably caused by the increase in the second language writing population in schools and universities in North America and the spread of the teaching of writing in English around the world. The institutional response to that growth and dispersion has been the production of specialists to teach doctoral students.

As a leading university program, IUP produced a significant number of dissertations in SLW during the last 35 years. I find this productivity largely to be the result of the design features of the program as well as the motives of its students, seeking to improve themselves as writers, teachers, and researchers while integrating themselves in the communities of SLW scholars. In this process, the doctoral advising relationship needs to be seen as a partnership. Programs need to provide richer support mechanisms. Power issues should be consciously considered by both faculty and students. These measures and those we might learn from other programs can serve to continue to build the field of SLW in doctoral education.

Programs in SLW—especially those with multi-disciplinary dimensions—need to lead the field to a clearer national identity that might enable greater resources and institutional standing to flow to doctoral dissertation recipients and their sites. Perhaps some reciprocal program development or at least more conversation and even collaboration among doctoral programs that focus on SLW might constitute a step in creating a more seamless and impactful community between the leading and the dispersed community of universities where SLW researchers have studied. Our ability to improve the collective status and visibility of SLW teachers and scholars may be one appropriate collective goal, as heard in Paul Kei Matsuda's call (in this volume) to "build the field" for the next generation's future in international post-industrial societies.

REFERENCES

Aboelela, S. W., Larson, E., Bakken, S., Carasquilla, O., Formicola, A., Glied, S.A., Haas, J., & Gebbie, K. M. (2007). Defining interdisciplinary research: Conclusions from a critical review of the literature. *Health Services Research, 42*(1), 329-346.

Ali, A, & Kohun, F. (2007). Dealing with social isolation to minimize doctoral attrition: A four stage framework. *International Journal of Doctoral Studies, 2, 21-33*.

Allen, C. (2011). A terrible time for new Ph.D.s. *Minding the campus: Reforming our universities.* Retrieved from http://www.mindingthecampus.com/originals/2011/02/a_terrible_time_for_new_phds.html

Belcher, D. (1994). The apprenticeship approach to advanced academic literacy: Graduate students and their mentors. *English for Specific Purposes, 13*, 23-34.

Bishop, W. (1998). A heart of gold. In D. Roen, S. Brown & T. Enos (eds.), *Living rhetoric and composition: Stories of the discipline* (pp. 25-35). Mahwah, NJ: Lawrence Erlbaum.

Boud, D., & Lee, A. (2009). Introduction. In D. Boud, & A. Lee (Eds.), *Changing practices in doctoral education (pp.1-9).* London: Routledge.

Bourdieu, P. (1972; 1977). *Outline of a theory of practice.* Trans. R. Nice. Cambridge: Cambridge University Press.

Bourdieu, P. (1984; 1988). *Homo academicus.* Trans. P. Collier. Stanford, CA: Stanford University Press.

Boyer, E. L. (1990). *Scholarship reconsidered: Priorities of the professoriate.* NY: The Carnegie Foundation for the Advancement of Teaching.

Buckingham, L. (2008). Development of English academic writing competence by Turkish scholars. *International Journal of Doctoral Studies, 3*, 18p. Retrieved from: http://www.ijds.org/Volume3/IJDSv3p001-018Buckingham29.pdf.

Carnegie Foundation for the Advancement of Teaching. (2010). Classification descriptions Retrieved from: http://classifications.carnegiefoundation.org/descriptions/.

Conference on College Composition and Communication. (2001; 2009). *CCCC Statement on Second language Writing and Writers.* Retrieved from: http://www.nwcte.org/cccc/resources/positions/secondlangwriting.

Cumming A., & Gill, J. (1991). Learning ESL literacy among Indo-Canadian women. *Language, Culture and Curriculum*, 4, 181-200.

Dirks, K. T., & Ferrin, D. L. (2002). Trust in leadership: Meta-analytic findings and implications for research and practice. *Journal of Applied Psychology*, 87(4), 611-628.

Golde, C. M., & Dore, T.M. (2001). *At cross purposes: What the experiences of today's doctoral students reveal about doctoral education.* Philadelphia: Pew Charitable Trusts. PDF available from: http://www.ssc.wisc.edu/~oliver/sociology/PhDEducationreport.pdf.

Hirvela, A., & Belcher, D. (2007). Writing scholars as teacher educators: Exploring writing teacher education. *Journal of Second Language Writing*, 16(3), 125-126.

Grover, V., & Malhorta, M. K. (2004). A rough model for success in doctoral study. *Decision Line*, 23-25.

Johns, A. M., & Swales, J. M. (2002). Literacy and disciplinary practices: Opening and closing perspectives. *Journal of English for Academic Purposes*, 1, 13-28.

Krashen, S. D. (1985). *The input hypothesis: Issues and implications.* NY: Longman.

Leki, I. (2007). *Undergraduates in a second language: Challenges and complexities of academic literacy development.* Mahwah, NJ: Erlbaum.

Leki, I., Cumming, A., & Silva, T. (2008). *A synthesis of research on second language writing in English.* NY: Routledge.

Van Manen, M. (1990). *Researching lived experience.* Albany, NY: State University of New York.

Matsuda, P. K. (1998). Situating ESL in a cross-disciplinary context. *Written Communication*, 15, 99-121.

Matsuda, P. K. (1999). Composition studies and ESL writing: A disciplinary division of labor. *College Composition and Communication*, 50, 699-721.

Matsuda, P. K. (2003; 2006). Second language writing in the twentieth century: A situated historical perspective. In P. K. Matsuda, M. Cox, J. Jordan, & C. Ortmeier-Hooper (Eds.), *Second-language writing in the composition classroom: A critical sourcebook* (pp. 14-30). Boston: Bedford/St. Martin's.

McAlpine, L., Pare, A., & Starke-Meyerring, D. (2008). Disciplinary voices: A shifting landscape for English doctoral education in the twenty-first century. In D. Boud & A. Lee (Eds.), *Changing practices in doctoral education* (pp. 42-53). London: Routledge.

MLA Office of Research. (2011). Report on the survey of earned doctorates, 2008-09. *ADE Bulletin 150*, 1-7.

National Center for Education Statistics. (2006). *Report and suggestions from IPEDS Technical Review Panel #15: First-professional degree classification.* Washington, DC: Department of Education. Available at: http://nces.ed.gov/ipeds/news_room/trp_technical_review_02072006_18.asp

National Science Foundation. (2012). *Doctorate recipients from U.S. universities: 2010.* Special Report NSF 12-305. Arlington, VA: National Center for Science and Engineering Statistics. Available at: http://www.nsf.gov/statistics/sed/

Power, K. A. (2012). *A social history of second language writing: First generation L2 composition scholars in the process era.* Unpublished doctoral dissertation, Indiana University of Pennsylvania, Indiana, PA.

Parry, K. (1998). Disciplinary discourse in doctoral theses. *Higher Education 36*, 273-299.

Rafoth, B. A., & Bruce, S. (Eds.). (2009). *ESL writers: A guide for writing center tutors*, 2nd edition. Portsmouth, NH: Heineman-Boynton/Cook.

Shaughnessy, M. (1977). *Errors and expectations.* NY: Oxford University Press.

Silva, T. (1993). Toward an understanding of the distinct nature of L2 writing: The ESL research and its implications. *TESOL Quarterly, 27*, 657-677.

Silva, T., & Leki, I. (2004). Family matters: The influence of applied linguistics and composition studies on second language writing— past, present, and future. *Modern Language Journal, 88*, 1-13.

Silva, T., Leki, I., & Carson, J. (1997). Broadening the perspective of mainstream composition studies: Some thoughts from the disciplinary margins. *Written Communication, 14*(3), 398-428.

Silva, T., Brice, C., & Reichelt, M. (1999). *Annotated bibliography of scholarship in second language writing: 1993-1997.* Stamford, CT: Ablex.

Strain, M. M. (2000). Local histories, rhetorical negotiations: The development of doctoral programs in rhetoric and composition. *Rhetoric Society Quarterly, 30*(2), 57-76.

Swales, J. (2004). *Research genres: Explorations and applications.* Cambridge: Cambridge University Press.

Tannacito, D. J. (1995). *A guide to writing English as a second or foreign language: An annotated bibliography of research and pedagogy.* Alexandria, VA: TESOL, Inc.

Tannacito, D. J. (2013). *English language teachers as program administrators.* Alexandria, VA: TESOL, Inc.

Warde, A. (2004). *Practice and field: Revising Bourdeusian concepts.* CRIC Discussion Paper No 65. Manchester, ENG: Center for Research on Innovation & Competition.

3 On My Initiation into the Field of Second Language Writing

Karen A. Power

Literacy practices of nonnative English speakers at the tertiary level as a topic of research has attracted the attention of second language writing (SLW) specialists since the late 1980s (e.g., Belcher, 1989). The publication of Belcher and Braine's (1995) *Academic Writing in a Second Language* formally brought concepts like "academic literacy," "academic discourse," "discourse community," and "initiation" into the second language writing research arena. Reports and case studies like those of Belcher (1989; 1994) and Casanave (1995; 2002) asked: How do nonnative speaker apprentices in their designated fields interact with local and global community members? What obstacles do they face? How do they negotiate those obstacles?

The literature in SLW is dominated by the initiation process of the nonnative speaker. Some nonnative newcomers in the field of composition studies have written personal accounts (e.g., Shen, 1989). Second language writing composition scholars George Braine (1999), Suresh Canagarajah (2001), and Ulla Connor (1999) wrote autobiographies of their own professional literacy experiences. Others in L2 writing wrote of the experiences of their students (Blanton, 2005; Leki, 2007; Spack, 1997a, 1997b; Zamel, 1995; Zamel & Spack, 2004). These studies and other firsthand accounts of nonnative speakers have given us vivid, and often poignant, descriptions of the socialization of the newcomer, nonnative speaker to the world of academe.

The *rite of passage* for any newcomer, native or nonnative speaker, typically involves the production of a written text that satisfies a set of pre-conceived expectations of a specialized audience. For the doctoral candidate, this written text is a dissertation. The successful completion of the dissertation pre-supposes a mode of interaction between teacher and learner, advisor and advisee, expert and novice mediated through language and occurring within the perceived boundaries of the academic territory. This direct communication between the novice and expert is organized in a social hierarchy that serves to develop the learner, or what Leki (2006) calls a *socioacademic relationship* when it takes place in a classroom.

A socioacademic relationship is formed when learning activity takes place within both an academic context—an instructional environment with an established set of goals and learning outcomes mediated by course assignments and grades—and a social context that facilitates the dialogic and dialectic exchanges, both verbal and written, that take place between expert and novice. A socioacademic relationship can best be understood as the social dimension of the academic experience, and one that plays an influential role in the positive and/or negative experiences of the novice learner, as Leki's (2006, 2007) work suggests.

What does that experience look like for initiates into the field of SLW? As Braine (1999), Canagarajah (2001), and Connor (1999) affirm, initiation into the world of academe is a grueling process of proactive engagement even for the most successful initiates. But what is that experience like for a native speaker? The native speaker experience is the one that I'd like to share—my own initiation into the field of SLW that occurred over the course of my dissertation research and writing.

My apprenticeship experience was unique in that opportunities were created that allowed me to research the SLW community not as a sideline observer, but as an active would-be member. Over the course of my research and writing, I was able to find a voice in the SLW community not only among members within my own local academic context, but also across the spectrum of the members of the SLW academic discourse community.

In the course of this narration, I do not attempt to separate, extract, and interpret the social from the academic in the socioacademic context and describe each as a distinct experience. To do so would be impossible because they are inextricably intertwined and interdependent; the context of one was never apart from the context of the other. However, there were moments when one context was foregrounded. Those are the moments I have chosen to describe

Apprenticeship Foregrounded in the Academic Context

Apprenticeship into SLW began in full measure in the academic context of a doctoral program. I selected a program that best suited my talents, interests, and goals. I had graduate training and teaching experience in composition. I was a veteran first year composition teacher of nineteen years with an MA in Composition and Rhetoric from Wright State University, a midsize public university in southwest Ohio. I had undergraduate training and teaching experience in TESOL and Spanish education. I taught Spanish at my university and was also the director of the teacher-training program in TESOL. Plus, the year I applied for doctoral studies, I published an article in *ESL Magazine* on how to teach 5th grade, nonnative speakers to compose an academic essay. The article was based on my teaching experience in a six-week elementary school summer migrant program the previous year. With my background and experience, the Composition and TESOL program at Indiana University of Pennsylvania (IUP) was ideal. I was IUP's exemplar teacher-scholar model student (see Tannacito, this volume).

The academic environment was familiar to me. I was fairly adept at the analysis and interpretation of information and the organization and development of ideas. I was the classic academic over-achiever: dedicated, serious, and endowed with a healthy intellectual curiosity. Over two summers, I took courses in writing, language, literacy, and teaching as well as courses in TESOL, and a core of required courses, including two courses in research methods. Some classes were more useful than others in terms of content; some professors more adept at delivering content than others. It didn't seem to matter. I was adept in adjusting my learning style to fit the professor's teaching style.

Selecting A Topic: The Back Story

My interest in writing began as a junior high school English teacher in the mid-1980s when I discovered the process approach to composition. Despite process writing's cool reception in writing classes at the college level, it was the rage in grade 5-12 classroom settings, and I was an enthusiastic convert. What we teachers loved about the process approach was that, by breaking down the general cognitive process of composing into identifiable units, we were able to teach it. Any task broken down into manageable steps is easier. What researchers loved about process approach was that, by breaking down the general cognitive process of composing into identifiable units, they were be able to look at writing behaviors in a more detailed way. It was an attractive topic of study.

By the mid 1990s, however, when I started an MA program in composition and rhetoric, process writing had morphed from a tool for creative expression into an instructional tool for internalizing content information. Classroom teachers of math, science, social studies, and foreign language were using writing to help students better understand subject matter. My interest in second language writing began here as I saw the connection to ESL writers.

The professor in the research class for my MA program, Chris Hall (whom I later invited to be a member of my dissertation committee), nurtured my newfound interest in second language writing by handing me articles outside of the course material that he thought would interest me. Chris also had recently published an article on the revision processes of non-native writers in *TESOL Quarterly*, the flagship journal for all of us interested in ESL. He encouraged me to investigate the way process writing research, popularized in composition studies, could be applied to second language writing. For my final research paper in his class, he suggested I investigate the influence of first language (L1) on second language (L2) writing. I found allure in the topic's practical application. Is L1 proficiency a good predictor of a quality written product in L2? Should teachers forbid the use of native language in the English language writing classroom or should they welcome and encourage it? The research for that paper gave me a solid grounding in Cognitive Process Theory, contrastive rhetoric, transfer, and the Threshold Hypothesis.

It was another decade before I returned to school, this time as a doctoral student. I had been teaching full time and advancing professionally by doing conference presentations on a regular basis and writing/editing a column for the *Ohio TESOL Newsletter*. By the time I revisited the influence of L1 in the L2 composing process, process writing as a topic of research had become history, victim to the social turn in writing and the literacy movement. There were still researchers out there interested in the cognitive side of composing, but the research venue had shifted from North America to Europe (See the work of Roca de Larios, Murphy, & Marín, 2002). So, I considered researching the historical perception of the role of the L1. I liked the idea of doing historical research. First, history had always sparked my imagination. It was, in my thinking, a series of meta-events that spanned the scope of time and transcended the everyday human experience. Second, and less romantic, it was practical. Historical research employs, for the most part, stable sources of data collection. Professional books, journals, conference papers/proceedings don't depend on the variable dynamics associated with human subjects who may renege on their willingness to participate or are unable to fulfill their commitment for one reason or another. But was this a viable topic? Even after writing up a dissertation proposal, I didn't know for sure. I needed guidance.

Selecting A Dissertation Advisor

Selecting a dissertation advisor is a process, and as Tannacito (this volume) admonishes, must be done carefully and wisely. He artfully describes the dynamic complexity of the practice of dissertation advising and the many roles an advisor fills: s/he is mentor to the advisee, manager of the dissertation committee, and expert in the knowledge of department policy and institutional procedures. Equally important, an advisor must have certain personal characteristics: s/he must have a measure of scholarly authority and knowledge in the field and be trustworthy, dependable, and willing to relinquish power and control over the mentee in order to nurture his/her mentee's autonomy. A checklist of what to look for in an advisor or having a list of pre-set questions for prospective advisors to answer is useful in selecting an advisor.

Unfortunately, I didn't have a list or a plan, nor did it occur to me that I needed one. The process of selecting an advisor for me was more like the aviator who, without instruments or flight plan, flies by the seat of her pants, using her best judgment and intuition. So flying by the seat of my pants, I took an ad hoc approach that mostly involved conferring with the members of my cohort and other IUP doctoral students wherever and whenever I had the opportunity.

One of our popular meeting spots for conversation during summer classes was on the Oak Grove, a central, open grassy space on the IUP campus filled with oak trees and benches and crisscrossed by sidewalks. Lining its circumference are the main academic buildings. On Wednesdays at lunchtime in the Oak Grove, dining services prepares an outdoor lunch of hamburgers and hotdogs and makes seating available in the form of folding chairs. I would grab a chair and find my classmates in a shady spot in the grove. It was a pleasant place to sit, eat, and socialize with other graduate students. It was here we talked about classes and shared everything we knew about professors, inside and outside the classroom. In this way, I got to know Dan Tannacito vicariously through the experiences of others.

Dan's name surfaced as the top expert on second language writing. He was smart; he had a PhD and a DA. He held clout on campus as the founder of the American Language Institute, IUP's wildly successful intensive English program. He had also directed the most dissertations in the program, which to me meant that he was willing to put his own scholarship on the back burner in order to devote time to his students. He held the respect of his colleagues and his students. More importantly, Dan was willing to take me on board.

The result of our first conversation as advisee-advisor redirected my research topic. My initial research proposal articulated my intent to develop a comprehensive theory of L2 writing based on historical research that would uncover not only the role of L1 in the L2 writing process, but would also explain the reason for the variety of seemingly contradictory approaches for teaching writing *and* the reason why the hundreds of studies that queried the composing process of L2 writers yielded contradictory results. In an unassuming way, I saw my research as answering the call for a unified theory of L2 writing as described by William ("Bill") Grabe's (2001) "Notes Toward a Theory of Second Language Writing."

Dan recognized the difficulty of the task. In order to account for the dozen or so variables (i.e., learner characteristics, learner processes, learning context, historical context, and social context), sub-theories would need to be identified from bilingual education, foreign language education, second language acquisition, applied linguistics, and composition. He pointed out that because the research could take me in a hundred directions, it would be exhausting, and he suggested that I save such a grand historical narrative for another time. His recommendation was to circumscribe the project by focusing on a general history of second language writing. Directing me to investigate the important themes and the key scholars of the field, Dan helped to set the course for what became the first dissertation offering a comprehensive history of the field of SLW (see Power, 2012).

Researching the Dissertation

By the time I finished coursework, I felt prepared for doctoral research. Yet, I still had a lot to learn about SLW: Who was privileged to speak? When, how, and on what? What interpretative paradigm overlay L2 writing research? What ontologies, epistemologies, and methodologies were applied to the interpretative framework that characterized the field?

Getting started was a struggle. I felt like a plane taxiing in a circular pattern on a runway. I just couldn't seem to get off the ground. The major holdup was that I could not make heads or tails of what defined the field of SLW. I sensed what Ferris and Hedgcock (2005), Kroll (2006), and Silva (1990) meant when they described the field as bewildering, confused, and chaotic. The more I read, the more the concepts became ambiguous. I was inundated with a myriad of terms and phrases associated with L2 writing.* The confusion was compounded by the fact that the literature was filled with dueling dichotomies that stimulated controversy and debate.† The disagreements that encom-

---

* Here is a partial list of terms associated with L2 writing: audience/discourse community, academic literacy, cognitive approach, contrastive rhetoric, comprehension hypothesis, content-based instruction (CBI), critical literacy, dialogue journals, discipline-specific rhetorical forms, English for Academic Purposes (EAP), English for Specific Purposes (ESP), expressivism, genre, linguistic process, literature/learning logs, notional-functional, pragmatic, process approach, reader-centered pedagogy, reading-writing connections, traditional rhetoric, new rhetoric, socio-cognitive, socio-cultural, sheltered instruction, social constructionist, social constructivisit, socioliterate approach, social process, text analysis, whole language, Writing Across the Curriculum (WAC), Writing in the Disciplines (WID), writing to learn, and writer voice/identity.

† Debates topics included: academic writing v. personal writing, accuracy v. fluency, direct v. indirect feedback, general v. academic literacy, composition v. literature, formative v. summative feedback, general v. subject-specific writing, inductive v. deductive teaching, peer v. teacher feedback, product v.

passed the time frame of my study centered on the best way to teach writing.

Here is a specific example. Early on, I read first generation L2 composition scholar, Joy Reid's (1984) "Radical Outliner, Radical Brainstormer: A Perspective on Composing Processes." It is about the differing approaches writers employ during the pre-writing process. Using outlining to illustrate her point, Joy argues that the pre-writing process is not the same for everyone. Some writers like to brainstorm or "bleed" on paper before starting the formal writing process and others, like Joy, prefer to let ideas percolate internally, outline, and then write. The point of the article, that the traditional concept of *outline* was evolving and that pre-writing is unique to every individual, certainly wasn't anything controversial. However, Joy's article was a Forum piece in *TESOL Quarterly*.

The Forum was (and still is) a popular site for author-to-author commentary, response, and critique. Comments and rebuttals published in the Forum have an editorial-like flavor—opinionated and many times highly critical. The style of writing was direct, personal, and comments were brief, under 3,000 words, but typically scholarly in presentation and highly entertaining to readers who enjoyed the intellectual sparring that often took place. So, by nature, Forum pieces represented opposing, or at least alternate, views.

Ruth Spack (1985) reacted to Joy's piece as a reader. Ruth agreed with Joy that students should be allowed the time and space to compose as they see fit. She agreed with Joy that the meaning of the term "outline" had changed with the advent of recent research on the composing process. And even though outlining in the traditional sense of Roman numerals and sub-points wasn't inherently bad and even though Joy clearly wasn't advocating outlining in the traditional sense, Ruth penned an argument against the use of traditional outlining in ESL classrooms. She concluded by commending Joy on her personal outlining process and ended with this definition of *outline*:

> To outline today means not to organize ideas *before* writing, but to organize ideas *after* generating them by means of thinking and writing—a complex, recursive series of mental

---

process, research-based v. practitioner knowledge, segregate v. mainstream, teacher-centered v. student-centered, student-centered v. discipline-centered, quantity v. quality.

and scriptural procedures writers undergo each time they confront an assignment. (p. 398)

So, was there a disagreement in there somewhere? It appeared so. In Joy's response to Ruth, she issued a call to teach formal outlining to ESL students of the kind that bore a "surface resemblance to the traditional concept of outlining" (p. 399). Formal outlining? Surface resemblance to the traditional concept of outlining? Wasn't it the traditional outline that the authors had just, each in her own way, condemned as passé? Or was "surface resemblance" a reference to outlining in the sense of "a complex, recursive series of mental and scriptural procedures writers undergo each time they confront an assignment" (p. 398), which Ruth had just suggested? And was Joy talking about outlining *before* or *after* writing? It struck me as a bit of a frivolous argument. What I mean is, did the type of pre-draft outlining really matter? Was the issue here even *about* outlining?

It wasn't just Spack and Reid. The more I read, the more befuddled I became. I was suffering from intellectual cognitive dissonance caused by what Silva and Leki (2004) later described as overlap, appropriation, and direct importation of concepts into SLW from other fields. I could see ideas from recent developments in applied linguistics, bilingual education, composition, foreign language education, second language teaching, and sociolinguistics surfacing in the literature. Distinctions were blurred, and I was having difficulty sifting through the way approaches were being integrated, synthesized, and applied to L2 writing. I wondered how in the world I was going to be able to write a dissertation proposal let alone a dissertation if I didn't even understand what I was reading. I wasn't sure what to do. So, I sought out the person I had chosen to guide me through this process, Dan.

I remember sitting anxiously in Dan's office at the American Language Institute (ALI) at IUP on a wintry February day waiting for him to finish a phone call. Then I sat patiently as he switched his attention to a fellow graduate student standing at the door waiting to see him. Dan was a busy guy. He was the director of the ALI, a faculty member in the English department with teaching responsibilities, and also a much sought-after dissertation advisor among the doctoral students.

The relaxing ambiance of Dan's office—the computer screen saver of a Caribbean island of white sand set against the backdrop of a cloudless sky and a peaceful blue ocean accompanied by the soothing music of Enya playing softly in the background—wasn't helping to calm my fears. As I sat there, my career as a doctoral student flashed before my eyes. I was standing on the edge of graduate student purgatory—that imaginary no man's land where all unsuccessful doctoral students go (a.k.a. ABD). If I were to write a social history of L2 writing, I needed to be able to explain and account for the ambiguities and contradictions I uncovered.

As I began to convey the depths of my confusion and frustration caused by what I was reading, I remember that in between my rapid-fire narration of the various examples of blatant ambiguities and disagreements, I kept repeating, "I just don't get this. I just don't get L2 writing!" Dan, as was his custom whenever I started my outpour of anguish, listened quietly, waited until I had stopped and then crystallized the problem for me: "These scholars are looking at different parts of the same elephant and championing their respective viewpoints. Each viewpoint holds a different degree of truth depending on the context and the student population" (personal communication, August 2, 2007).

Dan had pinpointed the source of my confusion. The elephant was an analogy that had surfaced before in issues relating to TESOL. In a 1979 TESOL plenary, Peter Strevens first invoked the image of Saxe's elephant and the blind men of Indostan to analyze the various applications of the term "ESL." Later, first generation L2 composition scholar Linda Blanton in her 1995 article in *College ESL*, "Elephants and Paradigms: Conversations about Teaching L2 Writing" used the metaphor to describe the disagreements on method, materials, and classroom practice that characterized SLW. Different scholars held telescopic and, on the whole, non-contradictory views on ways to teach writing.

The philosophical disagreements in L2 writing were most visibly apparent by the topics. Outlining was a good example of a disagreement that, to the novice apprentice, seemed easily resolved. Yet, the more seasoned scholars of the field were well aware that debates like outlining were reflections of deeper L2 writing issues. As I reread the Spack-Reid debate, words that triggered disagreement bubbled to the surface of my consciousness: "product" and "process"; "rigidity" and "complexity"; "rhetorical form and "creativity"; "reader-based" and "writer based"; "prescriptive" and "descriptive"; "imitate" and "create"; "pragmatic" and "spontaneous generation" (Reid, 1984, 1985; Spack, 1985). These terms spoke volumes not just about differing viewpoints of how or when to commit ideas to paper, but about philosophies and characteristics of very differing approaches to writing instruction. Below is a post-epiphany excerpt of an e-mail I sent to Dan when that realization hit me:

Here's a conclusion that is a surprise—while the research [of first generation L2 writing scholars] may have represented them in a certain light, their classroom practices were uncannily similar across the board. They may have used different terminology, but they were in essence saying and doing pretty much the same things in the classroom. The other thing I suspect is that some people were insistent about setting up dichotomies for the sake of debate (personal communication, Aug. 12, 2007).

This was a significant conclusion on my part. That L2 writing scholars were generating debate for the sake of debate is activity that characterizes intellectual communities. The purpose of debate is to energize community members. Strongly stated positions in the literature nurture alliances and antagonize the opposition. This attracts interest and attention and, more often than not, fruitful debate. I realized that I was witnessing not just the birth of a field, but of a discourse community. It was pretty exciting.

Apprenticeship Foregrounded in the Social Context

I became an anthropologist, a gatherer of information about a new academic territory and its inhabitants. With a much better understanding of the tensions that permeated L2 writing, my goal was to interview the entire L2 writing community, or as many of its scholars as was humanly and pragmatically possible. During the course of my research, I managed to interview 35 scholars, a number very close to the entire community of core members.

History needs to be studied in its social context. The purpose of the interviews was to capture firsthand accounts of events taking place in the fledgling field. I read about past events that shaped the field of SLW; they lived them. I set up as many face-to-face interviews as I could, sometimes in conjunction with conferences, which were usually sidewalk snatches and cafeteria chats. I developed the socially ill-mannered habit of following "my people" (as I called them) around at conferences asking seemingly random questions. I had a knack for finding people by attending conference sessions that I suspected would be of interest to them. I knew, for example, that I could always find Bill Grabe at Fredericka Stoller's presentations.

When I wasn't attending conferences, I arranged personal trips. These were special opportunities—private and uninterrupted time of dedicated, serious discussion. There was just something magical about chatting for hours with Ruth Spack in the sitting room of her colonial-style home in Boston, sitting in Vivian Zamel's office at UMass, overlooking the Boston Harbor and soaking in the atmosphere of the room—the books overflowing the shelves, the hundreds of personal photographs pinned to the wall above Vivian's desk, the red watering can next to the radiator on which sat a small cactus plant, or surveying the magnificent view of the Pacific Ocean from Joy Reid's Maui home. After dropping my sandals beside the front door below the sign that read "Mahalo for removing your shoes," I enjoyed the interview with Joy in my bare feet. I was creating social networks and professional friendships. I was engaged in social apprenticeship.

Gaining access to the community via the interview process had its challenges. The first was securing the interviews. In one case, I cornered an L2 writing scholar, who had been particularly reticent to agreeing to an interview, in a restaurant bar after a national TESOL conference. After a moderate quantity of consumption, he finally consented to an interview for a time "in the future." Another scholar, who was unresponsive to emails and phone messages, was quite put out that I phoned him during his office hours to request an interview. My perseverance finally wore him down, and I enjoyed one of the best interviews in my study.

Once interviews were secured, other challenges arose. Some informants spoke willingly and freely. Others were suspicious of my motives and perhaps somewhat skeptical of my capabilities and/or qualifications. Some were irritated by my persistent inquisitiveness. Some ignored emails. One informant once denied an answer to a general information question because she deemed it unessential to my research.

I often asked interviewees to interpret events for me. I was very interested in how the members themselves accounted for disagreements. Most were willing to offer opinions. A few, however, pointed out that analysis and evaluation was my job. Every once in a while, I unwittingly broke interview etiquette and was reprimanded with, "I can't believe you asked me something so ignorant" (a rough translation). I was usually quickly forgiven and the *faux pas* forgotten. Some participants spoke at length or wrote lengthy, detailed email messages. Most found the experience of consciously reflecting on their work during the interview process personally gratifying; they were delighted to participate and expressed genuine enthusiasm over my commitment to L2 writing. I was delighted at being so warmly welcomed into the inner circle of these luminaries in the field.

I felt an affinity toward my participants as they shared their stories, relived historic debates, and reminisced about past events. It was a feeling I once described to Barbara Kroll as a kid on Christmas morning. The interviews produced a feeling of excitement, exhilaration, and intellectual energy that kept me enthused throughout the duration of my study. These scholars shared not only their professional insights, but also their favorite personal stories and memories that they had carried with them for years.

Ann Raimes, one of my interviewees, was the first British transplant onto the American SLW scene. She began her teaching career in the US at Cornell University and later moved to the University of Massachusetts, Amherst where she taught German literature. According to Ann, she "slipped in sideways" to her career in ESL when she decided to leave Boston in 1963 for a sojourn in England to teach ESL. She returned to the US in 1967 and found a part-time job teaching ESL methodology in New York City at the New School for Social Research. Ann would later establish a very successful career at Hunter College of the City University of New York (CUNY), the largest of the CUNY system senior colleges. But in the late 1960s, while she was teaching at the New School, she needed a full-time job. When an ESL position became available at La Guardia Community College, Ann was recommended to the ESL program director, Don Byrd. "Why don't you hire Ann Raimes at the New School?" a former student of Ann's suggested.

"Oh, no!" Byrd replied. "We only hire native speakers" (A. Raimes, personal communication, July 14, 2010).

British English speakers didn't qualify as native speakers? Both Ann and I laughed with delight at this unabashed expression of American English linguistic pride. But, I came to realize that what I had recorded was a remembrance that shouldn't be lost because this extant piece of micro-information better conveyed the reality of the field in the 1960s than I could have ever found in the written records. This bit of local history of a British English ESL teacher who was denied a job in the ESL teaching community at La Guardia because she *was* British is funny, but it is also an early reflection of one of the many issues of politics and power in the field of TESOL.

Another memorable incident that demonstrates the politics of power of a different sort happened to Robert ("Bob") Kaplan. In the early 1970s, Bob met Professor C. M. Yang, a senior academic in Taiwan and a distinguished scholar. Professor Yang was a houseguest of Bob's neighbor, Ed Cornelius, the founder of English Language Services. Kaplan and Yang forged a personal connection. Yang was responsible for English teaching and English Teacher Training at Taiwan Normal University (TNU). He was dubious of the effectiveness of English language education and its supporting teacher training program at TNU. A discussion of the problem led Yang and Kaplan to conceive a language survey to be distributed widely across Taiwan: to secondary school English teachers, to a sample group in the Education Department, to business owners who employed English education graduates, and to select others from whom they hoped to gather feedback regarding attitudes toward English and English education. The project was cleared with the President of USC (Bob Kaplan's home university), the United States Information Agency (USIA) Chief in Taipei, and the Director of the Education Department in Taiwan. With the permission of these high-profile officials, the US government and the Education Department in Taiwan entered into a contractual agreement to study the English language teaching practice in Taiwan and to draw up a list of recommendations for its improvement.

Bob became the study's director. A small team was put in place in Taiwan in the early 1970s. As Professor Kaplan tells it, the team assembled a detailed report intended for submission to the Education Department. After months of work, the report was ready for presentation on a Friday afternoon; its presentation, which included a plan for an elaborate analysis of the report by an international team of language planning specialists, was scheduled for the following Monday.

As luck would have it, on the intervening Saturday afternoon, a high-ranking official was enjoying a casual drive when he encountered a group of Chinese Boy Scouts in need of a ride. Out of kindness, the President picked up the boys and delivered them to their destination. As the boys left the car, wishing to demonstrate what good students they were, they thanked him profusely in English. The generous benefactor, in Kaplan's words, "went up in smoke!" So incensed was he that Taiwanese children would address their president in English that he wrote a scathing editorial that was published in the government-controlled press on Sunday. Early Monday morning, the Americans on the team were invited to leave Taiwan as soon as departure could be arranged, and all activity on the project came to a sudden halt. Upon the hasty end to the efforts, recommendations for the improvement of English language instruction were shelved for the next five years, apparently a reaffirmation of Chinese linguistic pride (R. Kaplan, personal communication, June 15, 2009).

Other nuggets of information I gleaned from interviews created a fuller picture of what factors and experiences shaped their interests. Bob's editing experience prior to his founding of the *Annual Review of Applied Linguistics* included editing the 24th Infantry Division newsletter for a year during the Korean War. Bob worked "from a tent in the field near the town of Chunchon in central Korea, operating with a portable power generator and occasionally under fire" (personal communication, Sept. 7, 2011). What an initiation into professional editing!

Experience wasn't the only shaping influence. Sarah Benesch felt that, for her, one's professional interests were a manifestation of one's temperament. She was raised in the politically charged atmosphere of Washington D.C., and, as a teen, joined the masses in protest against the Vietnam War. Her attraction to critical pedagogy grew out of her interest in politics and civil rights.

I was charmed by the experiences that were shared with me. The stories made me feel connected in an intimate way to the members of the L2 writing community. But, how was I to interpret these mini-narratives as part of the overall meta-narrative of the field? How would the history of SLW have been different if Sarah Benesch had grown up in a small town in the Midwest or Ann Raimes had decided to teach ESL in England or Bob Kaplan's neighbor had not introduced Bob to his Taiwanese house guest?

The biographies I collected were representative of three controlling factors of any social formation, what Strain (2000) has identified as the "operative factors": 1) external factors over which there is no control (e.g., growing up in the Washington D.C. area); 2) individual choices (e.g., deciding to reside in the US to teach ESL); and 3) serendipity (e.g., a chance acquaintance with a Taiwanese diplomat). The biographies were important to me because they opened many small windows to the dynamic, complex, multi-layered socially constructed environment that represented the discipline of SLW and its membership, and ultimately helped me to make sense of the data I was collecting.

Apprenticeship Foregrounded Again in the Academic Context

Writing the Dissertation

The 35 interviews I conducted yielded at least one thousand pages of provocative information. Conducting interviews motivated additional study and research, but invariably, the information I gathered, both from the interviews and from my extensive reading of the literature, had to come together into a tangible product with a certain structure and rhetorical shape, a document that had to meet the pre-conceived expectations of a panel of experts who would judge its merit.

Chris Hall, my former professor and a dissertation committee member, was always generous with his time in answering questions, but Dan had the greatest influence on the shape of the dissertation. He read literally every word of every draft I sent including footnotes, appendices, and bibliography. His comments were copious and his suggestions specific. Dan addressed every dimension of the document I was producing: style, organization, form, and content. Here is a sample excerpt in which he commented on the manuscript for style, form, and clarity:

> Sometimes your writing style is too telegraphic and too direct ("dear reader") which went out with the eighteenth century novel. Try to be more discursive and expository. Don't introduce new info without first having prior mention. Avoid running compound semi-coloned sentences together. It all conveys breathless haste which makes for reader uneasiness. When you are meaning narrative, stick with that and don't convert to exposition. (personal communication, August 13, 2010)

Dan evaluated even the manuscript conventions: "The MS needs to follow APA 6 style (the newly adopted Department and Grad School standard). Revise your headings, reference list, etc., accordingly" (personal communication, August 13, 2010).

In addition to the mechanics of the document, Dan commented on global organization. He was able to see emergent historical themes when I could not. His suggestion to thematize was a stroke of genius on his part that enabled me to develop a coherent strategy for presenting the wealth of information that I had accumulated. Here is a sample excerpt:

> Thematize the section on NYU. Here it is (a) [the] role of practice in developing the emerging field, (b) the discovery of the subject, i.e. immigrant and gen 1.5 L2 writers, (c) [the] commitment to change the status quo of composition to student-centered processes and research, (d) the role of [composition studies] in shaping the path in L2 writing. (personal communication August 13, 2010)

These were practical suggestions that brought a much-needed unity to the entire dissertation. Dan had firsthand knowledge of the happenings in the field. He filled in gaps in the content, directing me to investigate key people or concepts in more depth. Here is an example:

> There are areas of the field that are largely missing from your account. They are not really major omissions but it would be nice to somehow acknowledge their inclusion.
>
> As I mention, there was an "applied" linguistics movement in English education, which was supported by NCTE. This included the work of Mellon (syntactic maturity), O'Hare, and later Daiker, Kerek, and Morenberger (sentence combining).
>
> Also, when you discuss the Dartmouth Project, please talk about Albert Kitzhaber's *Themes, Theories, and Therapy: The Teaching of Writing in College* (1963) which was based on the Dartmouth College Study *of which he was the director.* I studied under Kitzhaber at the University of Oregon where I first taught composition. According to the *Teachers College Record* (65,5, 1964, p. 469) "This book, in short, is in a sense subversive—subversive at least from the point of view of most college English departments." Kitzhaber also wrote a middle and

high school curriculum in Oregon known as the Oregon Project which applied transformational grammar to the teaching of English writing. So we have two themes here (i) the influence of "applied" linguistics (ii) the influence of L1 composition. (personal communication August 13, 2010)

The intersection of the parent disciplines of applied linguistics and composition studies, even though relatively brief, is important to the history of SLW. I witnessed the social transmission of ideas through Dan's personal connection to Albert Kitzhaber. More importantly, the extended exchanges between Dan and me on style, organization, and content helped to sharpen my awareness of community expectations. Dan was coaching me on ways to best represent myself to the L2 writing community. In this way, my own disciplinary identity was starting to form. It was another step in the initiation process.

Dan was not only my textual mentor, but he was also a key participant in the study. He was an informant whose role in the study of SLW was that of *field builder* or, as Paul Kei Matsuda termed these individuals, *field engineers*. Dan's (1995) *A Guide to Writing in English as a Second or Foreign Language: An Annotated Bibliography of Research and Pedagogy* spans a 60-year period beginning in 1934, listing 3,461 entries; it was the first comprehensive review of research in L2 writing. Dan's annotated bibliography made a unique contribution to the field in that it provided concrete evidence of a growing scholarly community and was an objective record of the development of a body of knowledge that represented L2 writing. It also served to identify people who were researching and writing about L2 writing. In a reflection of the significance of his own work, Dan compared the beginnings of SLW with an inaugural ball. By identifying the L2 writing community members in the bibliography, he had drawn up what he called a "guest list" and, according to Dan, the "party" was thrown by Tony Silva, Ilona Leki, and the *Journal of Second Language Writing* (personal communication, August 2009). Dan played a unique role in the development of the dissertation and the entire apprenticeship process. I knew I could test ideas and hypotheses on him and get un-biased, critical, comprehensive feedback.

Another mentor who added a unique dimension to my initiation into SLW was Bob Kaplan. At age 86, Bob is the oldest member of the SLW community, and the first of the first generation scholars. I was deeply gratified when he took an interest in my research. He edited my writing for clarity, mailed material he thought I could use, and emailed articles and citation information. Bob had an incredible ability to recall names, dates, and details when I needed them. He provided a wealth of historical information. Bob also read, commented on, and corrected parts of the dissertation that related to Applied Linguistics. His insight was always welcomed.

Bob pointed out to me that like any sensible person, I assumed that a field like SLW came together in some sort of orderly and logical process. He assured me on more than one occasion that it did not. Historical accounts that appear neat and tidy don't necessarily reflect reality. Bob did his best to supply me with the reality of events as they transpired in Applied Linguistics (personal communication, Oct. 5, 2011). Below is a short email excerpt in which Bob recounted one of those less-than-orderly-and-logical processes in the editing of the *Annual Review of Applied Linguistics*:

> The board and I tried to keep in control, and for the most part we did, but in truth we were often all amazed that [the journal] kept working. To tell the truth the first minutes at every Board meeting were spent in self-congratulation that we had collectively produced yet another volume. (personal communication, Sept. 3, 2011)

These and other accounts privileged me with an insider view of events on the way knowledge was disseminated to the greater community and the challenges that were overcome to do so. Such accounts demonstrated that despite the elusive nature of the nascent discipline of L2 writing, its existence was indeed palpable, realized by what its members did and how they did it.

Bob and I emailed often. He was prompt at answering my questions. Sometimes he emailed just to check my progress. Sometimes he emailed to encourage me along. At one point near the end of the writing, I had, what I can best describe as, a doctoral student identity crisis. I felt censored and restrained in what I could and could not write, ever mindful of my place as a junior scholar and my limited authority to speak. One email exchange, in particular, expressed my frustration:

> I really like my research topic and am fascinated with the events. I wish that my writing was better able to capture the

excitement I feel when I write. Part of it is that I don't feel like I have the authority to speak like Maureen Goggin speaks in *Authoring a Discipline*, for example. When I first read Ilona Leki's *ARAL* 2000 piece [in which she questions the subordinate position of SLW in relation to applied linguistics], I got the sense that she was bold and passionate [about the independent status of SLW] on the one hand, but hesitant to be too bold or be too adversarial on the other in order to try to maintain her objectivity. But I don't feel I can say that. "Fraught with tension" is as close as I get. And notice that Silva and Leki's (2004) call to the field in "Family Matters" is prefaced with "...it *might be best* [I added the italics here] for L2 writing to think of itself as a discipline in its own right." It was as if they were trying to be polite by hedging the statement with "it might be best." It is obvious to me that these were clarion calls for the self-assertion of the field, but I don't feel that I can say that either. During the course of my research, I have read many dull dissertations. I think other doctoral students really struggle with the issue of voice and identity, too. (personal communication, Oct. 5, 2011)

I was attempting to manufacture what Ken Hyland (2012), in his work on disciplinary identity, would call a credible academic identity, constructing my identity for L2 writing readers by "appropriating and shaping the discourses" (p. 1) that linked me to their community. Through my linguistic choices, I wanted to appear reasonable in my argument and plausible in my claim. I was learning through the interaction with my mentors that readers evaluate academic discourse through the lens of their disciplinary proclivities. I wanted to follow the rules of engagement; yet, I felt confined.

Here is Bob's response:

> Lord knows, there are literally thousands of dull dissertations; part of the problem lies with the form of the dissertation itself—dissertations are not expected to be groundbreaking. Dissertations are an appeal for a union card; they are designed to require the author to demonstrate that s/he knows how to dig out facts, arrange them in some reasonable order and draw them together into some sort of workman-like synthesis. Note: the words *exciting, interesting, useful, important*

do not appear in my definition. On the contrary, the incipient doctor is required to be cautious, careful, inoffensive, and to observe all the constraints on the research article. (personal communication, Oct. 5, 2011)

Bob went on to cite Atkinson (1999) who researched the historic origin of *hedging* in science writing. He added at the end, "[K]eep going, and remember that your ultimate objective is directed to your readers, not yourself." I found the email reassuring, especially since it came from such a prestigious member of the L2 writing community. It was also a reminder that the dissertation was a ritual in the apprenticeship process through which each initiate must pass. More importantly, however, Bob reaffirmed the existence of the unwritten code of discourse conduct and encouraged me to respect the community social norms in order to satisfy the expectations of my readers. I heeded his advice.

CONCLUSION

I have now been successfully apprenticed into the SLW community. The reflections of my socioacademic experience that I shared here were not the only opportunities I had to interact with the members of the L2 writing community. I still remember my first conference presentation on the social history of SLW. I presented in a slot reserved for graduate study research. I knew that my thoughts on the topic were only roughly defined and my research still in the embryonic stages of discovery. It was risky especially in the presence of SLW luminaries—Dwight Atkinson, Paul Kei Matsuda, and Tony Silva—who were sitting together in the fourth row from the front in a very crowded classroom where the presentation was held. The presentation was not stellar, but the audience was sympathetic and it was a memorable apprenticeship experience. It was thrilling for me to be able to answer questions from the fellow graduate students in the audience about the field.

The L2 writing community created this opportunity for me. It was the first, but not the last of other opportunities to come. By interacting directly with Dan Tannacito, Chris Hall, Bob Kaplan, and other members of the SLW community, I was able to carve out my own unique apprenticeship space. It was a space in which I thrived. Perhaps my entry was a little tangential in its approach. I was apprenticed not by a handful of experts in a single university context, but by an entire community of extraordinary scholars whose collective knowledge and experience spanned the globe and four decades. My journey was unique, but everyone's journey into academia is. Each of us has a story to tell.

References

Atkinson, D. (1999). *Scientific discourse in sociohistorical context: The philosophical transactions of the Royal Society of London, 1675-1975.* Mahwah, NJ: Lawrence Erlbaum.

Belcher, D. (1989). How professors initiate nonnative speakers into the academic discourse community. Paper presented at the 40th Annual CCCC Meeting, Seattle, WA.

Belcher, D. (1994). The apprenticeship approach to advanced academic literacy: Graduate students, and their mentors. *English for Specific Purposes, 13*, 23-34.

Belcher, D., & Braine, G. (Eds.). (1995). *Academic writing in a second language: Essays on research and pedagogy.* Norwood, NJ: Ablex.

Blanton, L. L. (1987). Reshaping ESL students' perceptions of writing. *ELT Journal, 41*(2), 112-118.

Blanton, L. L. (1995). Elephants and paradigms: Conversations about teaching L2 writing. *College ESL, 5*(1), 1-21.

Blanton, L. L. (2005). Student, interrupted: A tale of two would-be writers. *Journal of Second Language Writing, 14*(2), 105-121.

Blanton, L. L., & Kroll, B. (Eds.). (2002). *ESL composition tales: Reflections on teaching.* Ann Arbor: University of Michigan Press.

Braine, G. (1999). From the periphery to the center: One teacher's journey. In G. Braine (Ed.), *Non-native educators in English language teaching* (pp. 15-27). Mahwah, NJ: Lawrence Erlbaum.

Canagarajah, A. S. (2001). The fortunate traveler: Shuttling between communities and literacies by economy class. In D. Belcher & U. Connor (Eds.), *Reflections on multiliterate lives* (pp. 23-37). Buffalo, NY: Multilingual Matters LTD.

Casanave, C. P. (1995). Local interactions: Constructing contexts for composing in a graduate sociology program. In D. Belcher & G. Braine (Eds.), *Academic writing in a second language. Essays on research and pedagogy* (pp. 83-110). Norwood, NJ: Ablex.

Casanave, C. P. (2002). *Writing games: Multicultural case studies of academic literacy practices in higher education.* Mahwah, NJ: Lawrence Erlbaum.

Connor, U. (1999). Learning to write academic prose in a second language: A literacy autobiography. In G. Braine (Ed.), *Non-native educators in English language teaching,* (pp. 29-52). Mahwah, NJ: Lawrence Erlbaum.

Ferris, D., & Hedgcock, J. (2005). *Teaching ESL composition: Purpose, process, and practice* (2nd ed.). Mahwah, NJ: Lawrence Erlbaum.

Grabe, W. (2001). Notes toward a theory of second language writing. In T. Silva & P. K. Matsuda (Eds.), *On second language writing* (pp. 39-58). Mahwah, NJ: Lawrence Erlbaum Associates.

Hyland, K. (2000). *Disciplinary discourses: Social interactions in academic writing.* New York, NY: Cambridge University Press.

Hyland, K. (2012). *Disciplinary identities: Individuality and community in academic discourse.* New York, NY: Longman.

Kitzhaber, A. (1963). *Themes, theories, and therapy: The teaching of writing in college.* New York: McGraw Hill.

Kroll, B. (2006). Toward a promised land of writing: At the intersection of hope and reality. In P. K. Matsuda, C. Ortmeier-Hooper, & X. You (Eds.), *The politics of second language writing* (pp. 297-305). West Lafayette, IN: Parlor Press.

Leki, I. (2000). Writing, literacy, and applied linguistics. *Annual Review of Applied Linguistics, 20,* 99-115.

Leki, I. (2006). Negotiating socioacademic relations: English learners' reception by and reaction of college faculty. *JEAP, 5,* 136-152.

Leki, I. (2007). *Undergraduates in a second language: Challenges and complexities of academic literacy development.* New York, NY: Lawrence Erlbaum.

Power, K. (Dec/Jan 2005). Talking about writing: Collaborative writing for young ELLs. *ESL Magazine, 43,* 18-21.

Power, K. A. (2012). *A social history of second language writing: First generation L2 composition scholars in the Process Era.* Unpublished doctoral dissertation, Indiana University of Pennsylvania, Indiana, PA.

Reid, J. (1984). The radical outliner and the radical brainstormer. A perspective on composing processes. *TESOL Quarterly, 18*(3), 529-534.

Reid, J. (1985). The author responds to Spack. *TESOL Quarterly, 19*(2), 398-400.

Roca de Larios, J., Murphy, L., & Marin, J. (2002). Critical examination of L2 writing process research. In S. Randsdell & M. Barbier (Eds.), *New directions for research in L2 writing* (pp.11-48). Boston: Kluwer Academic Publishers.

Shen, F. (1989). The classroom and the wider culture: Identity as a key to learning English composition. *College Composition and Communication, 40*(4), 459-466.

Silva, T. (1990). Second language composition instruction: Developments, issues, and directions in ESL. In B. Kroll (Ed.), *Second language writing research: Insights for the classroom* (pp. 11-23). New York, NY: Cambridge University Press.

Silva, T., & Leki, I. (2004). Family matters: The influence of applied linguistics and composition studies on second language writing studies—past, present, and future. *The Modern Language Journal, 88*(1), 1-13.

Spack, R. (1985). Comments on Joy Reid's "Radical outliner and the radical brainstormer: A perspective on composing processes." A reader reacts. *TESOL Quarterly, 19*(2), 396-398.

Spack, R. (1997a). The acquisition of academic literacy in a second language. *Written Communication, 14*(3), 3-62.

Spack, R. (1997b). The rhetorical construction of multilingual students. *TESOL Quarterly, 31*(4), 765-774.

Strain, M. M. (2000). Local histories, rhetorical negotiations: The development of doctoral programs in rhetoric and composition. *Rhetoric Society Quarterly 30*(2), 57-76.

Strevens, P. (1979). Differences in teaching for different circumstances or the teacher as chameleon. In C. A. Yorio, K. Perkins, & J. Schachter (Eds.), *On TESOL '79: The learner in focus: Selected papers from the thirteenth annual convention of Teachers of English to Speakers of Other Languages* (pp. 2-11), Boston, MA, Feb. 27-Mar. 4, 1979. Washington, DC: TESOL.

Tannacito, D. (1995). *A guide to writing in English as a second or foreign language: An annotated bibliography of research and pedagogy.* Alexandria, VA: Teaching English to Speakers of Other Languages.

Zamel, V. (1995). Strangers in academia: The experiences of ESL Students and faculty across the curriculum. *College Composition and Communication, 46*(4), 20-35.

Zamel, V., & Spack, R. (1998). *Negotiating academic literacies: Teaching and learning across languages and cultures.* Mahwah, NJ: Lawrence Erlbaum.

Zamel, V., & Spack, R. (2004). *Crossing the curriculum: Teaching multilingual learners in college classrooms.* New York, NY: Lawrence Erlbaum.

4 Doctoring Yourself: Seven Steps

Alister Cumming

Undertaking doctoral studies is an enormous commitment, involving consequential choices and extensive time and effort to establish distinct abilities, knowledge, and relationships that profoundly affect a person's scholarly potential and career prospects. For these reasons, like parenting or retirement, there is much individual variability in how people prepare for, perform in, and make use of a doctoral degree, even within a particular field like language and literacy education.

Reflecting on my own experiences, I can see seven basic steps that people tend to take prior to, during, and after completing a PhD:

1. Shopping
2. Investing
3. Studying
4. Researching
5. Proposing
6. Reporting
7. Establishing

I do not want to suggest anything mystical or doctrinaire about this number nor the substance or stages of these steps, which overlap and interact. The tune of Miles Davis's 1963 recording "Seven Steps to Heaven" kept coming into my head (in a manner right out of Sacks, 2007) as I mulled over what advice I might offer to people planning or doing a PhD or working in other PhD programs related to second language writing. I wonder, though, in hindsight, if that tune was appearing in earnest or in irony, as heaven is scarcely the location to which one should expect doctoral studies might lead. At any rate, I was led to formulate these steps by asking myself, in my experience with PhD students (and of course as someone who once did a PhD myself, from 1984 to 1988):

- What processes do I usually see?
- What issues emerge?
- What advice can I offer?

Thinking about these matters as well from the perspective of professors teaching in graduate schools, I also asked myself, and I conclude this article with, the question: How might these issues and suggestions be addressed effectively in a university PhD program related to second language writing?

My observations are based on doctoral programs that involve course work, usually full-time for two years, prior to embarking on a thesis or dissertation study, as is the norm in North America. This context differs from many programs in Europe, Australia, New Zealand, or some parts of Asia, where doctoral students begin to work on a thesis from the start of their programs and without the benefit of preparatory courses. So I should caution readers about the contextual bias of my observations and experiences, based on my working at various universities in Canada (Toronto for the longest period but also British Columbia, McGill, Carleton, and Concordia) as well as shorter periods as a visiting professor at the universities of Auckland, Beijing Foreign Studies, Copenhagen, Hong Kong, Hong Kong Polytechnic, Macquarie, Michigan, Nagoya, and Pennsylvania State. My sense, from now having supervised, read, and/or examined hundreds of PhD theses in Canada and around the world, is that the format and substance of the final written documents for a PhD thesis are fundamentally consistent, but the requirements and nature of doctoral programs vary greatly from place to place in terms of preparatory courses, exams, and relations between students and professors as well as the types and qualities of supporting services and resources available locally.

I should note, as well, that the Ontario Institute for Studies in Education at the University of Toronto, where I have worked since 1991, and where I did my own doctorate in the mid-1980s, has Canada's largest, most established set of PhD programs in education, involving 835 PhD students (as of September 2012). Usually, each year, about 45 PhD students continue, and five to seven incoming students begin, the specific program in Second Language Education where I teach, alongside a slightly larger number of students doing several types of Masters degrees either full-or part-time.

SEVEN STEPS

Shopping

Before embarking on a PhD program, a person has to decide on a particular program, make an application for it, and be accepted into it. Easier said than done. Only a certain number of universities around the world have certified, reputable PhD programs related to Language Education, Applied Linguistics, or Composition Studies, though most major research-oriented universities do have at least one (in various types of departments in faculties of arts, social sciences, or education). An increasing number of such programs have appeared each year over past decades. However, entry into the best, established programs is highly competitive and selective, primarily because programs are (virtually) obliged, because of the long-term commitment to full-time specialized studies (i.e., four to seven years), to offer scholarships or some form of guaranteed funding such as teaching or research assistantships; and for reasons of available resources, both financial and human, programs can only provide a few of these annually.

So a person preparing to enter a PhD program necessarily has to shop around to identify the program best suited to one's goals and interests, personal financial resources and commitments to family and/or work, and geographical or societal location (i.e., close to or far from home; in the same or different society). Moreover, the competitive nature of program selection requires most people to apply to several PhD programs and be willing to accept a second or third choice if a first choice is not available.

How does one do this specialized kind of shopping? Internet sites offer extensive, detailed information on established PhD programs (and if they do not, then one might well be wary). Many programs also publish brochures, distributing them at conferences or around their own or nearby campuses, and they may advertise in relevant journals, newsletters, or discussion groups. At a more personal level, the reputation (both positive and negative) of PhD programs can be ascertained by talking to graduates of the programs, seeking advice from one's current professors, attending conferences to see professors or graduate students present their work, and reviewing key journals and other publications to identify scholars doing research or discussing ideas of interest. The choice for individuals is, fundamentally, determining what has recently been done by professors, current students, and recent graduates of PhD programs, and then deciding whether one wants to learn studiously from and emulate those accomplishments or not. Someone told me long ago, look around carefully at the professors in the program, and see if you like what they do, because eventually you will become one of them. A scary thought, yes, but in my experience all too true.

To evaluate the suitability and desirability of a PhD program, one wants to consider its institutional capacity and history. Is the program widely recognized by others to be of good quality, producing a certain number of successful graduates within reasonable periods of time, and involving a critical mass of experienced professors and courses to provide substantial courses in a range of relevant topics? Do the professors actively engage in high quality research sufficient to guide or support thesis studies effectively? Is the program firmly established, or might it be new and emerging or be declining from its former glory? There are advantages and disadvantages to all three of these states, and historical cycles through which all programs and universities inevitably pass. You also need to ask yourself personal questions like: What intrigues me? What does the program excel at? Why should I want to go there? What will I become if I do?

I recall asking myself these kinds of questions before I decided to apply to the University of Toronto, among several other possible universities in Canada, to do my own PhD as well as while talking with, and obtaining valuable advice from, professors I had met at conferences who had themselves established successful research careers after graduating from the same program in Toronto, specifically, Robert Anthony at the University of Victoria, Sima Paribakht at the University of Ottawa, and especially the late Craig Chaudron at the University of Hawaii. I took the opportunities as well to see conference presentations and talk with professors from the doctoral program at the University of Toronto, including Patrick Allen, Jim Cummins, and David Stern, and I was impressed by all of them, though in different ways.

Everyone applying for a PhD program does so from the vantage point of a Master's degree, and often with the benefit of teaching or research experience. So various personal questions need to be asked too: Will the PhD program build on, extend, complement, or differ from my Master's degree, teaching experiences, and research interests? Firm advice I was given by several professors during my Master's degree (at a point in my life when I had no particular inclinations to do a PhD) was to do a doctoral degree at a university different from the one I was then attending. It took me some years, observing others, to see the wisdom of their advice: Doing both graduate degrees at different institutions greatly expands one's experience, knowledge, and capacities, which can easily become saturated if a student takes full advantage of a Master's program and thesis research.

Investing

After deciding where to apply, one has to make a commitment based on the criteria mentioned above and, particularly, a sincere appraisal of what one wants to do and to become. One has to buy firmly into the program, if I may extend the shopping metaphor. Everyone working in language or literacy education benefits visibly—in terms of knowledge, abilities, and ways of reasoning—from completing a Master's degree. But only a few people really need to make the long-term commitment needed to complete a doctoral degree. The fundamental reason to do a doctoral program is to become a university professor, though a few people do take up careers in related fields of research or scholarship such as policy analysts in governmental or non-governmental agencies or researchers in school boards or educational administration. The commitment to become a scholarly researcher is what drives successful doctoral candidates through the four to seven years of intense, full-time work needed to complete the degree. There are options for part-time doctoral studies, particularly for those with positions of employment they want to retain while they study and develop themselves, but everyone I have seen embark on that option has struggled severely for seven to ten years to complete the degree and not been satisfied with the experience, and many have decided to opt out in order to maintain commitments to work and/or families rather than to complete the degree.

The material realization of commitment to a doctoral program appears in the statement of purpose or intent that accompanies an application to the degree program. Professors judging applications to PhD programs pay particular attention to these statements alongside other information such as recommendation letters, grades from previous courses, and the quality and relevance of prior degrees and work experience. For this reason, in preparing a statement of purpose, a person should take special care to assess and state one's goals and future aspirations clearly and sincerely, relate these logically to one's prior education and work experience, and align them all directly to what the program can offer in terms of professors' interests, course offerings, and institutional reputation. Doing this requires self-examination, some familiarity with the specific program (e.g., at a minimum through Web searches), and clarity of thought and intention. However, accomplishing all this can be tricky if a person is applying to several different PhD programs at once, as the orientations, faculty members and their interests, and program content inevitably differ between programs.

As noted above, the competitive nature of admissions to PhD programs, plus annual cycles of admission and funding decisions, require that most applicants apply to several different institutions at the same time, expecting to be accepted into one or more of their top choices. I should observe here, though, that under conditions of competition, decisions about admissions may depend heavily on an assessment of the relative fit between an applicant's statement of purpose and the available offerings, capacities, and orientations in a specific program, above and beyond grades, recommendations, and prior experience. For these reasons, applicants may never be able to know exactly why they have, or have not, been accepted into a particular PhD program beyond the most basic, advertised qualifications (just as in applying for employment for university faculty positions, hiring committees decide on applicants based on complex criteria and sets of interests that are difficult to ascertain outside of the context of deliberations within a committee).

Another type of investment made earlier in one's academic studies, in preparation for a PhD program, is to do a thesis during one's Master's degree. The research, writing, and analytic skills and knowledge acquired in the process of conducting the more minor, focused research typically done for a Master's thesis provides a distinct, useful foundation to plan for and conduct a more extensive thesis study for a PhD. This foundation research experience can, nonetheless, be acquired in professional circumstances too, for example, through conducting and writing up various types of research in one's workplace such as program evaluations, action research, or curriculum innovations. Indeed, I have to acknowledge that the latter route was what I did in the several years that I taught ESL between completing my Master's degree (without a thesis) and then deciding that I needed to do a PhD (in order to learn to do research effectively and to obtain a full-time, tenured position at a university). I thereby compiled over those years a portfolio of research-oriented reports and publications that I could submit in place of a Master's thesis when applying for the PhD program.

Most Master's degrees now involve courses only, rather than a thesis, for the benefit of the majority of people who do a Master's degree to develop their professional abilities—for example, as educators—rather than to embark on a scholarly career by spending the extra half year or year needed to complete a Master's thesis. Entry into the better PhD programs around the world now usually requires completion of a Master's thesis or comparable portfolio of research-oriented accomplishments. Over the years working with many doctoral students, I have come to see that this advance preparation during the Master's degree is useful, and perhaps even necessary, as PhD students plan thesis research, engage in rigorous analytic methods, and do the writing and assembly of the large document that typifies a doctoral thesis, experiential abilities that do not come just from writing short papers for courses during either a Master's or PhD program.

Studying

There are diverse ways in which learning occurs, and multiple opportunities for different kinds of professional development that appear, in a specialized program of advanced studies. In selecting from the myriad possible choices for courses, part-time work, and other activities, one simple principle that I have always adhered to in graduate studies is to "follow your interests!" Interests are what motivate a person to acquire new knowledge and abilities and to persevere though the long stretch of independent studies and thesis research. But that principle also entails defining one's interests and relating them to available opportunities and resources. I also advise doctoral students to specialize in one or two areas, and to aim to know everything (quite literally) that is known about them from reading and from interacting with others. At the same time, it is important to develop a general, comprehensive knowledge about the field of one's studies, not only in order to be informed across the field and related domains, but also because after completing the PhD, newly hired professors are usually expected to teach basic introductory courses (such as teaching methods, curriculum organization, or language or literacy acquisition) in addition to teaching and doing research in their areas of specializations.

To achieve these aims, talk with knowledgeable others, and read extensively and strategically; I suggest about three times more than may be prescribed in courses and well beyond the basic level that students do in Master's programs. Read, read, and read. Plan to become an expert, not just competent. Select courses that will expand your knowledge to include, but go well beyond, the ordinary. Do courses, as well, that lead to thesis research, focusing on relevant research methods, exploring new ideas and approaches to inquiry, and getting to know professors who may be a supervisor or member of your thesis committee. Establish groups of like-minded student peers in your courses, spend time talking with them outside of classes, and discuss mutual and differing professional and scholarly interests. These people will form a supportive resource during your studies as well as sympathetic colleagues well into the future. Exchange and comment on drafts of each other's course papers before submitting them, aiming to improve your sense of what makes for effective and interesting written texts in your field. During courses, while reading to know all that you can about topics, seek out principles and frameworks that relate theories to practical issues in education, policies, and empirical inquiry. Look for explanations of puzzling phenomena in order to make sense of, and while acquiring, information about them. Become a scholar not just a student.

Researching

Apprentice yourself, as well, into becoming a researcher. Courses in doctoral programs are expected to prepare students for thesis research, and knowing how to do research is a hallmark expectation of a person with a PhD in the social sciences and humanities. But the means to these ends vary as do the range of topics and approaches to inquiry that exist in a field as vast and diverse as language and literacy education. Within courses, do syntheses of recent research or meta-analyses on topics that will lead to your thesis research. At a more experiential level, orient your course assignments to try out preliminary tasks, develop research instruments, or practice methods of analysis that will lead to your thesis research.

To involve themselves in the broader professional community, doctoral students should participate often in (and even organize) scholarly colloquia, conferences, and study groups, not only locally but also nationally and internationally. The most profound apprenticeship types of research experience, however, can come from working with a professor and a team of other graduate students and researchers on a long-term project, either related to or different from one's thesis interests. As documented in several publications arising from some of my own research projects, graduate student researchers can work productively and supportively together to accomplish the aims of a project while also acquiring and practicing fundamental skills in preparing for, gathering, analyzing, interpreting, and reporting research data (Cumming, 2006, 2012; Cumming, Shi & So, 1997). For doctoral students who may not have opportunities to work in these ways with a professor, students themselves can organize small-scale projects focused on their own learning, teaching circumstances, or other interests. Opportunities to do research are what doctoral programs should provide and involve. Expanding one's repertoire of research activities beyond thesis inquiry itself also adds value to one's doctoral experience and employment prospects.

Proposing

Deciding on, refining, and conducting one's own thesis research is the central, consequential, and culminating element in a doctoral program. Preparing a thesis proposal is where doctoral candidates are wise to seek advice from as many people as are reasonably relevant. My advice to people at this stage of a doctoral program is as follows: Focus on a topic that intrigues you, answering a question to which you really want to know the answer (and nobody else really does). If you are an experienced teacher, language learner, or writer, consider an issue that has intrigued you but for which current explanations do not exist or are questionable. Aim to contribute usefully to current knowledge generally, as well, by relating theories and past research to fundamental issues in educational or societal policies and practices. Choose a supervisor who is knowledgeable about and interested in the topic as well as members of the thesis committee who have complementary expertise in key aspects of the topic or its research methods. These are all major decisions, not only because you will spend at least two or three years doing the research, but also because the thesis study will shape the following decade of your career, informing your publications and reputation as well as the subsequent studies you might expect to do.

Take the time to refine the proposal by showing it to and seeking suggestions from other graduate students and various professors, incorporating their questions or recommendations into your plan. Likewise, present the plan in local colloquia and study groups. Before embarking on a full study, try out the research methods and instruments in preliminary, small-scale, or pilot studies. Make sure that the methods of data collection are feasible and worthwhile, providing the quality of information, within reasonable time and conditions, needed to answer the research questions satisfactorily. Be certain the instruments to be used are valid, either by adopting them from published, recognized studies or validating them systematically yourself (recognizing that the process of creating and validating new research instruments such as tests or questionnaires is extensive and can, in itself, constitute the object of thesis research). Consider, as well, the methods for analyzing the data, ensuring that you know how to employ them competently and reliably if statistics or interpretive methods are involved.

Reporting

Write, write, and write throughout the doctoral program, and especially (but not only) to report on the thesis study:
- to inform yourself and others,
- to become a participating member of the professional discourse community,
- to learn as much as possible in and about varied, relevant text genres and contexts,
- as a single and as a co-author (with peers and professors),
- to establish your scholarly reputation, and

- to know how to write better, conforming to and mastering conventional styles (e.g., such as APA formats) and relevant genres.

Present the findings from your thesis research in oral and written forms, in preliminary ways to your professors and peers, seeking their advice. Follow up with presentations at colloquia locally and conferences nationally or internationally, looking for responses from interested experts and then addressing their concerns systematically. Everyone who does a thesis has a professional obligation and substantive basis to publish a synthesis of the results of their study in the form of an article. For the sake of one's reputation, and to make the knowledge from a thesis widely known, leading international journals are undoubtedly the medium of choice, but regional journals, limited distribution book publishers, or even local venues that can be read and cited may be a fallback alternative if submissions to international journals do not pan out.

Indeed, getting the results of a doctoral thesis study into some form of print has become an implicit expectation for most job competitions or tenure decisions at universities. For recent PhDs, the comments of journal reviewers on a manuscript, however, can at first impression seem unduly harsh. So, we all need to be reminded of principles like the following: Every response to a manuscript or conference presentation signifies something worth addressing in some way. Professors and journal reviewers always want, and strive with considerable effort, to make things better. Everyone engages in the professional discourse community to contribute to current knowledge and to the community itself. Quality and reputation matter. Moreover, they appeal to and interest people. It has always surprised me how many people read, quote, and send me messages from around the world about publications I have written.

Establishing

Graduating with a PhD is a major, distinctive accomplishment, but it is just the beginning of establishing an academic career. The final stages or upshot of a doctoral program, therefore, extend several years after a thesis has been submitted, defended, and accepted. Optimally, while completing the thesis most doctoral candidates will want to apply for a university faculty or related position. My advice on this stage is as follows: Apply for positions you are uniquely qualified for and sincerely interested in. Use all available professional networks to seek these out: professors, conferences, associations, listservs, and student peers. Above all else, publish as much and as well as possible. People read, cite, and respect journal articles. To an extent that has often surprised me, they are the principal means of, and commodity for, gaining respect and professional recognition in scholarly circles. Most hiring committees at universities want to hire a new professor who they can be certain will obtain tenure and contribute productively to their program and reputation, both of which require ample, notable publications.

Once in a university or similar position, persevere to continue to publish, while also learning to teach well and perform university and professional service. I reiterate, people read and respect journal articles and other publications. Publish, publish, and publish. To provide the substance for new publications, embark on new research projects, small and large, following from your thesis research. At the same time, create a culture around your research interests and expertise through ongoing seminars, study groups, and preliminary projects leading to larger ones. As a professor, link the courses you teach to your developing research program so that they build on and inform each other rather than pull in different directions. Collaborate, as well, with professional colleagues, near and afar, based on new as well as established contacts. Needless to say, become a mentor and model for masters' and doctoral students yourself.

Concluding Remarks: How Can University Programs Facilitate These Seven Steps?

For a doctoral student to be able to engage in any of the seven steps outlined above necessitates that a university program is able to facilitate, promote, and sustain these processes. Doctoral programs exist in and as institutional contexts, rather than through individual initiatives, though institutional and individual efforts and activities should ideally work together to serve complementary purposes. A university program for doctoral studies bears several responsibilities to make these things happen. One is to build a cultural community focused on research and doctoral studies. Doing so may be a slow and challenging development process. I have observed this in various programs with established teacher certification and masters' programs that decide to expand into doctoral studies as well. Unlike short-term educational programs, doctoral students take many years to complete their degrees, requiring unique and specialized resources and attention along the way. These may include support from writing tutors, short courses, or centers; reference librarians; peer groups of graduate students; models of effective research completed; and copy-editors of thesis drafts. Creating a vibrant culture of thesis-oriented research can, likewise, be a challenge, for example, requiring the coordination of ongoing seminar series, both formal and informal, in which doctoral students, professors, and visiting scholars share their ongoing and completed research in ways that are professionally engaging and fulfilling.

Administrators of doctoral programs are, of course, obliged to attract the most talented and able students locally and internationally by promoting the program on the Internet, through participation and interactions at conferences, and ongoing email communications with prospective, current, and completed students—while making clear requirements and expectations for students and faculty alike. Perhaps the most effective way to attract the best students, however, is for professors to publish significant research and theoretical work. As I reiterated above, people respect, and are drawn to, published research and influential ideas. Applicants to doctoral programs often want to study with professors whose reputations they have read about in publications and discussed in previous courses or professional circles. An equally important element is to ensure the long-term success of student graduates in their careers. Success breeds success. Prospective students appeal to the opinions and experiences of recently graduated students. Doctoral programs also need to plan for long-term development and renewal of faculty and resources, considerations that are increasingly difficult under conditions of economic constraint.

Each doctoral program also has to a establish unique niche, to distinguish one program from other competing programs, while at the same time establishing a breadth of expertise across topics relevant to the field in order to provide courses that fulfill conventional expectations and provide a range of domains of and orientations to scholarly inquiry. For example, the graduate program in Second Language Education at the Ontario Institute for Studies in Education has strived (though faculty appointments, research projects, and admission of doctoral students) to maintain a focus on the interface between theories, research, and educational practices in respect to language learning, teaching, and policies in relation to both English and French, aiming in this way to continue to distinguish the program from many others in North America and internationally, despite an increasing emphasis over past decades on English in education in Toronto and around the world. At the same time, we have tried to diversify the faculty complement—as senior professors retire and new professors are hired, and as our student population has increasingly included people from around the world or with interests in international issues—to include scholars from countries other than Canada and of varied ethnicities or cultural backgrounds. At the same time, we have tried to retain and foster expertise in the breadth of academic areas central to the program such as discourse analysis, research methods, assessment, and teaching methods.

REFERENCES

Cumming, A. (Ed.). (2006). *Goals for academic writing.* Amsterdam: John Benjamins.

Cumming, A. (Ed.). (2012). *Adolescent literacies in a multicultural context.* New York: Routledge.

Cumming, A., Shi, L., & So, S. (1997). Learning to do research on language learning and teaching: Graduate assistantships. *System, 25*(3), 425-423.

Sacks, O. (2007). *Musicophilia: Tales of music and the brain.* New York: Alfred A. Knopf.

5 Doctoring Myself: Observation, Interaction, and Action

Luxin Yang

Undertaking a doctoral degree entails a movement from the periphery of a community of practice toward full participation in it. Participation involves acquiring a community of practice's shared repertoire of tools such as its language and artifacts to engage in "actions whose meanings [members] negotiate with one another" (Wenger, 1998, p. 73). Participating in this way, however, requires doctoral students to construct and negotiate their own unique identities within the existing community. In other words, new doctoral students need to be clear about what it means for them to participate in the community of a graduate program. Many new doctoral students have painful experiences at the beginning of the process of participation because they are uncertain about what they need to do or how they can 'perform' well with professors, especially their advisors or supervisors, and lack of the language, styles of reasoning, and tools necessary to engage others in the community (Simpson & Matsuda, 2008). Some students appear to know the "ropes" of performing properly as doctorate students, based on their learning experiences as master's students. That is, they have observed what senior graduate students are doing to complete their graduate studies, or they have acquired a sense of how to do research from a mini-project, or MA thesis, or they have learned how to present their thoughts in proper academic English through doing various course assignments (e.g., literature review, book review, critique, designing research instruments). In this article, I describe my experiences of "participatory practice" (Casanave, 2008) from China to Canada as a graduate student and then from Canada to China as a returnee, especially my struggles of learning to do research and present my research in both academic English and Chinese.

SOCIALIZATION INTO BEING A GRADUATE STUDENT IN CANADA

In my case, my initial participation in the academic community started when I was a Master's student. Perhaps all doctoral students need to go through this preliminary stage prior to their doctoral studies. With a Master's degree from a Chinese university and having been a full-time English teacher for four years at a university in Beijing, I started my MA studies in the TESL (Teaching English as a Second Language) program at the University of British Columbia (UBC) in September 1999. It was at that time I became a graduate student in the Western sense of academia. I was not confident in my previous academic training in research that I received in the early 1990s in China because I was not offered any courses on research methodology but courses on British and American literature, linguistics, English grammar, and ancient Chinese philosophy. Therefore, I applied for the Master's program instead of a Doctoral program when I decided to study abroad. My decision was wise, as I indeed faced many challenges that I could not imagine when I was in China. The fundamental challenge, as Kuwahara (2008, p. 188) noted, was "an inability to perform up to standards".

I was excited to receive the acceptance letters from the three Canadian universities I had applied to, as it was quite difficult for Chinese students to get opportunities to study abroad due to unfavorable financial conditions at that time. I decided to attend the University of British Columbia (UBC) for its reputation and location. My excitement about joining the new academic community in Canada was soon replaced by a loss of direction after the first-week's classes. The professors of all the graduate courses that I took at the UBC voiced their expectations for students' participation in class discussions. At the very beginning, I was not comfortable with the casual style of Canadian classrooms, which was the complete opposite of the classroom culture I was familiar with in China (e.g., mainly lecturing and few class discussions). In my view, I came to Canada to learn from professors not from my classmates, and so I expected professors to dominate the classes and to lecture rather than ask students for their opinions or even initiate discussions in class. To meet the course requirements, I tried to speak up in class, but I often found myself unable to express my thoughts as quickly and clearly as my native-English-speaking (NES) peers did. This frustrated me, and I started to doubt my English language competence.

Moreover, reading through the course outlines, I found myself completely unprepared for the expectations for writing requirements as a graduate student in this TESL program. Although I had publications in both my first (Chinese) and second (English) languages in China, most of my work had been translations between the two languages and English textbooks for high school students. In addition, my previous training in English writing was to write short responses to questions or short essays based on my personal experiences. I had no clue about what I was expected to do for various types of term papers such as summaries, critiques, literature reviews, and research proposals. At the time, I felt embarrassed to ask my professors for clarification, as I thought I should have known how to write these kinds of papers as a graduate student.

Fortunately, I got to know two Chinese doctoral students, Gulbahar H. Beckett[*] and Yan Guo,[†] during the first month of my graduate studies at UBC. They soon became my friends and mentors. To make sure I was on the right track, I always asked them for advice on how to approach the topics I selected for my term papers before I started to write. Sometimes they showed me their previous term papers. After I finished my drafts, I usually would ask either Gulbahar or Yan (depending on their schedules) to read and comment on my drafts. Their candid and explicit comments (e.g., "What do you mean?" "Why do you think it is helpful?" "Please avoid long quotes unless absolutely necessary.") gave me opportunities to address problems before I submitted my papers. More importantly, their explicit comments scaf-

---

[*] Dr. Gulbahar H. Beckett is now Professor of Applied Linguistics and Teaching English as a Second Language in the Department of English and Director of the Intensive English and Orientation Program at Iowa State University.

[†] Dr. Yan Guo is now Associate Professor in the Werklund School of Education at the University of Calgary.

folded me, step by step, into the genres of the discipline. By the end of the first year, I came across common types of term papers in this TESL program and gained knowledge of how to approach them properly, though I still had some problems with my English vocabulary and grammar. I became confident in my studies because I knew what I was expected to do as a graduate student.

I learned to do research through my MA thesis study under the guidance of Dr. Ling Shi. I was fortunate to have worked with Ling at the beginning of my graduate studies in Canada. Originally from China, Ling was clear about the difficulties I might encounter in doing my MA thesis research, such as a lack of research experience and weak academic writing competence. At the end of the first year, Ling agreed to be my thesis supervisor, but she asked me first to find a research topic before I could discuss with her my plan for the thesis study. Despite two months of searching and reading journals and scholarly books, I failed to find my research focus. Desperately, I came to Ling's office, telling her my frustration and asking her to give me a direction. Listening to my story attentively, Ling looked at me calmly and thoughtfully. Then she gave me articles written by Campbell (1990) and Cumming (1989) and a book by Ericsson and Simon (1993) and suggested that I read them while thinking of my research plan. I was grateful to Ling for giving these suggestions. After reading the recommended literature, I got the idea of researching a summary task. Then I came to Ling again and told her that I wanted to find a few Chinese ESL students and give them a summary task to write. Instead, Ling suggested that I do a naturalistic study by collecting students' summaries submitted in their disciplinary courses. I agreed with Ling that this was a good idea, but I sensed that it would bring more challenges: Where could I find participants who happened to be doing a summary writing task? How could I manage the unexpectedness in the procedures for data collection in this kind of naturalistic study?

I decided to try the local network of Chinese students. I posted a message about my study to a listserv for Chinese students at UBC. Within a week I received responses from twelve Chinese students. I asked these students if they had any summary assignments in their academic courses and if they could recommend any of their classmates who were native English speakers as a comparison group. Three native-English-speaking students were recommended and also agreed to participate in the study. Therefore, I invited only three Chinese students to match the number of the comparison group for my MA thesis study. Then I discussed with Ling the procedures for data collection. This experience taught me how to search for and approach research participants, benefiting me a lot in my later doctoral studies and current position at Beijing Foreign Studies University. Ling also guided me through the process of data analysis and thesis writing step-by-step and further helped me publish an article from my MA thesis study (Yang & Shi, 2003). Working with Ling prepared me for my subsequent doctoral studies, as I was clear about what I needed to do to perform as a graduate student of TESL in the Canadian university.

I continued my growth as a novice researcher and scholar during my doctoral studies at the Ontario Institute for Studies in Education (OISE) under the supervision of Dr. Alister Cumming, whose guidance consisted of four aspects: 1) working on Alister's research project, 2) supporting my work as a coordinator for an informal seminar series, 3) supervising my doctoral research, and 4) collegial support after my graduation, which are illustrated in the following sections.

Working on Alister's Research Project

The best way of learning to do research is to work on a professor's project. While taking graduate courses to broaden my knowledge and deepen my understanding of second language education, I had an opportunity at the beginning of my doctoral studies to join the research team on Alister's project investigating goals for academic writing (published later as Cumming, 2006). This was truly a process of learning by doing. As a research assistant, I attended the research team's weekly meetings to discuss such issues as interviewing student participants, transcribing and coding interview transcripts, writing up data reports, preparing conference proposals, and drafting research papers. For example, a more senior doctoral student, Mike Busch, guided me through the process of transcribing interviews and coding interview transcripts. In an email to Alister and the research team, Mike said:

> Email 1: *Alister, I have a question to ask about transcribing. One of the girls that I interviewed has a habit of using ah, um, and, but, because extensively as connectors and continuatives. The problem is whether to transcribe these. If I omit them, it would involve cleaning up their speech, but at the same time making the*

> *transcript more readable. What do you think?* (personal communication, Oct 21, 2001)

Alister wrote back:

> Email 2: *Yes, I would be inclined to leave them in, Mike, particularly if they are obvious features of her speech. Thanks for checking.* (Personal communication, Oct 21, 2001)

This email exchange clarified my question about transcribing interviews and highlighted the importance of keeping the originality of data for later accurate analysis. Moreover, Mike gave me three training sessions to help me understand the coding scheme set up by the team prior to my participation and apply the scheme in my coding practice. In the first two sessions, Mike and I reached the inter-coder reliability levels of .31 and .68, respectively. At that moment, I was uncertain whether I should continue my coding or have another meeting with Mike, and so I wrote the following email:

> Alister, shall I continue coding or wait until Mike and I can get a higher reliability? ...As Mike indicated in his previous email, I am a little confused with 'self-regulation' and 'stimulation', or I am not completely convinced by Mike. The Chinese students that I interviewed said that, to improve their writing skills, they would 'see' or read more books or model essays and memorize the new words and sentence structures or essays [In Chinese, we can say 'see' and 'read' a book. So I interpret 'reading' when the Chinese students said that they 'see' the books or newspapers. Mike teased me that I over-interpreted it]. Extensive reading and memorization of well-written phrases, sentences and essays are widely used when we learn to read and write in Chinese. To me, memorization is not simply a studying technique but also a self-regulation strategy, because memorization is boring to some extent and the learners need to monitor and plan their learning processes. To comprise my belief, I like to code 'memorization' as both 'self-regulation' and 'studying'. What do you think? Which way should I take? (Email 3, Aug 16, 2002)

Alister responded:

> Thanks for the update, Luxin. I think it best to establish the inter-coder agreement before carrying on with any more coding. As for "memorization", I would have to say it is a studying, rather than self-regulation strategy, primarily because it is a way to improve one's knowledge not a way to regulate one's behavior or performance while writing. (Email 4, Aug 16, 2002)

After these exchanges, Mike and I decided to code a third transcript together and reached 78% agreement. Commenting on this result, Alister said that figure sounded reasonable to him because it was close to 80% agreement and was "what normally comes out of this kind of coding." He then suggested that I "go ahead with the coding" in his response email. Voicing my queries explicitly, I received explicit guidance from Alister and Mike and was able to complete the coding task on time. Transcribing and coding work is one of the daunting, challenging, and important tasks for qualitative research. Simply reading papers and books on qualitative research is far from sufficient for a graduate student or novice researcher to develop the ability to manage qualitative data. My experience convinced me that the best way to learn to do qualitative research is to participate in the research project of experienced researchers, performing and sensing each procedure while doing it under their guidance. This experience built up my competence in handling qualitative research data.

Alister later took the whole team to present our individual work at two conferences (TESOL Ontario 2003 in Toronto and AILA 2005 in Madison, Wisconsin). To prepare for these conferences, Alister organized a rehearsal session, during which I observed how other members presented their work, and also received useful feedback for my presentation from the team. This event taught me what a symposium was like in academic conferences. Most importantly, I noticed that all the individual presentations needed to serve the theme of the whole symposium and have smooth and relevant transitions between presentations.

Moreover, Alister guided us to write research papers based on the data analyses we had done for his project. For example, I worked with Kyoko Baba and Alister on a paper about three Chinese and three Japanese ESL students' writing goals (Yang, Baba, & Cumming, 2004). This paper started from my term paper for a graduate course co-taught by Merrill Swain and Sharon Lapkin. In that paper, I focused on one Chinese ESL student whom I had interviewed for Alister's project, reporting this student's changes in her English writing development. The paper got an A+ from Merrill and Sharon, which strengthened my confidence in writing up a qualitative case study. Later, I showed this paper to Alister, and he suggested that I could elaborate on it by including data from more Chinese students. I took Alister's advice and added data from another two Chinese students to this paper, which I then presented at the TESOL Ontario Conference the next year. After the conference, Alister indicated that the paper would be stronger if it could be combined with Kyoko's related paper on three Japanese students. Through our discussion, Kyoko and I figured out a way of combining our two conference papers. Knowing that Alister would have time for our paper during the winter holidays, Kyoko and I worked together and completed our joint paper by then. Alister worked on our draft paper and then emailed us back his revised version in three weeks. He expressed his satisfaction with this joint paper, which truly encouraged Kyoko and me to write more from the data for Alister's project.

> Luxin and Kyoko, I am forwarding in the attachment here the version of our co-authored paper for Angles that I have edited. I think it has come out well, though it is still a bit longer than they want, though perhaps it is also a bit better than they are expecting. So I think this version will be okay for this publication. If you have any revisions to suggest to this draft, can you let me know by early next week? ...Good to see this all coming together! (Email 5, Jan 21, 2004)

In my eyes, Alister is a responsible and efficient supervisor, always responding to his students' emails rapidly and addressing their questions explicitly. Under his guidance, I worked with Kyoko to combine our papers into an article that was later published. Alister read and edited our draft carefully. Reading his edited version, I noted the errors he corrected and the sentences he rewrote and revised, pondering why Alister wrote in certain ways and compared my version and his version. For example, regarding the unit of analysis in literacy research, my original version was:

> Therefore, when doing research into literacy development, it is important to shift our focus or unit of analysis from decontextualized variables to an activity system composed of individuals and their related contextual factors. Leont'ev proposes a three-level scheme of analyzing an activity system in terms of **activity, action, operation** and corresponding **motive, goal,** and **instrument conditions.**

Alister's edited version was:

> This theoretical framework shifts our focus of analysis from decontextualized variables (e.g., as in pre-constructed experimental tasks) to analyses of activity systems composed of individuals in their naturally occurring social contexts. Leont'ev (1978, 1981) proposed a scheme for analyzing an activity system in terms of **activity, action,** and **operation** and corresponding **motive, goal,** and **instrument conditions.** (Yang et al. 2004, p. 14)

The two versions kept the same meaning, but Alister's version was accurate and concise. In addition to editing, he seemed to be using a writing teaching method called 'reformulation', a technique of "having a native writer of the target language rewrite the learner's essay, preserving all the learner's ideas, making it sound as nativelike as possible" (Cohen, 1983, p. 4). I noticed the differences between my writing and Alister's writing, and then I tried my best to imitate him in my own writing. In other words, Alister actually taught me how to write in academic English.

Coordinator for Informal Seminars

At the beginning of my second year at OISE, Alister gave me the opportunity to organize a series of academic events in the Modern Language Centre (MLC) featuring presentations by graduate students and visiting scholars on their completed or in-progress research projects. In the email below, Alister explained the duties of being a coordinator and offered his suggestions for the potential presenters.

> Luxin, might you be interested in coordinating the MLC Informal Seminars this coming year? If so, I would be happy to talk with you about what is involved (basically just recruit-

ing fellow students to report on their work: e.g., I have a few people in mind who have just finished theses, and notifying the secretary about how to advertise the seminars). ...and we thought that you would be the best qualified person for this. Perhaps, you might also want to work together with another student on this, and if so, that would be a good idea, and something we could discuss. (Email 6, Sept 13, 2002)

Alister said I was "the best qualified person for this". This really touched me. If the professors in the MLC believed in me, why should I not believe in myself? So I decided to take on this obligation.

During my two years as a coordinator, I paid close attention to the research projects that other MLC graduate students were carrying out so that I could find potential candidates as presenters for the coming semester. Then I reported my tentative schedule to Alister and made adjustments according to his suggestions. Alister always encouraged me with his positive feedback and recommendations for potential presenters so that I could contact and invite them to present their work in the seminar series.

This experience taught me how to organize an academic event and interact with prospective presenters, which indeed benefited me not only in my doctoral research but also in my current work. For example, since returning to Beijing, I have participated in the organization of four academic conferences, including AILA 2011. I am often appointed in my current position as the person who contacts the presenters or keynote speakers, especially those from overseas, mainly due to my learning experience as an international student in Canada.

GUIDANCE ON MY DOCTORAL RESEARCH

With Alister's help, I went through the process of my doctoral studies smoothly at OISE, including such steps as preparing for comprehensive exams and a thesis proposal, gathering and analyzing data, writing up the dissertation, and preparing conference proposals. In the email below, I told Alister what I planned to do for Question 1 on the comprehensive exams, which I could prepare in advance, and asked him when was the best time for me to take these exams.

> I need your advice on my ideas on Comps question 1 and time-frame on taking COMPS. First, my proposal is still in process... In order to situate Second Language Writing (SLW) in the field of Second Language Education, now I am thinking a mini-proposal is not appropriate. What I am thinking now is to do a critical historical overview on SLW teaching and learning by drawing on the research of Adult ESL learners in formal academic settings. I will try to connect SLW and second language learning theories. ... Do you think it is appropriate for Comp question 1? Second, I am thinking whether I take COMPS this December or next May... Through the interviews, the five Commerce students don't have any writing assignments in their field-specific courses during the first year. I am thinking it may not be big difference that I start data collection next January or next September. By giving myself another half a year, I can get my proposal and my first question paper well done, I think. What do you think I should do? (Email 7, Nov 13, 2002)

In the response, Alister used the phrase "seem appropriate to me" to address my first question, and explained why he could not give me detailed comments. Regarding my second question, he said I was "the only person who can judge" when to take the exams. Alister's response reflected his professional ethics, which I gradually understood through our interactions. On the one hand, he explained to me what he could say as an examiner. On the other hand, he prompted me to make independent decisions based on my own judgments of situations. This earned my deep respect and, consequently, I have tried to follow his example in my own supervising practice.

To make my meetings with Alister more efficient, given his busy schedule, I usually emailed him my questions or sent him drafts of material to review beforehand. For example, I submitted my draft thesis proposal to Alister before I asked him for an appointment. Thus, he could have time to read it and know my current thinking about the research proposal, enabling him to give me suggestions or comments for my consideration before our meeting as shown in Email 8. In other words, I was always well prepared for my meeting with Alister and clear about what support I needed from him.

> Luxin, I read with interest this morning your thesis proposal. I like the scope, orientation, and purpose of the study, I can envision you doing this well, and the review of theories and previous publications are thorough and useful. There are various suggestions that I would like to make, though, and it would be worth talking them through. I could meet you next week to do that. Would Tuesday (April 15) at 11:00 suit you? If not, Wednesday at the same time would also be okay for me.
>
> A key thing I think we should talk through is to tighten up the logical relations between the (a) research questions, (b) data you will collect, (c) analyses you will do, and (d) results you expect to find. If we talk through these points next week, I expect you could adopt a more focused, systematic approach in the study (and not be overwhelmed by excessive data that may be difficult to interpret or interrelate). To help prepare for this, could you make, before we meet, a simple chart that outlines each of these four points, and shows how they logically interconnect?
>
> A related point concerns justifying the sample for the study. It makes good sense to choose the Chinese students in Commerce, but I wonder if you can develop a rationale or sampling plan for the data you will collect from them, particularly in regards to writing samples, course materials, and instructor interviews (and perhaps, as well, a perspective on the field of Commerce studies at university)? We should talk through how this could be done systematically so that you define clearly the scope and relevance of your study.
>
> Looking forward to talking with you about this and various other minor details in the proposal, Alister (Email 8, Apr 10, 2003)

I was also quite frank when telling Alister about my circumstances and plans so that he could arrange his time accordingly and give me the assistance I needed. For example, in the email below, I told him that I planned to go home in the summer for a family reunion when he approved my proposal and explained that I could still do my academic work at home.

Doctoring Myself

> ... I will go home this summer. I will book my flight when you approve my proposal. ... I've got to look after my daughter and help her review her school work this summer so that my mom can have some break. At the same time, I refresh myself and prepare for next-round efficient hard work. Even I am in Qingdao, I think I can spend average three to four hours every day on my work (reading, writing or thinking for the project). I can contact you via email and access to on-line journals...
>
> Hope you understand me, Luxin (Email 9, May 9, 2003)

Knowing of my research plan, Alister emailed me any relevant references that he came across, even when I was back home in China, as shown in Email 10. His suggestions saved me a lot of time searching the literature and pointed me in right directions for data analysis.

> Luxin, this is just to point you toward a journal article, when you return to Toronto, which I came across, which may be useful in providing a methodology for analyzing group talk in your thesis research: Resnick, L., et al. (1993). Reasoning in conversation. Cognition and Instruction, 11, 3 & 4, 347-364.
>
> The article is somewhat dated now, so there may be more recent articles on the project they describe, if you do a search for Lauren Resnick, who is the main researcher. Cheers, Alister (Email 10, July 15, 2003)

Furthermore, during the process of transcribing the group discussions for my thesis research, I encountered the issue of dual language use. I was not sure whether I should transcribe the data verbatim or translate them into English while transcribing, as shown in Email 11. Responding to my email, Alister suggested that I transcribe the data verbatim and analyze it as was (Email 12).

> Hi Alister, I am transcribing the first group discussion that I recorded last Saturday (Sept. 13). The group is made up of five Chinese students, including the focal student Ying Xue. They speak in Chinese 99% of time. I am afraid that my English translation might lose some information (pragmatic aspect), though I try to keep original meaning as much as possible. So what I am doing now is to write down the original lan-

guage that the participants were talking in and followed by English translation if the utterances are spoken in Chinese. In the future, I can go back and check my English translation according to original Chinese version. It appears to take more time transcribing in two languages. What do you think that I should do, transcribing as it is or transcribing and translating at the same time? (Email 11, Sept 16, 2003)

Interesting, Luxin. I would suggest transcribing the data in Chinese, and analyzing it in Chinese as well, if it is mostly in Chinese. Then, when you write up the thesis, and if you want give quotations, translate those into English for the benefit of readers of your thesis. (Email 12, Sept 16, 2003)

I think this was a judicious decision for handling data in multiple languages. Translation inevitably involves losing or distorting some information. I still keep this principle in my current research and my supervision of graduate students.

During the process of writing my dissertation, Alister responded to my draft chapters within two weeks with explicit suggestions. For example, he gave me suggestions for shortening Chapter 4.

Luxin, your draft of Chapter 4 looks good. Glad to see that. I think it would be a good idea to put Table 4.1 at the beginning of the section 4.2 so that readers know what to expect in the pages that follow. The information all looks relevant, and we need to know it, in order to understand your findings (in the next chapter). But the chapter is a bit lengthy. I wondered if there might be some way to (a) shorten or (b) streamline the presentation a bit? Two possibilities:

1. Could you put the detailed information about course assignments into boxes (naming them as Figures, perhaps), and smaller print, so that they do not take up so much space on the pages and are separated from the main text? You might also want to consider putting some of the details (if they are not necessary or integral) into appendices, but that may not be suitable in most instances.
2. For the information on courses, you might be able to streamline the subsections schematically, for example, with headings like Course, Assignments, etc. so that peo-

ple can read these quickly and see how they compare to each other (Email 13, Nov 16, 2004)

Alister's quick response saved me from further struggles with managing the length of details for the courses and assignments in Chapter 4 and pointed me in the direction of reorganizing this chapter concisely. In brief, Alister's efficiency and explicit comments eased the process of my writing, which in turn encouraged me to concentrate on writing the dissertation.

SOCIALIZATION INTO BEING A RETURNEE TO CHINA

After completing my doctoral studies in 2006, I immediately returned to China to join my family. I suddenly became a returnee, or *haigui* (海归)* in Chinese parlance, to my Chinese colleagues because of my overseas education. With the same pronunciation, haigui is often joked about as another haigui (海龟),† "sea turtle". As a returnee to an academic position at a university in China, I have gone through another process of socialization that was full of new struggles beyond my expectations, just as a "sea turtle" may go through when it decides to live on the "mainland" rather than in the "sea." First, I learned that it is difficult for a returnee to get a research grant from funding agencies in China because of his or her unfamiliarity with Chinese expectations and conventions. Initially, I wrote a grant proposal in Chinese according to Western academic conventions, with a specific focus and possible implications. I was very confident about my first research topic (on academic writing for training graduate students for publication in English) because of its general interest to second language (L2) writing researchers in Western academia. None of my colleagues worked in the field of L2 writing, and so I did not ask them to read my proposal. I was very disappointed when I got the news that I did not get the grant from the National Social Science and Humanities Research Council of China. In fact, I failed three times in this competition before I was awarded my current research grant. The three topics were all about academic writing in English, which sounded very specific but quite far from the government's current concerns or the list of recommended

---

* 海归, pronounced "haigui", means "return from overseas."

† 海龟, pronounced "haigui", means "sea turtle."

topics in the guide to writing grant proposals according to my present understanding of grant proposals.

I was frustrated and depressed about my inability to obtain this research grant, largely because I was under pressure to have some kind of funded project to continue to work in the research center where I was employed. Meanwhile, my colleagues trained in China all had their grant proposals approved and funded. This cruel reality forced me to reflect on my educational background and to examine more closely the social context in which I was working. This 'studying' process was similar to finding a research topic for my doctoral dissertation. I searched websites to read lists of funded projects and tried to figure out patterns and tendencies among them. I also asked my colleagues for their successful grant proposals to find out their 'secret weapons' for success. Gradually, I realized that the topic of academic writing in English was too specific and not of interest to the grant council, which favored the topics listed on the guide to grant application or the concerns addressed in the government's five-year development plan.

As time passed, some of my colleagues became my friends in a way that permitted me to feel comfortable to ask for help. One of my colleagues, who was skillful at getting research grants, told me that I'd better read carefully the list of recommended topics posted in the website for grant applications prior to deciding on a topic for a proposal. He told me that the topics in the list were priorities for the granting council and were most likely to succeed. This is the important lesson I learned: the topic for my research proposal should not be confined to my own research interests. Instead, I need to consider the needs or concerns of the government at the time of application. In other words, the results of the granted projects are expected to provide some constructive suggestions or useful information to related departments of the government for making judicious decisions regarding various issues such as education, agriculture, and environment.

This understanding was strengthened in one of our faculty meetings, in which the director said that our research center had an obligation to serve the needs of our country, such as offering suggestions on foreign language education and providing professional training to in-service English teachers because of the mission of the center when founded by the Ministry of Education of China as revealed in its name "National Research Center for Foreign Language Education". Therefore, each faculty member needs to develop an area useful for this purpose, which might be beyond his or her research interests. The relevant area of my training in L2 writing research was foreign language teaching and learning. Some of my colleagues have done a lot of research on foreign language teaching and learning at the tertiary level, implying that it was not a wise choice for me to get into an already established field. However, I noticed that none of my colleagues were studying foreign language teaching and learning at the primary and secondary school level. Moreover, this domain is important to our country, as English is a compulsory school subject in China, but continues to present many problems for teaching and learning it. To survive and find a unique, 'irreplaceable' position in the Center, I realized that I needed to do what my colleagues had not done, that is, research English education at the level of primary and secondary schools. Therefore, for my fourth grant proposal, I chose the topic of English education at the secondary school level and did a lot of 'homework' to prepare for it. For example, I studied the list of recommended topics carefully and asked my colleagues to comment on my draft proposal. The first draft was still written in the manner of an English research proposal. One of my colleagues read it and recommended that I 'exaggerate' the importance of my research topic to the needs of the county in order to gain the reviewers' attention. This was quite hard for me as I was trained to be specific in these aspects. Following my colleague's suggestion, I revised my grant proposal and sent it to him for further comments. I guess he realized that I was 'hopeless' in addressing his suggestion before the deadline for submission. He did a tremendous revision on this draft. The ideas were mine, but the way of writing was his. Comparing the two versions, I realized that my previous failure in seeking grants was not only related to my specific topic on L2 writing, but also to the style of grant proposal writing. With the help of my colleague, I got the research grant for this fourth proposal. This success meant that I had stepped into the academic community in China to become a successful novice player of the 'academic game' in my home country.

Second, as a returnee, it has been difficult for me to present and publish my research in Chinese. All my academic training in second language education was done in English and in Canada. I was unfamiliar with scholarly journals published in China and new to the academic network in China. I found myself resistant to reading papers written in Chinese, as I had to translate the concepts and literature review written into English to comprehend the terminology and ideas, and sometimes I failed to find equivalent terms in English. This difficulty in turn discouraged me from reading more scholarly papers in Chinese. I also noticed differences in writing styles between Chinese and English academic publications. For example, Chinese academic papers tend to have a short literature review section, and a majority report on quantitative studies. After going through a few issues, I lost interest in reading scholarly journals written in Chinese. My unfamiliarity with the discourse conventions resulted in my deficiency both in oral presentations and in writing up my academic work. For instance, during a faculty meeting in the first semester after I returned to Beijing, I was to report on a project on teacher qualifications assigned by the research center to my Chinese colleagues. I prepared the Power Point slides in English and gave the presentation in English, too, because I did not know how to do it in Chinese. I think this made my colleagues feel uncomfortable. As a Chinese person, I spoke to them in English instead of Chinese in this local Chinese context. They might think I saw myself more as an international scholar rather than a Chinese scholar. My way of presenting or talking actually created a distance between my colleagues and me implicitly. Over these years, I have observed how my Chinese colleagues presented their research in Chinese and paid particular attention to the language they used. Gradually, I have come to feel comfortable and am now able to give scholarly presentations in Chinese.

A few of my colleagues suggested that I should publish my research in Chinese so as to make my research known to a larger audience in China and consequently establish myself domestically in the academic field. I understood that their advice was good for me to survive and thrive as a returnee, but first I needed to break the block of writing in Chinese. The breakthrough for me was the success of my grant proposal. As I mentioned earlier, I studied carefully the differences between my version and my colleague's revised version. I suddenly developed a sense of Chinese academic writing through this careful comparison and transferred my sense of L2 (English) writing to L1 (Chinese) writing. Then I drafted a paper based on the data collected after I returned to Beijing and asked two of my colleagues to comment on the paper. This paper was eventually published (Yang, 2010a), and its success cured my fear of and resistance to writing in Chinese. At present, I have ten papers and a book published in Chinese. Moreover, I was invited to be the editor for a Chinese journal on English education.

Third, I found myself in a disadvantageous position to get published in English, too. Being far away from the academic community in which I had been educated, I lost the support and environment for me to write in English. For example, I could not access certain scholarly journals in China, as my university did not purchase the particular database. I had nobody with whom I could discuss my English writing in the Center, as my colleagues were not interested in publishing their work in English. The only support that I could seek was my former academic network in the West, but I knew they were quite busy with their own research and writing, and so I often hesitated to ask them for help. I felt like a kite that had lost the thread connecting it to the earth. On the one hand, I was resistant to writing in Chinese. On the other hand, I found it difficult to get my work published in English as I often received rejections of my writing from international journals. I struggled to find my way out of this difficult situation. I told myself that I had to be strong, to keep on writing in English, and to seek support from my former network in the West. I turned to my doctoral thesis supervisor, Alister, for his advice on writing papers from my dissertation. He wrote me the following after I informed him of the rejection news from a major scholarly journal. Alister comforted me about the disappointing news and suggested further actions to take:

> That is disappointing, Luxin. But I suppose all you (or anyone) can do at this point is to respect the Editor's decision and the journal's policy. I think the Editor's suggestions about other journals are good ones. My sense is to revise the manuscript to address his points below then try either TESOL Quarterly (if you are prepared to wait a while for reviews, and probably do more revisions for them) or try Language Teaching Research (which will probably accept your paper with minor revisions). I suspect either of these journals will accept your manuscript, but TESOL Quarterly is more of a gamble, and usually requests lots of revisions. (Email 14, Apr 28, 2008)

I decided to revise the paper to address the editor's points and submit it to another journal. Upon learning of my decision, Alister gave me positive feedback and also reminded me that "publication takes patience." The revised paper was eventually accepted and published in *Language Teaching Research* (Yang, 2010b).

Whenever I had a chance to talk to Alister at the international conferences I attended, I poured out my frustration about not getting published in English. He was a good listener and often shared his own stories of failures and his way of handling rejection letters and reviewers' comments. Talking with Alister has helped me face the rejection calmly and view it positively and, as a result, I have regained my courage to continue my efforts to publish in English. Up to now, I have five journal papers published in international journals since I returned to China.

Concluding Remarks

Looking back, I have gone through a dual process of scholarly socialization, going first from China to Canada and then from Canada back to China. The lessons I learned from the former socialization process formed a significant foundation for the latter one and, in fact, I continue to learn from these experiences. I think it is crucial for graduate students to take the initiative to communicate with experienced members of the community regularly to "develop a sense that they are allies, and to ask, watch, listen, and learn" (Liu et al., 2008, p. 181). It is also important for the community to provide additional support to international graduate students since it is already more complex and challenging for them to study in western academies than for their native-English-speaking counterparts. It is even more complex and challenging for international graduate students if they decide to return to their home country after graduation. To survive and thrive as novice researchers and scholars, these returnees need support not only from the larger academic community but also the local academic community and their families.

As a doctoral student and a returnee, I have benefited from a number of participatory practices (Casanave, 2008) such as taking part in my supervisors' projects, attending conferences, writing for publication in English and Chinese, and applying for grants. To me, learning to become a professional scholar, and to survive and try to thrive as a returnee, has been a gradual process, involving engagement in culturally embedded, even tacit, practices (Prior & Min, 2008), and, importantly, continual reflection. Through my continual reflection on the activities that I have participated in, I have often been able to learn from my previous experiences and see the more subtle aspects of the field to which these activities exposed me (e.g., getting support from Chinese colleagues, understanding the 'rules' of seeking grants in China). My reflections on the process of 'performing' doctoral studies and professional obligations have highlighted for me the intricate relationship between learning and identity construction in two differing social contexts (Canada and China), and the gradual process of developing my own professional identity as a researcher and writer in the field of second language writing in particular and second language education in general (Casanave, 2002; Wenger, 1998). It is through constant participatory practices that I have gradually gained a (novice) membership in both Chinese and Western academic communities. This learning is an ongoing journey full of observation, interaction, and action, accompanied by "joys and despair, relief and frustration, fear and confidence" (Prior & Min, 2008, p. 245). After all the ups and downs that I have gone through over the years, and with the support from both communities, I am now on my way to shuttling between them and starting to enjoy the benefits of multiple memberships (Canagarajah, 2002).*

REFERENCES

Campbell, C. (1990). Writing with others' words: Using background reading text in academic compositions. In Kroll, B. (Ed.), *Second language writing* (pp. 211-230). Cambridge: Cambridge University Press.

Canagarajah, S. (2002). Multilingual writers and the academic community: Towards a critical relationship. *Journal of English for Academic Purposes, 1*, 29-44.

Casanave, C. P. (2002). *Writing games: Multi-cultural case studies of academic literacy practices in higher education.* Mahwah, NJ: Lawrence Erlbaum.

Casanave, C. P. (2008). Learning participatory practices in graduate school: Some perspective-taking by a mainstream educator. In C. P. Casanave & X. Li (Eds.), *Learning the literacy practices of graduate school: Insiders' reflections on academic enculturation* (pp. 14-31). Ann Arbor, MI: The University of Michigan Press.

Cohen, A. D. (1983). *Reformulating second-language compositions: A potential source of input for the learner* (ERIC ED 228).

Cumming, A. (1989). Writing expertise and second-language proficiency. *Language Learning, 39*, 81-141.

Cumming, A. (Ed.) (2006). *Goals for academic writing: ESL students and their instructors.* Amsterdam: John Benjamins.

---

* This chapter was supported by the Program for New Century Excellent Talents in the University (NCET-12-0792), sponsored by Ministry of Education of China.

Ericsson, K. A., & Simon, H. A. (1993). *Protocol analysis: Verbal reports as data*. Cambridge, MA: MIT Press.

Kuwahara, N. (2008). It's not in the orientation manual: How a first-year doctoral student learned to survive in graduate school. In C. P. Casanave & X. Li (Eds.), *Learning the literacy practices of graduate school: Insiders' reflections on academic enculturation* (pp. 186-200). Ann Arbor, MI: University of Michigan Press.

Lave, J., & Wenger, E. (1991). *Situated learning: Legitimate peripheral participation*. Cambridge, UK: Cambridge University Press.

Liu, L., Weiser, I., Silva, T., Alsup, J., Selfe, C., & Hawisher, G. (2008). It takes a community of scholars to raise one: Multiple mentors as key to my growth. In C. P. Casanave & X. Li (Eds.), *Learning the literacy practices of graduate school: Insiders' reflections on academic enculturation* (pp. 166-183). Ann Arbor, MI: University of Michigan Press.

Matsuda, P. K. (2003). Coming to voice: Publishing as a graduate student. In C. P. Casanave & S. Vandrick (Eds.), *Writing for publication: Behind the scenes in language education: Insiders' reflections on academic enculturation* (pp. 39-51). Mahwah, NJ: Lawrence Erlbaum.

Prior, P. A., & Min, Y. K. (2008). The lived experience of graduate work and writing: From chronotopic laminations to everyday lamentations. In C. P. Casanave & X. Li (Eds.), *Learning the literacy practices of graduate school: Insiders' reflections on academic enculturation* (pp. 230-246). Ann Arbor, MI: University of Michigan Press.

Simpson, S., & Matsuda, P. K. (2008). Mentoring as a long-term relationship: Situated learning in a doctorate program. In C. P. Casanave & X. Li (Eds.), *Learning the literacy practices of graduate school: Insiders' reflections on academic enculturation* (pp. 90-104). Ann Arbor, MI: University of Michigan Press.

Wenger, E. (1998). *Communities of practice: Learning, meaning, and identity*. Cambridge, UK: Cambridge University Press.

Yang, L., Baba, K., & Cumming, A. (2004). Activity systems for ESL writing improvement: Case studies of three Chinese and three Japanese adult learners of English. *Angles on the English-Speaking World, 4*, 13-33. Copenhagen: Museum Tusculanum Press, University of Copenhagen.

Yang, L., & Shi, L. (2003). Exploring six MBA students' summary writing by introspection. *Journal of English for Academic Purposes, 2*(3), 165-192.

Yang, L. (2010a). Exploring Chinese university EFL teachers' beliefs and practices in writing instruction. *Foreign Language Learning Theory and Practice* (wai yu jiao xue li lun yu shi jian), 2010(2), 59-68.

Yang, L. (2010b). Doing a group presentation: Negotiations and challenges experienced by five Chinese ESL students of Commerce at a Canadian university. *Language Teaching Research, 14*, 141-160.

6 The Will to Build: Mentoring Doctoral Students in Second Language Writing

Paul Kei Matsuda

"The Competitor in Chief," read the headline of a *New York Times* article (Kantor, 2012) that Dwight Atkinson had sent me. Underneath the subtitle, "Obama Plays to Win, in Politics and Everything Else," was an image of President Barack Obama doing push-ups, accompanied by a caption: "Presidential Zeal: Whether shooting pool, reading to children or working to raise his bowling scores, President Obama cannot contain his competitive nature." It had been a standing joke between Dwight and me that I, like President Obama, took everything seriously—from cooking and photography to Karaoke and playing *Just Dance 2* on Wii. Call me an overachiever. I prefer not to think of it as competitiveness, but I am fully aware of my own perfectionist inclination—something I have been trying very hard to overcome.

The comparison does not end there. I tend to thrive when I am challenged (but not in a competitive way); when someone says, "You wouldn't be able to do it," my response is: "Yes we can." I became serious about learning English as a high school student in Japan when I learned about the notion of the Critical Period Hypothesis—that it would be impossible to acquire a high level of proficiency in a second language after puberty. People told me that I would have to live in an English-speaking country in order to learn to speak English; I decided to become a proficient user of English while in Japan. People also said

I would not be able to learn to write without first learning to speak; I was determined to learn English primarily through reading and writing. I studied journalism as an undergraduate student and became a writing specialist partly because many people seemed to assume that nonnative English users would not be able to do it. Writing was considered the last language skill—the most challenging of all language skills. That's my kind of challenge.

This "can do" attitude was at least partially responsible for my decision to specialize in second language writing as well as my strong desire to contribute to field building. When I decided to pursue my master's degree and become a writing specialist, a practicing ESL teacher told me that there was no such thing as a writing specialist; I found a master's program in composition and rhetoric where I could specialize in writing. In the master's program, it seemed that few, if any, graduate students at my institution were paying attention to issues related to second language writers; I decided to argue the importance of paying attention. At the Conference on College Composition and Communication, sessions on second language issues were few and far between; at TESOL, there were some writing-related sessions and publications (e.g., Kroll, 1990; Leki, 1991), but it still seemed like a minor topic that only a small group of dedicated specialists pursued. "I have to change the situation," I thought to myself. And that is how it all started.

LEARNING FROM THE MASTER

After finishing my master's degree, I went on to pursue my PhD studies at Purdue University. I chose Purdue primarily because of the presence of Tony Silva, who was engaging in the kind of field-building work that I wanted to be involved in. He had started the *Journal of Second Language Writing* with Ilona Leki (see Silva, 2012, for a story of the genesis of the journal), and was leading the effort to promote L2 writing at CCCC (Matsuda, 2012b). He also had authored a history of L2 writing pedagogy that resonated with my evolving understanding of the field (Silva, 1990). It was also important that he had started this line of work while he was a doctoral student. He was the kind of scholar and academic citizen I wanted to become. Before applying to Purdue, I visited his office and asked him where the field was going. "Up," he replied. His optimism undergirded by his broad knowledge and his commitment to field building made me want to learn from the master and help build the field with him.

For me, the best part of working with Tony was the opportunity to engage in real and meaningful professional activities. In his L2 writing seminar that I took during the first semester of my doctoral studies, he asked students to review a real manuscript submitted to the *JSLW*. He also asked us to write a book review; I published mine in *TESOL Quarterly* (Matsuda, 1997c). My seminar paper in that class, which extended my master's thesis, was also published in the *Journal of Second Language Writing* (Matsuda, 1997a). He also gave me a chance to write a five-year retrospective account of the journal (Matsuda, 1997b). Later, I served as Tony's editorial assistant for the *JSLW* and helped compile annotated bibliographies. He also listened to my ideas and helped me turn them into reality. One day, after a class discussion about professional conferences, I approached Tony and said we needed a conference for L2 writing specialists; a few years later, Tony and I organized the first Symposium on Second Language Writing to create a sense of identity as a field by bringing together L2 writing specialists who were often working in vastly different geographic, institutional and disciplinary contexts. We also edited two books that captured the historical development (Silva & Matsuda, 2001a) and the state of the art (Silva & Matsuda, 2001b). He also gave me opportunities to teach graduate-level practicum courses for first-time teachers of second language writing.

For my dissertation, I chose to conduct an historical study of L2 writing in North American higher education. My goal was two-fold: to give the field a sense of identity and to communicate the importance of L2 issues to mainstream rhetoric and composition specialists, who at the time seemed more receptive to humanities oriented scholarship than social scientific research. Choosing a historical study was not an easy decision because I was aware of how it would position me more in line with composition studies than with second language studies, which seemed to favor empirical research in a social scientific tradition. At that time, applied linguists seemed to regard history as mere chronological literature review or personal reminiscences only senior scholars were entitled to write (Matsuda, 2006). At the same time, it became increasingly clear to me that historical and theoretical studies were needed in order for L2 writing to establish its identity as a field. When I told Tony about my decision, he smiled encouragingly and said that I was going to become the "first fulltime theorist and historian of second language writing." That reassurance gave me the courage to proceed. I also decided to balance my professional profile by pursuing some data-driven projects (e.g., Matsuda, 2001; 2002).

By the last year of my doctoral study, my career goal was firmly established in my mind—to teach in a doctoral program where I can teach the next generation of L2 writing specialists. I reaffirmed that goal at the TESOL convention in March 1999, where Terry Santos organized a colloquium entitled "On the future of second language writing." The colloquium was later published in the *JSLW* (Santos, Atkinson, Erickson, Matsuda, & Silva, 2000). In that colloquium, Dwight Atkinson suggested the field of second language writing was "dying before our eyes" (p. 2) because only a small number of L2 writing specialists were preparing the next generation. Although I did not believe the field was dying, I did see the need for more systematic reproduction of L2 writing specialists at the PhD level. At that moment, my mind was set: I must work at a doctoral-granting institution with strong PhD programs in rhetoric and composition, applied linguistics, or both.

The decision to be involved in the education of doctoral students intensified my will to publish. Although I was already driven to write for publication—not just to have published but to influence the ways in which L2 writing is conceived, studied and taught in various disciplinary contexts (see Matsuda, 2003)—I made extra efforts to place my work in high-profile publications in both composition studies and second language studies in order to develop a profile appropriate for a PhD advisor. In making the decision to focus on doctoral education, I also had to contend with my passion for teaching. Although I enjoyed both teaching and researching writing, I found balancing the demands of the two activities to be a real challenge because they seemed to stretch my intellectual and creative muscles in different ways. At some point, however, I made a conscious decision to focus on field building through research and teacher education rather than classroom writing instruction. If I taught writing courses, I reasoned, I would be able to help 15 to 20 students at a time; if I worked with teachers and researchers, I would be able to improve the conditions for a much larger number of L2 writers. I later realized that I would always be teaching writing even in working with graduate students and professionals—as they learn to write articles, dissertations and other professional documents in various genres.

When I went on the job market in 2000, the market was particularly strong in both applied linguistics and rhetoric and composition. Because of my dual specialization in the two booming fields, I was able to find over 60 positions for which I qualified—and that I would have accepted had an offer been extended—at a wide variety of institutions across the United States. My determination to be involved in graduate education must have been obvious; all of the campus interviews and job offers came from masters' and doctoral-level institutions.

Building My Own Nest

On The Tenure Track

My first tenure-track job was Assistant Professor of Composition and Linguistics at Miami University of Ohio, which had a well-established PhD program in Composition and Rhetoric. In addition to teaching undergraduate linguistics courses and writing courses, I taught a graduate seminar on linguistics and writing. The graduate course was my initial attempt to promote the integration of language and writing issues at Miami. The course enrolled only two students, both of them from the PhD program in composition and rhetoric. I was disappointed by the low enrollment, but the department was kind enough not to cancel my class—perhaps because it was my first year. In addition, Christina Ortmeier-Hooper, who was just beginning her doctoral study at the University of New Hampshire (UNH), participated in the course for independent study credits (see Ortmeier-Hooper, this volume). She participated in online discussion of readings and a chat session with Ken Hyland about his corpus-based research on disciplinary discourses. I also invited Ulla Connor as a guest speaker to discuss issues related to contrastive rhetoric.

While I taught my first graduate seminar at Miami, I was also applying for a position at UNH to be closer to my spouse. In the following year, I joined the faculty at UNH, teaching in a small PhD program in Composition Studies. UNH had a long-standing reputation as the cradle of the writing process, especially through the work of Donald Murray, Donald Graves and Thomas Newkirk. The program went through some major transitions during my six-year tenure. My position was a replacement for Robert B. Connors, a renowned historian of composition who was killed in a motorcycle accident. A few years after my arrival, two of the core faculty members, Patricia A. Sullivan and Cinthia Gannett, moved to other institutions. Except for a few years when Jessica Enoch was with us, Tom and I were the only core faculty members.

Given the strength of the program and the availability of courses and teaching opportunities at UNH, I decided to focus on developing specialists in composition studies with an expertise in second language writing. When I arrived, there already were two students who were interested in second language writing: Christina Ortmeier-Hooper and Michelle Cox (see Ortmeier-Hooper, this volume). The program had always had a large pool of applicants, but after a few years, we began to see a growing number of applicants who were interested in L2 writing, including Steve Simpson and Elisabeth Kramer-Simpson. Since the program was relatively small, I was able to work closely with all students in various capacities. I provided additional mentoring for students specializing in L2 writing on an individual basis, collaborating with them on projects and encouraging them to play leadership roles at professional organizations and conferences. The process of mentoring while at UNH is described in Simpson and Matsuda (2008).

Teaching in a small program of a few faculty members and about a dozen PhD students had its advantages. Graduate classes were relatively small, enrolling 8 to 10 students. I was involved in the admission decision of every student, and I served on everyone's dissertation committee. Since I also taught most of the core courses—such as composition theory, history of composition and research methods—I was in close contact with all of the students. By the dissertation stage, all the students were well prepared by my standards. I was also able to create a dual-level (undergraduate/graduate) introductory survey course on second language writing theory, research and instruction, which was offered every other year with a healthy enrollment of students from undergraduate linguistics, MA in TESOL, PhD in education, and PhD in Composition Studies. (The course is now being taught by Christina.) Being in a small program also had its limitations. Although UNH offered a range of courses in rhetoric and composition as well as TESOL, the number of faculty members was small. The availability of teaching assistantships was also rather limited, and we were able to admit only a few PhD students each year. UNH also did not offer a specialization in applied linguistics or TESOL at the doctoral level. The institution did not have a large number of second language writers, enrolling only about 600 international students and a small and unidentified population of resident students. It was a great place to establish my career, but by the time I went up for tenure at UNH, I was feeling I had outgrown this institutional context.

The New Frontier

As I continued to build my professional profile, I began to receive recruitment offers. In September 2006, just after I was tenured at UNH, I received a phone call from Neal Lester, who at the time was the chair of the English department at Arizona State University (ASU). "How would you like to spend a few years in the desert?" he asked. As he explained, it was a strategic hire to upgrade and further strengthen the PhD program in Rhetoric, Composition and Linguistics. ASU already had a strong reputation in the field of rhetoric and composition, and it was also in the process of creating an interdisciplinary PhD program in Applied Linguistics. ASU also had a concentration of students and faculty engaging in cutting-edge research on various topics in applied linguistics, literacy, rhetoric and composition, and TESOL. It also offered teaching and internship opportunities in first-year composition as well as a robust intensive English program. ASU is also rich in linguistic diversity, enrolling numerous users of Spanish and Native American languages as well as one of the largest groups of international students in US higher education. Doctoral students would be able to specialize in second language writing in several disciplinary contexts and to engage in various research projects. The opportunity was too good to pass up. I decided to make the move but offered to continue to work with UNH students as a committee member and informal mentor. To my relief, UNH hired Christina to replace some of my functions and to add a stronger emphasis on literacy at various educational levels (see Ortmeier-Hooper, this volume).

Building an L2 writing community at ASU went much more smoothly than I had expected. ASU already had a track record of producing PhDs who had written dissertations on L2 writing (see Tannacito, this volume), and when I arrived in 2007, several students were already interested in second language writing. Tanita Saenkhum was one of them (see Saenkhum, this volume). Also teaching at ASU was Mark A. James, a former student of Alister Cumming's whose research interests included learning transfer from the L2 first-year composition course to other writing contexts (James, 2008, 2009, 2010). The number of students interested in second language writing grew rapidly. I now supervise over a dozen doctoral students who are working on various topics related to L2 writing in two doctoral programs: Applied Linguistics, and Rhetoric, Composition and Linguistics. (In 2014, the plan was approved to reconfigure these programs into Writing, Rhetorics, and Literacies, and Linguistics and Applied Linguistics.) In addition, an increasing number of students who do not see themselves as specialists are opting to take L2 writing courses to expand their repertoires. There have also been a growing number of master's students in TESOL with an interest in writing research and instruction. Each year, I also sponsor several visiting scholars who bring to the community their interest, experience and expertise in L2 writing.

Having a critical mass of students and colleagues with various levels of interest in L2 writing has created some opportunities for curricular innovations. I started with a catchall graduate-level L2 writing course similar to the one I taught at UNH, but it quickly became apparent that the demand was larger than what a single course could accommodate. To meet the diverse needs of graduate students at different levels, I decided to develop three separate courses—an introductory course focusing on teaching, a practicum for first-time teachers of L2 writing courses, and an advanced course focusing on theory and research. The introductory course is offered every year. The practicum, which is required for first-time L2 writing teachers at ASU, is offered every semester. The advanced course is offered at least every other year with different topics to allow all PhD students to have a chance to take it at least once, if not twice, during the course of study. I have also sponsored group independent studies on topics that are important to my students. In addition, there is a course called cross-cultural discourses; I have taught it with a focus on writing, integrating insights from contrastive or intercultural rhetoric, comparative rhetoric, and genre studies, among other areas.

One of the advantages of a large program is the ability to create a local community of L2 writing specialists. In addition to individual advising—by email, via Skype, and in person—I schedule regular meetings with small groups of students who are at the same stage of professional development. To foster a sense of community, I host potluck dinners at the beginning and at the end of each academic year, and a few additional gatherings in between. These events are primarily for my advisees, visiting scholars and, occasionally, prospective students. They are sometimes combined with workshops on topics such as proposal writing and finding a research topic. During a semester when I was not able to offer L2 writing-related courses, I asked Tanita to organize a monthly reading group, which was open to a larger community of graduate students. Students also seem to have developed their own support network as well—they get together regularly to play tennis, go hiking, and socialize over food and drinks. I also try to visit countries some of my students come from and meet up with them to understand the contexts in which they grew up, worked or will be working in the future.

An Approach to Mentoring

My approach to mentoring combines my interest in applying situated learning theories (Simpson & Matsuda, 2008) as well as my own experience as a graduate student (Matsuda, 2003), both of which I articulate explicitly and share with my advisees at the beginning of the mentoring relationship. I have also been influenced by my own mentors, especially Tony Silva and Janice Lauer. Both of them provided valuable opportunities, support and advice at various points of my own professional development, but they also represented two very different approaches—almost two different ends of the spectrum. Tony was a hands-off mentor, which I appreciated very much because, like Tony, I am an autonomous learner—I don't like to be told what to do. Whenever I met with him, he would ask me what I was working on at the time. I explained my projects, and then he would give me words of encouragement and suggestions, and send me on my way. As I mentioned earlier, he provided opportunities for professional engagement, but he gave me plenty of elbowroom. Still, he took the time to read most of what I wrote while at Purdue and provided encouraging comments and a few pointed pieces of advice as well as editing suggestions. In contrast, Janice was a highly systematic and hands-on mentor. Every course, every reading and every activity had a clear and specific purpose, and I could feel the direction towards which she was steering me. At the same time, she was warm and encouraging. She genuinely cared about her students and the field of rhetoric and composition. Although I was not used to her directive mentoring style, I learned much because I trusted and respected her deep and personal knowledge of the field of rhetoric and composition as well as her commitment to mentoring her students.

Having experienced and appreciated both approaches to mentoring, I have tried to incorporate these approaches into my own mentoring, varying my strategies depending on individual student needs and stages of professional development. In general, my approach to mentoring can be summarized with four keywords: *Exemplify, expose, engage* and *encourage*.

Exemplify

A good first step toward mentoring is to have your own house in order—to establish your own career and to continue engaging in the kind of activities that I want to encourage my students to participate in. Although I collaborate with my students regularly, I also try to engage in my own individual research and publication efforts. Keeping up with my own research and other professional activities is also important so I can carve out opportunities for my students to take part in. Thinking about my own possible research projects also helps as I suggest possible topics for my students.

To help students gain a situated understanding of professional practices, I often use my own examples, both the process and product. I also encourage them to share theirs with one another. I have created a password-protected Web space for my advisees, where I post various documents that I produce, including conference proposals, presentation slides, handouts, human subject protocols, as well as manuscripts under development, under consideration and in press. I also share rejection letters for my manuscripts and proposals—as well as my honest reactions to them. For students who are on the job market, I share my own examples of job application materials, teaching portfolio, and tenure and promotion documents.

I also use blogs and social media to share my own activities, such as having written a manuscript, being stuck in the drafting process, meeting or not meeting deadlines, and so on. I also share my personal life—stories and photos of food, places I visit, and other activities—

to remind others (and myself) that it is important to have a balance in life. This is something that was completely missing when I was a graduate student; I focused almost exclusively on my academic life. Although I do not regret that part of my life—in fact, I still miss being a graduate student when I was able to focus on my own work without having to worry about anything else—I try to set a positive yet realistic example by sharing my attempts to have a life outside academia, including some failed attempts.

I am aware that the example I set can sometimes be intimidating, as a number of students have mentioned to me. Although I set the bar high for myself, I try to be realistic about my expectations for my students. It is quality, not quantity that matters. A related issue is that of identity construction in an interdisciplinary field like second language writing. My goal has always been to position myself as a *bona fide* member of multiple fields, including applied linguistics, rhetoric and composition, and TESOL, among others. That kind of multidisciplinary positioning was important for my own agenda—to help build the field of second language writing. I do recognize, however, that it is not necessary for everyone who works in the field. Indeed, some of my students identify themselves primarily as applied linguists while others situate themselves in rhetoric and composition. What I try to facilitate is an awareness of various identity positions that are available for second language writing specialists, each with its own potential and limitations. I also try to encourage students to continue to branch out even while grounding themselves firmly in one of the disciplines they can call home.

Expose

As I share my own work, I also try to explain the back-stage stories. One of the major obstacles for beginning graduate students and early-career professionals is the wide array of tacit assumptions and practices in academia that are passed down from one generation to the next without explicit instruction or even explanation. While many graduate programs and mentors are getting better at providing orientations and occasional workshops to demystify graduate school and academic careers, graduate students are still expected to figure out the rules of the game mostly by trial and error. Just as some people find it helpful to have some aspects of language and genre described and explained explicitly, many students and early-career professionals seem to find it helpful to hear explicit discussion of various assumptions, practices and strategies that are often tacitly passed down from one generation of academics to another.

While figuring out the tacit assumptions and practices is hard for all students, they are especially inaccessible to those who come from non-dominant linguistic, cultural and educational backgrounds. The real significance of this point is often lost on those who have never been marginalized in society in significant and sustained ways. As a first-generation college graduate and nonnative English user from Asia in Anglophone dominated academia, I have faced many of the challenges that some of my students face as they seek to enter the academic community. Fortunately, I have been able to figure out many of those assumptions and practices through my experience and observations, by reading various books and articles about the academic profession, and with the help of my mentors. I consider it my mission to make those insights (and more) available to the next generation of L2 writing specialists. Some of my publications reflect this belief (Matsuda, 2003; Silva & Matsuda, 2005; Simpson & Matsuda, 2008). The piece you are reading right now is another example.

I also make a conscious effort to tell the stories behind my own work. They are not all success stories. In fact, I make a point of sharing my own narratives of frustration, failed attempts and negotiations as well as my honest reactions to these experiences and coping strategies. I strongly believe these behind-the-scenes stories are important as a way of contextualizing and complicating the neat and clean appearance of published works, which only tells a small part of the real story (see Matsuda & Silva, 2005). I also encourage advanced graduate students to share their documents and talk about their experiences, not only for the benefit of others but also as a way of gaining experience in mentoring.

I constantly tell my students that I have very high standards but will provide strategies to help them meet those standards. I try to expose the assumptions, practices and strategies of academia both in and out of class: when I explain assignments, when I provide feedback on student projects, when I engage in conversations about conferences, when I collaborate with my students, and when I have social gatherings with my students. Sometimes I conduct workshops focusing on specific aspects of professional development, such as finding research topics and writing conference proposals. I also try to make some of the information available beyond the community of my advisees. To this end, I keep a blog that provides unsolicited advice on various professional matters. If I were a magician, I would be labeled a rogue magician for revealing the secrets of the trade. But I am no magician, and I am not worried about competition. I strongly believe that the field will be better off when everyone has access to metadisciplinary knowledge.

Engage

One of the most effective ways I know of mentoring graduate students is to engage them in real professional activities that I am involved in. As I have described in Simpson and Matsuda (2008), I am constantly looking for ways to carve out collaboration opportunities with my advisees from my own ongoing professional activities. Depending on the level of experience, students engage at different levels and in different ways. When the task is a challenging one, I may take the lead and ask my advisees to play supporting roles. At an early stage of development, students may mostly watch what I do: as I talk through a plan, draft and revise the text, respond to feedback, and so on. As they gain more experience, I gradually try to shift the responsibility to students in order to give them more agency. The transition is not always predictable. Sometimes I start by talking through the aim and scope of the project, outlining key components, and identifying key sources before sending students off to develop a draft. In many cases, I ask students to draft a text and then I ask them to watch me as I revise or completely rewrite each sentence and each paragraph, explaining my rationale every step of the way. For more advanced students or colleagues, I may ask them to take charge as I monitor their progress and provide feedback along the way.

Delegation has not always been my strong suit, but with experience, I have become better at trusting my student-collaborators, especially those who are more advanced and accomplished. In putting together *Second Language Writing in the Composition Classroom* (2006), I asked two of my advisees, Michelle Cox and Christina Ortmeier-Hooper, to be co-editors. I also asked Jay Jordan, then a graduate student at another institution, to join the team. One of my motives was to expose Jay to the discourse of second language writing. Although he was already incredibly well versed in the literature for someone who was studying at an institution without an L2 writing specialist, I felt that he would benefit from the socialization experience that his interactions with Michelle and Christina would provide. At the same time, I wanted to give Michelle and Christina an opportunity to be exposed to the discourse outside the local university community.

My role in this project was to conceptualize the overall aim of the project and the framework, and to propose and negotiate the project idea with the publisher. I also provided feedback on the selection of articles for inclusion and on drafts of the overall introduction and section introductions. Although I had my own ideas about articles to include in this collection, and although I did provide guidance in developing the categories, I tried not to play a central role in choosing the readings. Instead, I asked each of my collaborators to be responsible for a few sections and to develop a list of readings for each of the sections, which we would then discuss as a group. My primary intention in asking them to take charge was to encourage more autonomy. At the same time, however, I was hoping to get fresh perspectives on the issues that I was becoming too close to. The collaborative effort resulted in a much more diverse and well-rounded collection than what I would have been able to put together by myself. The success of this project helped me become better at controlling my own impulse to take charge and to let my students and collaborators work at their own pace, while monitoring progress and providing guidance along the way.

In addition to research and publication projects, I have also been seeking ways to carve out opportunities to gain administrative experience. At ASU, I have been able to create the title of Assistant Director of Second Language Writing for graduate students who wish to gain some administrative experience. While this is not a paid position (at the time of drafting this piece), it provides opportunities to engage in various projects for doctoral students who are interested in writing program administration or those who wish to obtain additional professional experience with first-year composition. Tanita Saenkhum, who specialized in L2 writing program administration, was the first to hold this position, and she worked on improving the placement practices for L2 writers in the first-year composition program (see Saenkhum, this volume). The Symposium on Second Language Writing also provides additional opportunities for professional development, allowing students to gain hands-on experience in planning and organizing a conference.

Encourage

Encouragement is something I struggle with the most. I have extremely high expectations—for myself and for my students—and I let my students know that from the beginning of the mentoring relationship. Although I do believe that encouragement is important, I do not like to give or receive empty praise. I tend to be rather straightforward in describing issues and concerns in students' work, but I try to provide a sense of direction and resources to help them move forward. I also tend to provide a large amount of feedback, which I know can be overwhelming. I do expect graduate students to develop a thick skin that can withstand the challenges of manuscript reviews, and tenure and promotion reviews. In providing my critique and suggestions, however, I consciously try to separate the quality of work from the person who created it.

I do provide positive feedback when it seems appropriate. On a regular basis, I try to verbalize my students' strengths and accomplishments when I see them, however big or small they may be. Beyond those positive observations, I often visualize the distribution of my encouragement as an arc, much like the narrative arc, which starts by setting the stage, developing the plot, reaching the climax, and ending with a resolution. I use this principle in writing courses as well: The beginning of the semester sets the tone for the course, with a bit of anxiety and excitement for what is to come. The story unfolds with each class meeting and assignments, each challenging students in small ways but providing resources and encouragement to move on to the next stage. Then comes the climax—the most challenging assignment for the semester—and the semester ends with a sense of accomplishment, resolution and satisfaction. My praise for student work is strategically placed along this arc of encouragement. This principle also works for each writing project as well.

For graduate students, the arc of encouragement plays out differently. Unlike undergraduate students in writing courses, graduate students have bigger goals and longer-term relationships with me and with their colleagues. The main arc is the entire degree program, not just a semester or a project. In providing feedback on course projects, for example, I do not necessarily seek to provide a sense of resolution or accomplishment (unless it is deserved) beyond the satisfaction of having completed the assignment sufficiently and on time. Instead, my feedback often leaves students with a sense of dissonance that can lead to further thinking, reading, writing, and revising that gives them a sense of where they are and where they need to go next along the trajectory. The irresolute ending is not just my discursive construction; students do need to know that most course papers (even "A" papers) do not meet the expectations for publishable manuscripts. There are exceptions, of course; I managed to publish most of my graduate course papers, and some of my students have also been able to publish revised course projects successfully (e.g., DePalma & Ringer, 2011).

So, when do I offer my encouragement and how? The key is found in the words of my daughter's piano teacher. At the recital for her students, she always makes the point of asking the audience to provide words of encouragement to other people's children. "When parents praise their own children, they don't believe it," she explains, "but when it comes from other people, it's real." I encourage my students to attend and present at conferences not only to be socialized into the profession and to establish themselves in the field but also to expose them to real and meaningful assessment of their professional development. Many students come back from conferences excited that their work was recognized by peers and senior members of the field. When someone tells me my students are impressive, I make a point of conveying the message to the students. When they receive awards and other forms of recognition, when they pass exams, when their proposals and manuscripts are accepted, and when they reach other significant milestones in their careers, I congratulate them and share the news on my blog and through social media. I also announce and celebrate those accomplishments at the potluck dinners with my students at my house.

Coda

I have high expectations for myself and for my students, and my students know that. I expect them to work hard, but I also do everything I can to provide the support and resources to help them succeed. I tell my students that, if they can meet my expectations, they will be fine out there in the field. I also tell them that my mentoring comes with a lifetime warranty. It takes an enormous amount of time and effort for me to sustain this type of mentoring relationship, especially with the growing number of students, and I imagine working with me requires a serious commitment on the part of my students. But can we do it? Yes, we can.

REFERENCES

DePalma, M. J., & Ringer, J. M. (2011). Toward a theory of adaptive transfer: Expanding disciplinary discussions of "transfer" in second-language writing and composition studies. *Journal of Second Language Writing, 20,* 134-147.

James, M. A. (2008). Learning transfer in second language writing education: The impact of task similarity/difference. *Written Communication, 29*(2), 133-147.

James, M. A. (2009). "Far" transfer of learning outcomes from an ESL writing course: Can the gap be bridged? *Journal of Second Language Writing, 18*(2), 69-84.

James, M. A. (2010). An investigation of learning transfer in English-for-general-academic-purposes writing instruction. *Journal of Second Language Writing, 19*(4), 183-205.

Kantor, J. (2012, September 2). The competitor in chief: Obama plays to win, in politics and everything else. *New York Times.* Retrieved from http://www.nytimes.com

Leki, I. (1991). *Understanding ESL writers: A guide for composition teachers.* Portsmouth, NH: Boynton/Cook Heinemann.

Matsuda, P. K. (1997a). Contrastive rhetoric in context: A dynamic model of L2 writing. *Journal of Second Language Writing, 6*(1), 45-60.

Matsuda, P. K. (1997b). The first five years of the JSLW: A retrospective. *Journal of Second Language Writing, 6*(2), iv-v.

Matsuda, P. K. (1997c). [Review of the book *Theory and practice of writing: An applied linguistic perspective,* by W. Grabe & R. B. Kaplan]. *TESOL Quarterly, 31*(2), 375-377.

Matsuda, P. K. (2001). Voice in Japanese written discourse: Implications for second language writing. *Journal of Second Language Writing, 10*(1-2), 35-53.

Matsuda, P. K. (2002). Negotiation of identity and power in a Japanese online discourse community. *Computers and Composition, 19*(1), 39-55.

Matsuda, P. K. (2003). Coming to voice: Publishing as a graduate student. In C. P. Casanave & S. Vandrick (Eds.), *Writing for publication: Behind the scenes in language education* (pp. 39-51). Mahwah, NJ: Lawrence Erlbaum Associates.

Matsuda, P. K. (2005). Historical inquiry in second language writing. In P. K. Matsuda & T. Silva (Eds.), *Second language writing research: Perspec-*

tives on the process of knowledge construction (pp. 33-46). Mahwah, NJ: Lawrence Erlbaum Associates.

Matsuda, P. K. (2012a). Historiography. In C. Chapelle (Ed.), *Encyclopedia of applied linguistics*. Oxford, UK: Wiley-Blackwell.

Matsuda, P. K. (2012b). Teaching composition in the multilingual world: Second language writing in composition studies. In K. Ritter & P. K. Matsuda (Eds.), *Exploring composition studies: Sites, issues and perspectives* (pp. 36-51). Logan, UT: Utah State University Press.

Santos, T., Atkinson, D., Erickson, M., Matsuda, P. K., & Silva, T. (2000). On the future of second language writing: A colloquium. *Journal of Second Language Writing, 9*(1), 1-20.

Silva, T. (2012). JSLW@20: The prequel and the inside story (with several previously unpublished bonus texts). *Journal of Second Language Writing, 21*(3), 187-194.

Silva, T., & Matsuda, P. K. (Eds.). (2001a). *Landmark essays on ESL writing*. Mahwah, NJ: Lawrence Erlbaum Associates.

Silva, T., & Matsuda, P. K. (Eds.). (2001b). *On second language writing*. Mahwah, NJ: Lawrence Erlbaum Associates.

Simpson, S., & Matsuda, P. K. (2008). Mentoring as a long-term relationship: Situated learning in a doctoral program. In C. P. Casanave & X. Li (Eds.), *Learning the literacy practices of graduate school: Insiders' reflections on academic enculturation* (pp. 90-104). Ann Arbor: University of Michigan Press.

7 Choices in Identity Building as an L2 Writing Specialist: Investment and Perseverance

Tanita Saenkhum

I begin this chapter with an anecdote. In the spring of 2006, while I was in an early stage of my master's thesis work, I wrote an email to an established second language writing scholar asking for suggestions for readings focusing on second language writers in first-year composition classrooms. A few minutes later, I received a reply to my email to which three articles were attached. I was very surprised and impressed by that speedy reply. When I applied for my PhD study, the university where this professor worked at that moment was one of my top choices. Unfortunately, I could not submit my application to this institution because my GRE scores had not arrived and it was impossible to meet the deadline. I was really disappointed because I thought that I lost my opportunity to work with this professor.

But everything happens for a reason, and I do feel thankful for not being able to submit my application. In the fall of 2007, when I started my PhD study at Arizona State University (ASU), I was surprised (again) by the presence of this same professor at an annual Linguistics/TESOL social gathering. I learned at the event that this professor had recently joined ASU's Rhetoric, Composition, and Linguistics program, and I took that opportunity to introduce myself to him, to explain that I was interested in second language writing, and to show interest in working with him. A week after our discussion about my research interest and career plan, this professor agreed to take me on as his mentee. Ever since then, Paul Kei Matsuda has been my mentor, teacher, and dissertation director. We have also collaborated on research projects and publications.

In this chapter, I discuss my perspective on going through doctoral education in second language (L2) writing, highlighting choices in identity building as an L2 writing specialist, and my decision to choose a tenure-track position in the United States. I graduated in the spring of 2012 and was subsequently hired as a tenure-track Assistant Professor of English with a specialization in second language writing in the Rhetoric, Writing, and Linguistics program at the University of Tennessee, Knoxville (UTK).

My background had nothing to do with teaching. A journalism major, I first worked as a columnist for a women's magazine and later as a journalist for an English newspaper, both in Thailand. Through many years of such experience, I discovered how much I loved writing, even though it was challenging to write in a language that was not my mother tongue. As a journalist, I worked under deadlines and pressure, writing on variable subject matters for a wide audience. Being able to write as a journalist was a big stepping stone to my other career goals. At that point, I thought about changing my career since I no longer wanted to write as a reporter; rather I wanted to pass on my knowledge of writing to those who were interested. All of a sudden, the idea of teaching came into sight; I wanted to be a writing teacher. But I did not have a teaching degree; "How could that be possible?" I asked myself. A year later, after researching various teaching degree programs and getting accepted to an institution in the United States, I decided to quit my job in order to pursue my master's degree in Teaching English to Speakers of Other Languages (TESOL) at Southern Illinois University Carbondale (SIUC) with a clear goal of learning how to teach writing. This is where the serious journey of my academic career began.

I first came into contact with the term "second language writing" when I took a course on teaching English as a Second Language (ESL) composition in my first semester at SIUC. That course was required for all new graduate teaching assistants who would be teaching first-year composition to ESL students for the first time. I first heard of Paul Kei Matsuda, Tony Silva, Ilona Leki, Dana Ferris, and other prominent L2 writing specialists from reading their work in that course. In addition to teaching first-year composition to international students,

I had the opportunity to assist the Director of the ESL Writing Program at SIUC in administering written placement tests, evaluating essays, and deciding course placement for students. I also co-organized a one-week training session for new graduate teaching assistants in the Linguistics department, where I mentored one writing teacher who was teaching second language students for the first time. Since then, I knew that L2 writing was going to be my area of specialization; I chose to focus my thesis on how L2 undergraduate students transferred what they learned in first-year L2 writing courses to writing in the disciplines (Saenkhum, 2007a). Later, when pursuing my PhD in Rhetoric, Composition, and Linguistics at ASU, I chose to specialize in L2 writing with a focus on writing program administration in order to broaden my scholarship in these two related fields.

Identity Building As An L2 Writing Specialist

Over the course of my graduate career, I participated in various communities of practice (Lave & Wenger, 1991) that, in turn, helped develop my identity as an L2 writing specialist. I took on extra responsibilities, instead of just completing coursework, writing a dissertation, graduating, and having a doctoral degree. In what follows, I discuss how my identity has been shaped by my involvement in professional organizations, engagement in collaboration, and apprenticeship as a writing program administrator (WPA). In all of these capacities, Paul, my mentor, played a significant role in supporting and helping me build my L2 writing specialist profile, providing me with various professional development opportunities.

Involvement In Professional Organizations

In order to learn more about the field of L2 writing, I actively attended and presented at regional, national, and international conferences related to second language writing. My professional debut was at the Annual Illinois Teachers of ESOL & Bilingual Education Conference in March of 2006, where I delivered a teaching demonstration based on a project entitled "Journalistic Interview: Promoting Better ESL Writing" (Saenkhum, 2006), originally developed in a course called "Teaching Composition in a Second Language" at SIUC. My teaching demonstration adapted the one-on-one interviews used in journalism to teach L2 students how to better organize their writing. The rationale behind this teaching demonstration was that a successful journalistic interview requires solid research, question planning, and strategic organization of material to make the resultant article interesting and readable. My second professional presentation was at the Conference on College Composition and Communication (CCCC) in 2007, where I presented a paper on characteristics of ESL writing in the disciplines of business and engineering (Saenkhum, 2007b). The paper was part of my master's thesis, which investigated knowledge transfer from first-year ESL writing classes to writing in the disciplines (Saenkhum, 2007a)

I became more involved in professional organizations through working with Paul, serving as a symposium assistant for the Symposium on Second Language Writing (SSLW), which Paul and Tony Silva co-founded, between 2008 and 2011. I have also given presentations at SSLW since 2008 and served as a proposal reviewer since 2009. I was more actively involved in SSLW when I served as Associate Chair for the symposium in 2009 that took place at ASU (see Matsuda, this volume). Together with Paul, Tony, and Mark James, who also served as Associate Chair, I worked on the symposium planning, programming, and scheduling. Through this valuable experience, I learned how to collaborate with other professionals in the field and ultimately enhanced my understanding of the possibilities for a professional career. In addition to helping me develop my leadership skills, this opportunity allowed me to expand my professional network; I was able to get to know researchers from other universities who share my research interests, and I continue to collaborate with a number of them on conference proposals and presentations.

Apart from being involved in SSLW, I, as a graduate student, participated in other professional organizations such as the Second Language Writing Interest Section (SLW-IS) of TESOL and the CCCC's Committee on Second Language Writing. I attended their business meetings and took part in other scholarly activities, including working on workshop proposals for CCCC. As a result, I gradually developed my own academic community. My work commitment and involvement in the field of L2 writing have become more formal when I, as an assistant professor, was elected in March 2014 to the steering committee member-at-large for the SLW-IS and was invited to join the CCCC Committee on Second Language Writing, both for three-year terms.

Engagement in Collaboration

Apart from being involved in professional organizations, I had various opportunities to work collaboratively with my mentor and other graduate students. Paul and I published an Annotated Bibliography of Second Language Writing and Writing Program Administration in the *WPA-CompPile Research Bibliographies* (Saenkhum & Matsuda, 2010) and a review essay of three books in *WPA: Writing Program Administration* (Saenkhum & Matsuda, 2011). Along with Steven Accardi, we revised and resubmitted a manuscript based on an institutional survey of writing teachers' perceptions of the presence and needs of multilingual writers to the *Journal of Second Language Writing*, and it was accepted for publication (Matsuda, Saenkhum, & Accardi, 2013). We also presented findings from this institutional survey study at different conferences, such as CWPA, SSLW, CCCC, and AAAL.

In addition to publication and presentation collaboration, Paul and I also submitted a proposal to the CCCC and won a 2010-2011 CCCC Research Initiative for our project on the placement of multilingual writers in college composition programs, which collected data from a survey of writing program administrators across the country. The goal was to examine various US colleges' and universities' placement of multilingual writers in order to generate information that could help improve the quality of placement practices in college composition programs. This was an excellent hands-on experience for me; I learned how to write a grant proposal by doing it myself, with Paul providing comments and suggestions, and together discussing revisions. Enabled by the national grant, we are in the process of data analysis and writing up an article to be submitted to a major journal in the field of rhetoric and composition.

Working collaboratively on these research projects helped immensely to develop my research skills and, in turn, strengthen my dissertation, which investigated the role of agency in multilingual writers' placement decisions. By learning how to design questionnaires from the nationwide survey, I was independently able to craft different sets of interview questions and use them when conducting a series of four in-depth interviews with multilingual student participants. My prior experience in analyzing data from the institutional survey study informed my ability to understand this new data for my dissertation

Through working on these collaborative projects, I also learned that Paul sets high standards and expectations, which was evident from the constructive, critical, and thoughtful feedback he provided on various working drafts of each project (see Matsuda, this volume). Paul read every single line, and his feedback was both thorough and prompt; I always received it within one or two days, sometimes even one or two hours. This prompted me to be fast in my response as well; I tended to work on revisions right away, and I usually would not let his comments sit for long. At first, I would count how many times I revised a draft; eventually I came to see it as a fluid, ongoing part of the writing process and adopted the mantra: Keep Revising. Paul's high standards encouraged me to achieve more and do better. From receiving his feedback, I learned to analyze my audience, understand genre, and establish a coherent argument. These skills helped me win two competitive awards: TESOL's Albert H. Marckwardt Travel Grant in 2009 and CCCC Chairs' Memorial Scholarship in 2012. The former was judged on an applicant's statement that addressed his or her scholarship, personal attributes, involvement in and commitment to ESL/EFL teaching and the profession, and financial need. The latter was judged on the quality of the proposal submitted for the annual CCCC. Both the statement and proposal were evaluated based on the quality of writing, among other things.

To be honest, I found that my biggest challenge in revision was my own tendency to become frustrated at my inability to express myself clearly and fluently. I learned that I could not force myself to write or revise if I felt upset. I came to the conclusion that I could revise more productively when my mind was clear, and I had a good sense of what my final product would look like. As a writer, I have come to deeply value feedback, and as a professor I tend to be explicit with my students about how I view it. I often share with them feedback I receive from colleagues and peers. I want them to understand that feedback is not only common but also necessary in the academic arena. One thing I learned from Paul that I use when providing feedback to student writing is to ask what types of comments students want from me. This encourages them to think about their own writing and allows them to engage with and be responsible for their own texts. I find this practice very helpful in the way that it allows me to meet the needs of my students.

Apprenticeship

In my last year at ASU, while finishing up my dissertation, I served as the Assistant Director of Second Language Writing in the Writing Programs. Paul created this position for graduate students who were interested in program administration and wanted to have administrative experience (see Matsuda, this volume). As the Assistant Director of Second Language Writing, I helped improve the placement procedures for multilingual writers—including international visa students and US residents or citizens who are nonnative English speaking students—by providing recommendations for increasing communication between the writing program, academic advisors, writing teachers, and multilingual students. This initiative was based on part of the results of my dissertation that showed academic advisors' lack of an accurate understanding of first-year composition placement and available placement options, as well as multilingual students' misunderstanding about placement information (Saenkhum, 2012). To increase first-year composition placement communication, I designed a brochure and handout that contained information about available first-year composition placement options, test score cutoffs, and a brief description of available courses. The writing program later distributed these documents to first-year multilingual students and academic advisors. I also recommended that the writing program disseminate placement information to other related academic units, such as ASU's freshman orientation and the office of international students.

In addition, I served as a member of the ASU Writing Programs Committee and presented a proposal to change course titles and descriptions of multilingual composition courses that caused the misplacement of multilingual writers, especially resident, nonnative English students. This proposal was based on data that Paul, Steven, and I collected from the institutional survey of writing teachers' perceptions of the presence and needs of multilingual writers in first-year composition courses. The survey also showed what teachers needed in order to work effectively with multilingual writers. As a result, the Director of Second Language Writing established a mentoring program for those who teach multilingual composition, as well as for mainstream teachers who have multilingual students in their classes.

Through the apprenticeship, I gained hands-on experience in program administration for multilingual writers. I also developed my understanding of the kind of work that WPAs do. This valuable opportunity has prepared me to effectively work with multilingual students who are part of college composition programs in US higher education.

Being Hired as an L2 Writing Specialist

Before I go into detail on my job search, I will briefly discuss my preparation for understanding the job search process in the United States. I started reading academic job advertisements on a listserv I subscribed to during my first year of doctoral study, participated in workshops on job application preparation, and attended candidates' job talks. One aspect of the job search I found especially helpful was when I had the opportunity to assist job candidates during their campus visits to ASU. I had seen what their schedule looked like, whom they had to have lunch or dinner with, and what they had to wear, among other things. These tiny yet important details helped me become prepared when I became a job candidate myself.

I went on the job market in the fall semester of 2011, but I had been thinking about applying since I entered the fourth year of my doctoral study because I was uncertain about where I wanted to work: here in the United States or in Thailand, my home country. It was a tough decision; I kept going back and forth between these two choices. At the end of my fourth year, a professor from a well-known university in Thailand approached me and encouraged me to apply upon completion of my degree. I was tempted by this potential offer for two main reasons: I could go back home and live with my family, and I could secure a position at one of the top two universities in the country. That temptation was only dampened by the fact that I had invested for so long in my academic career here in the United States. My research had been based here, and I wanted to continue it. I found it difficult to make a decision myself, so I discussed with Paul all the possibilities, advantages, and disadvantages of working in those two locations. Finally, I made a decision to apply for jobs in the United States with my own rationale: to continue my scholarship of second language writing with a focus on writing program administration for second language students.

Once the decision was made, I worked with Paul closely during my job search period, beginning with preparing job application materials before moving on to job interviews, campus visits, job talks, and accepting and negotiating job offers. Job applications require a lot of work in putting materials together: CV, cover letter, research statement/agenda, teaching philosophy, teaching portfolio, and description of experience in writing program administration. Like other job applicants, I did not just produce these documents once because I applied for multiple positions, and I tailored each application to each position. To increase my odds of success, I sent out 49 job applications, which I felt was crazy. I applied for everything: research and teaching institutions, tenure and non-tenure track positions, renewable and full-time positions. Later, I realized what I did was not unusual. Many of my friends did the same thing; some of them even sent out 60-70 job applications.

Sometimes, you do not know exactly what you want to do in your career. For me, I just knew that I wanted to do research on L2 writing and train prospective teachers to work with L2 students. In my case, it became clear when I saw a job advertisement from the University of Tennessee, Knoxville. Paul had forwarded the advertisement to me and left a brief message at the end: "This is Ilona's replacement." The full email reads as follows:

In case you haven't seen this:

> U of Tennessee, Knoxville
> English, 301 McClung Tower, Knoxville, TN 37996
> http://www.utk.edu
> Assistant or Associate Professor, Second Language Writing in English. [15577]

>> The University of Tennessee, Knoxville, is seeking applications for a tenure-track position as Assistant or Associate Professor of English, with specialization in L2 writing in English. The successful candidate will teach in areas such as language acquisition and other domains related to TESL. In addition, he or she will play a significant role in course and program development and administration. Position requires PhD in Rhetoric/Composition with L2 writing specialization/concentration, Applied Linguistics, or related field, experience or

strong interest in directing a writing program for multilingual students, a record of teaching excellence, and publications appropriate to the rank. Duties include active participation in graduate and undergraduate programs, both in the English department and in conjunction with relevant L2 faculty in other departments, plus significant research and publication. UTK features the BA, MA, and PhD in English with an emphasis in Rhetoric, Writing, and Linguistics. Salary and teaching loads are competitive, and our endowment provides ample support for research and travel. UTK, a "Doctoral/Research Extensive" institution, is the flagship university in the state system. Applications due by November 1, but the search will remain open until the position is filled. Send letter of application and dossier (including detailed description of current project(s), a statement of philosophy of teaching and a description of interest and/or experience in program administration, and vita) to Misty Anderson, Associate Head, Department of English, University of Tennessee, Knoxville, TN 37996-0430. The University of Tennessee is an EEO/AA/Title VI/Title IX/Section 504/ADA/ADEA institution in the provision of its education and employment programs and services. All qualified applicants will receive equal consideration for employment without regard to race, color, national origin, religion, sex, pregnancy, marital status, sexual orientation, gender identity, age, physical or mental disability, or covered veteran status.

This is Ilona's replacement.
P

I responded to Paul's email and let him know that: "This position is exactly what I was looking for." I read the job advertisement over and over, and my heart kept beating. What was written in the job advertisement was exactly what I had been trained to do during my graduate school career.

When working on job application documents for this and other positions, I realized how everything I did in graduate school came together; it helped prepare me for the "real work world." I was able to draw on my various experiences and professional involvement in the field of second language writing to compose application materials. I also realized how Paul's high standards and expectations of quality of writing came into play. Certain job application documents required a great deal of genre and audience analysis, as well as a well-written and established argument. My understanding of these issues and my experience in writing with Paul helped ease the process of working on these documents. I did not start from scratch; rather I utilized what I learned from receiving feedback and applied those skills to the production of my job application materials.

When I learned that I was invited for a campus interview, I was thrilled and nervous. Fortunately, those feelings of uncertainly did not linger as long as I expected, though I did have butterflies in my stomach until the last day of my visit. Yet I was able to feel at ease because I knew what a campus interview and its process would look like, thanks to my prior experience in taking care of job candidates and attending their job talks. I found my job talk the most challenging part of the process because the majority of the audience was not from the field of L2 writing and was not familiar with my topic. I did my homework about the department and knew who would be my audience so that I could deliver my presentation in a way that everyone could understand. Again, this confirmed for me the importance of being able to know and analyze one's audience. I had the good fortune to be hired for what I felt like my dream job.

I started my tenure-track Assistant Professor position in the Rhetoric, Writing, and Linguistics program in the Department of English at The University of Tennessee, Knoxville (UTK) in the fall of 2012 with a 2-2 teaching load. My position is a replacement for the renowned L2 writing specialist Ilona Leki, who retired in 2010 and stayed post retirement through 2011. I am grateful for this opportunity, as it allows me to continue to do research on L2 writing and train prospective teachers to work with L2 students. In my first two years, I taught both graduate and undergraduate courses on L2 writing, teaching English as a second/foreign language, pedagogical grammar for ESL teachers, sociolinguistics, and second language acquisition.

My appointment has a component of administrative work, but I did not take over UTK's ESL Program until my second year. Because of the administrative duty, my teaching responsibilities have been reduced to a 1-2 load beginning in the fall of 2013. Before I assumed the director position, I took my first year to observe one of its co-directors administering an English placement exam to L2 students (international students are the majority), evaluating exam essays, deciding placement for students, and coordinating with other related academic units. My apprenticeship as a WPA at ASU has perfectly prepared me for my current position; what I used to do there makes my tasks here at UTK easier. As the director of ESL Program, I handle first-year composition sections for L2 students; determine the English placement exam policies; recruit, prepare, and supervise L2 writing instructors; serve as a liaison between the ESL program and other related stakeholders across campus; and lead faculty-development workshops within the English department and across campus, among other duties.

Nevertheless, as a pre-tenure writing program administrator, I find this administrative role the most challenging. First and foremost, since I am new to the institution, I am still in the process of navigating and articulating the institutional cultures and the department's system, among other things. Second, administrative work takes a considerable amount of time, energy, and effort. As one can imagine, I have to juggle my own research, teaching, administrative work, and other departmental service, including advising both undergraduate and graduate students. Third, as the director of ESL, I have been asked by other departments and units on campus to serve on various committees related to ESL. While I cannot take on additional roles since I already have a lot on my plate, I am in the process of learning to say "No."

In grappling with those challenges, I have developed some strategies while negotiating the workloads in order to balance my work. I hope what I share here will be helpful to those who currently are or will be working as pre-tenure writing program administrators, a position that an increasing number of junior faculty have been asked to take on in their early-career (Saenkhum, 2014). Assistant professors need to be protected, and I believe everyone realizes this. First, I seek help and advice from my faculty mentor and department head. Every new tenure-track assistant professor at UTK is assigned to a faculty mentor who serves as his or her academic advocate. In my case, I always communicate with my faculty mentor, keeping him informed about my research progress, teaching, administrative work, and other related issues and concerns. For example, when I was asked to serve on a search committee for another department and did not think I could take it on. I did want to say "No," but saying it to the head of that department was difficult for me. To be honest, I did not know how to respond to that request and so decided to consult my mentor and department head who both knew about my situation. They said since I was over extended, it was perfectly fine for me not to take on this additional role. In the end, I was confident enough to decline that request. Yet, I am learning to say "No."

Second, because I do not want to lose my writing momentum, it is crucial that I save an entire day or two (during regular semesters) for my research and writing. This is something that I can control. So, I set a time and concentrate on my writing, and I do not open emails until I am done writing on that day. I know it is easy to say. In fact, it is the hardest thing to do. In addition, I have a writing buddy who is also an assistant professor in the same department. We get together and write for four to five hours a day once a week. Having a writing companion has helped me immensely. We encourage each other to write since we are both working toward to same goal of getting tenured and promoted.

Third, I find support from my fellow assistant professors, both within the department and outside the institution. It is important for junior faculty to have someone who is in the same situation to share things with and to talk to. As I mentioned earlier, I have my own academic community, and folks from this academic circle are my friends who share research interests. We used to be graduate students, and we currently are assistant professors. I still keep in touch with all of them and continue to collaborate on conference presentations and publications. In addition to working collaboratively, we discuss and share with one another what we have encountered and gone through as junior assistant professors. By discussing and sharing, we have learned from one another and have developed a better understanding of how the academy works.

All things considered, I find time management the most challenging part of the tenure-track career. I am learning to strike a balance between research (working on my writing), administrative work, and teaching; at the same time, I want to make sure that I have a well-rounded, healthy life.

This may seem like a story with a happy ending, yet the real story has just begun. What I have shared with you so far is just a prologue. I cannot know what will happen over the next five or ten years, but one thing I can do is to continue to invest, commit, and persevere.

Coda

I would like to emphasize the essential nature of participating in communities of practice, which can help one become prepared when she or he is on the job market as well as when she or he enters the real academic work world. Graduate students, talk to and consult your mentors about your career plan. Mentors are great resources for your professional development; they can even help open the door to opportunities for you. Yet, you are the one who needs to take the initiative and walk through those doors.

Acknowledgments

I am grateful to Paul Kei Matsuda, Christina Ortmeier-Hooper, and Richard Hermes for their helpful comments on an earlier version of this chapter.

References

Lave, J., & Wenger, E. (1991). *Situated learning: Legitimate peripheral participation.* Cambridge, UK: Cambridge University Press.

Matsuda, P. K., Saenkhum, T., & Accardi, S. (2013). Writing teachers' perceptions of the presence and needs of second language writers: An institutional case study. *Journal of Second Language Writing, 22*(1), 68-86.

Saenkhum, T. (2006, March). *Journalistic interview: Promoting better ESL writing.* Paper presented at the Illinois Teachers of ESOL & Bilingual Education Conference, Naperville, IL.

Saenkhum, T. (2007a). *Transfer of knowledge from first-year ESL writing classes to writing in the disciplines: Case studies of writing across the curriculum* (Master's thesis). Retrieved from ProQuest Dissertation and Theses database. (UMI No. 1448819).

Saenkhum, T. (2007b, March). *Characteristics of ESL writing in WAC.* Paper presented at the Conference on College Composition and Communication, New York, NY.

Saenkhum, T. (2012). *Investigating agency in multilingual writers' placement decisions: A case study of the writing program at Arizona State University.* (Doctoral dissertation). Retrieved from ProQuest Dissertation and Theses database. (UMI No. 3505626).

Saenkhum, T. (2014, March). *Exploring ways to balance research, administrative work, and teaching as a pre-tenure writing program administrato*r.

Paper presented at TESOL International Convention and English Language Expo.

Saenkhum, T., & Matsuda, P. K. (2010). Second language writing and writing program administration, WPA-CompPile Research Bibliographies (No. 4). *WPA-CompPile Research Bibliographies*. Retrieved from http://comppile.org/wpa/bibliographies/Saenkhum_Matsuda.pdf.

Saenkhum, T., & Matsuda, P. K. (2011). Second language writers in college composition programs: Towards awareness, knowledge and action. *WPA: Writing Program Administration, 35*(1), 199-203.

8 From Doctoral Education to the Tenure Track: Lessons and Observations from the Journey

Christina Ortmeier-Hooper

In 2007, I completed my PhD. Currently, I am an advanced assistant professor at a research institution, which also happens to be my alma mater. I work with graduate students with interests in composition, literacy studies, linguistics, and second language writing, and I have gone from being the advisee to the advisor. As a doctoral student, though, I remember finding guidance and confidence in talks given by Dana Ferris (2005), Linda Lonon Blanton (2005), Stephanie Vandrick (2006), and Christine Tardy (2010), among others. These talks, and subsequent book chapters, welcomed me as a graduate student to look behind the curtain of the profession and provided insights into publishing, research, and theory building in the field. This chapter is written in that tradition. The chapter begins with a narrative of my early journey to the field. Then I'll draw upon my experiences through graduate school and along the tenure track in order to highlight how perseverance, previous professional identities, and a broadened sense of professional community can augment graduate students' movement into disciplinary discussions, traditions, and norms. I'll conclude with some reflections derived from writing this chapter and consider how my own experiences impact my current role as an advisor to new doctoral students in the field.

My Journey Into Doctoral Education

Casanave (2008) once wrote that "learning how to 'do' graduate school does not come naturally to most people" (p. 14). The ways in which we enter academia and our fields are not always smooth or clearly delineated. My own story begins with the fact that I was a first-generation college student, whose parents immigrated to America without any knowledge of English and no experiences in higher education. My father always taught me to take chances and to hold onto the mantra that anything was possible, but in our family, the idea of earning a PhD or working in academia was an unheard of proposition.

My journey into the field of second language writing, and academia more generally, did not begin with an unwavering sense of certainty. In many ways, I stumbled upon the field of second language writing, and it was an irregular and unexpected path that led me to work with my dissertation advisor, Paul Kei Matsuda. Like many of my colleagues, I came across the world of L2 writing through my students. I began my work as a teacher with secondary school ESL students at an urban school in the Northeastern US. My portable classroom was far from the main building, and on cold winter days, the wind off the playground made it feel like a mile. As the only dually licensed English language arts and ESL teacher at the school, my job was to teach all the sections of ESL Reading and Writing. I had no budget and limited textbooks.

Early on, I knew writing was essential to my students' success. I had seen myself as a writing teacher. Books and lessons from Lucy Calkins (1986), Don Murray (1995), and Nancie Atwell (1987) lined my shelves, but at that time, the theories and practices for teaching writing in the dominant fields of composition and literacy studies didn't address the complicated act of writing in an L2. In researching my Master's thesis on teaching ESL writing at the middle school level, I had come across the works of Sarah Hudelson (1989) and Carole Edelsky (1986); only their works offered me a glimmer of hope that some other answers might be out there.

Those answers began to come in 1999 when I attended my first TESOL conference in New York City. It was the largest, most international conference that I had ever attended. I had to commute to the convention from a friend's house in New Jersey, because I could not afford to pay for a hotel room. But I didn't mind, and the experience was eye-opening, thrilling. After I presented a poster session on a curriculum unit I'd developed, I went to all the sessions I could manage, grabbing every handout and good teaching idea I could find. But one session caught my eye in the program book: "On the Future of Second Language Writing." I circled the title and underlined those last three words: Second Language Writing. It was the first time that I had seen the term, and it resonated with me. I wondered: were other people asking similar questions about writing and ESL?

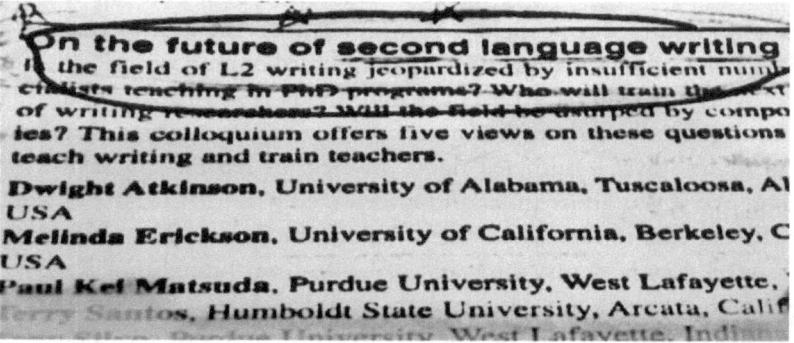

Figure 1. From the TESOL 1999 Program Book.

As I stepped into the session room, I saw a panel that included some of the biggest names in the field today: Terry Santos, Tony Silva, Melinda Erickson, Dwight Atkinson, and this other guy—Paul Kei Matsuda. I knew none of them, and truth be told, much of the conversation that day went over my head. I was not immersed in the discourse yet, and like so many new graduate students, I felt lost. But bits of the conversation stayed with me. In my journal, I wrote: "It seems like there may be more questions, than answers here." I didn't find the lack of answers frustrating; instead, I was intrigued, fascinated by the work that needed to be done. It seemed like a world teeming with possibilities. I wanted to engage in these conversations and seek more answers to the kinds of questions that kept arising from my work in the classroom. But I had no idea how anyone "did" this kind of work. The session ended historically with Matsuda and Atkinson in disagreement about the future of the field (see Santos et al., 2000). I only saw the future. I left the session and met Tony Silva at the bottom of the stairs. He generously listened to my questions, handed me his card, and told me about the PhD program at Purdue. As he headed to the next session, I sat in the lobby, tucking his card away with a sigh. I could almost hear the sound of a door closing in my mind.

At that time in my life, there was no way that Purdue could have been a possibility for me. Indiana was a world away from our house and mortgage, my husband's business, my elderly parents, and my growing family. The same was true of the few other doctoral programs in the US that had scholars working in L2 writing. Still, I went back to my students with renewed enthusiasm for teaching. I had learned that I wasn't alone in my questions or my interests. In my classroom, my students and I continued to work on their writing, trying out new workshop strategies and new projects. In the evenings after teaching, I would reread Hudelson's work. I began to buy books by Barbara Kroll (1990), Ilona Leki (1992), and Joy Reid (1993). I wrote an article about a writing curriculum that I'd developed, and I sent it to *TESOL Journal*. I continued to work with local workgroups on ESL issues. The following fall, *TESOL Journal* accepted my article for publication. I began to struggle with the reality that I was the only teacher in the school building that was allowing my ESL students to write extensively. I began to wonder if I might be able to create more change from another vantage point. I returned to the idea of a research degree, and I began to think creatively about my more local options, including the University of New Hampshire.

The PhD program in Composition Studies at UNH was well known for its scholars' interests in writing and literacy studies. Through my teaching, I'd met professors from the program and asked about pursuing a self-designed path in writing studies, ESL/immigrant literacy, and teacher education, if I were accepted. The graduate director told me 'yes,' and several linguists in the English department offered encouragement. So I took a leap of faith and send out some applications to UNH and few other regional programs. Later that spring, I was accepted into the UNH doctoral program. Two days after receiving my acceptance letter, I learned that I was pregnant with my first child; the intertwining of my personal and professional life would be part of this journey from the start. Six months later, pregnant and nervous, I would leave the stability of my full-time teaching position to start commuting to the PhD program in New Hampshire. There was no reason that this should work, I whispered to my husband at two in the morning. Looking back now, I can see that I had only a vague sense of where this new path might lead me.

At UNH, I had all the support I needed to learn about composition, writing-across-the-curriculum, writing centers, and more. But becoming immersed in L2 writing would be a solo mission at the start, and I would need to build my own opportunities. Luckily, I met Aya Matsuda, UNH's new linguist, and her interests in ESL and World Englishes were compelling. We serendipitously served together on the state-affiliate for TESOL. One day after a local conference, we had coffee. I shared my concerns that many of the writing initiatives at UNH didn't seem to acknowledge ESL writers. Aya mentioned that she had fielded numerous calls from faculty asking for assistance with UNH's growing international student population. Fueled by caffeine and a wonderful sense of synergy, we began to brainstorm. By the end of my first year, that conversation (and partnership) would turn into a small survey study of faculty and a collaboratively-designed series of faculty workshops that focused on culture, ESL, and writing, funded by the University's WAC program. For me, these initiatives, though not part of any formal coursework, helped me to become more familiar with ESL conversations in higher education. They would also be some of my first forays into building workshops and presentations for university faculty. Aya Matsuda would remain an important mentor, and that collaboration would soon unlock other doors.

As Aya and I worked together, I learned that Paul Kei Matsuda—that guy from that TESOL panel—was her husband. He was then an assistant professor at Miami University in Ohio. When he visited, Aya would invite me to join them for bagels. We had some great talks about L2 writing and my own interests in immigrant literacy. But geographically, Paul was far away from New Hampshire. Undeterred, I continued with my course work, studied my growing reading list, and developed my first seminar papers around my interests in immigrant literacy and the rhetoric of citizenship. One day via email, I took a chance and approached Paul to see if there was any way I might virtually sit in his upcoming seminar titled "Linguistics and Writing." It was a long shot, but his fondness for technology meant that aspects of the course would be on-line, and I was eager to participate in conversations with others who had similar interests. Paul graciously agreed to add me into the spring course as a guest. At UNH, I finagled, lobbied, begged, and finally persuaded the graduate director to allow me to participate in Paul's class for credit, as part of an independent study. That spring, in front of my computer screen and sometimes while bouncing my newborn on my lap, I took my first seminar with Matsuda. Only later would I learn that UNH was interested in hiring Paul for the composition program. Paul's arrival at UNH would add new dimensions to my journey in doctoral education.

I tell this narrative at length because, like many other people's tales of graduate education, it is marked by moments of doubt and setback, as well as moments of confidence and conviction. For many of us, we fluctuate between variations of these extremes throughout our graduate years, though we don't often talk about them. The obstacles that we encounter in graduate school are also part of the learning, though. Personal and institutional obstacles do not stop when we reach the tenure track, or even, I'm told, after tenure. But I encourage doctoral students to embrace these challenges with a sense of perseverance and even a bit of entrepreneurial spirit. My father used to quote an old line, often attributed to the philosopher Seneca, that there is no such thing as luck; rather, luck was what happened when hard work met opportunity. He also taught me to embrace the fact that many opportunities don't often come about in straightforward ways; sometimes you have to be open to discovering less traditional pathways and making them work for you. In the remainder of this chapter, I'll expand on these sentiments by sharing some of the lessons I've learned through my own doctoral experiences and the tenure track.

LEARNING THE ROPES OF THE ACADEMIC WORKPLACE: LESSONS FROM THE JOURNEY

Paul's coming to UNH as a faculty member certainly solidified my commitment to the field of L2 writing. His presence also marked the beginning of my more nuanced understanding of the workplace of academia and my own moves toward a new professional identity. As Paul has shared in earlier publications, he is a firm believer in facilitating mediated learning and creating authentic participation (see Simpson & Matsuda, 2008; Matsuda, this volume). His philosophy, which draws on situated learning theories (Lave & Wenger, 1991), is evident throughout his graduate courses and beyond them. But, for me, one of the most valuable aspects of his instructional stance has been his willingness to provide some transparency to the work and workplace dynamics of academic professionals. Paul spoke candidly about the academy *as a workplace*, offering students a sense of transparency on the day-to-day responsibilities of faculty members, the inner workings of academic institutions, and insights into administration, proposal writing, presentations, networking, editorial work, and publication. In classes and casual conversations, he helped to decipher how a person might move from one stage of a career to the next. In doing so, he demystified the academic work environment, often only discussed in ethereal terms of knowledge and remaining somewhat clandestine to those outside of it.

One result of his tutelage was that throughout my doctoral education, I was always keen to learn more about navigating and contributing to the communities that were all intrinsically part of this new "workplace" that I was entering. Although I learned a great deal working with Paul and my other professors throughout my doctoral program, four lessons from these conversations and experiences continue to reverberate for me in very salient ways as I navigate the tenure track. Drawing on examples from my own journey, I'll expand on them in the pages ahead, but in brief, they include the following: (1) Every experience can be a learning opportunity, even the challenging ones; (2) New professional identities don't have to be disconnected from old professional identities; they can be built upon them; (3) Be an ethnographer of the new workplace; and (4) Understand the importance of community and invest in the communities that surround you.

Lesson 1: Every Experience Can Be Seen as a Learning Opportunity, Even the Challenging Ones

Sometimes as doctoral students, we have successful moments, and other times, we don't. On one occasion, I turned an early bibliographic essay on the status of immigrant L2 writers in US contexts into an article, and Paul suggested I send it to the journal, *Written Communication*. Months and months later, it was returned with a letter of rejection and four pages of detailed commentary—commentary that closely mirrored the intense scrutiny that Paul often gave in his feedback to our seminar work. I'll confess that that envelope from the journal sat in my car's glovebox for over two weeks. I wasn't sure how to handle the rejection. Mostly I felt embarrassed and those "imposter" doubts surfaced again, making me question what I was trying to accomplish.

I questioned how I would ever find a voice and a way of writing that would be good enough for this new academic world.

Around the same time, though, Paul shared some of his publication woes and the critical feedback he received from a piece that he was working on. He wasn't thrilled, but—and I think this was most enlightening—he wasn't devastated either. After a seminar one day, he shared his thoughts and brainstormed aloud how he might respond with revision, or even resubmission to other journals. It made me realize that these kinds of rejection might be par for the course in this profession, and I had to develop productive ways of responding to them.

That realization allowed me to step back and take stock of what I might learn in the moment. I turned back to the editor's feedback with renewed curiosity and an intention to learn from their concerns. The article never did make it into that journal, but elements of that early piece would become part of a CCC article in the future. Now, as an editor and reviewer myself, I recognize the generosity of those four pages and the rich, detailed feedback they contained. I also remind myself of the significance of those editors' final sentences, which kindly and sincerely encouraged me to continue writing and sending my work out. That encouragement helped me to believe that my voice and my interests mattered, and I continued to hone my writing skills.

Lesson 2: New Professional Identities Don't Have To Be Disconnected from Old Professional Identities

Lave and Wenger (1991) have theorized the importance of apprenticeship models, a concept that informs much of the current literature on graduate education. Academic apprenticeship models, however, often seem to rely on the idea that the apprentice is always a novice, a *tabula rasa* of sorts. Many doctoral students, though, are actually transitioning and transferring *across* professional identities, not just entering new ones. Current discussions don't often address how individual students can and do transfer knowledge and identities across their experiences as they navigate into new professional conversations and identities. For example, before I began my studies, I had an established teaching career in K-12 and a rich professional identity derived from that experience. As I entered my doctoral program, I saw all my efforts not just as a program of study, but as an extension of my professional career. I knew I had a great deal to learn, and I was eager to do so. Yet, my "new job" of graduate school, along with the tenure-track positions that came later, was not completely severed from my old job, and I continued to draw upon the professional profile that I had already established.

Throughout graduate school, I used my earlier professional identity and communities to propel me forward, to maintain my confidence, and to prepare me for later opportunities. For example, I continued to work with many of my secondary school teaching colleagues, sometimes returning on breaks to teach classes on writing to their students. During three summers, I served as a curriculum consultant to a local literacy program for ESL students. I remained active on the steering boards for local teacher organizations, including my local TESOL affiliate. I furthered these roles by joining ongoing school-university collaborations that were already taking place at UNH, particularly by working at the writing center and serving as a Steering Board member for the local chapter of the International Writing Center Association. In summers, I joined with fellow graduates to do workshops for local school teachers and students. Whenever possible, I continued to present at local conferences on writing, literacy, and teaching. My local initiatives, often emerged from connections established by my earlier professional work, and I firmly believe that these earlier connections and support networks helped me to have confidence in starting new initiatives and participating more actively in new disciplinary conversations.

When Paul and others began to approach me with opportunities for more national and international work in the field, I drew strategies and support from these past successes, experiences, and professional relationships. For example, when I started to collect signatures in 2004 to form the Second Language Writing Interest Section (SLW-IS) at TESOL, some of the very first signatures on that petition, along with letters of support, came from old colleagues, area teachers, and regional TESOL leaders that I'd known through my work as a K-12 teacher. Looking back, my continued engagement in local actions and networks helped me to build a stronger sense of my growing expertise and a more insider's sense of the demands that were part of the broader academic community.

Throughout my doctoral program, Paul and my other professors encouraged me to draw upon my past professional experience and expertise as I ventured into new professional territory. They reminded me that, although I was a student again, I was not an empty slate. That realization was empowering. Through the years, I have continued to value and benefit from the fact that my earlier professional identity was not lost; it has become an integral part of a unique professional profile that I continue to build upon as I move forward in my academic career.

Lesson 3: Be an Ethnographer of Your Field and Your Job (Transitioning to the Tenure-Track)

Since completing my dissertation, I have held faculty positions at two PhD granting programs: first, at the University of Massachusetts, and now at the University of New Hampshire. It is an interesting transition to move from being the student to being the advisor. During the early years of graduate school, we can get comfortable in our role as students, participating and rising to the challenge set forth by our professors, the experts in the room. Then, the roles change, and newly minted PhDs "officially" become the experts. But in many ways, the tenure-track position is a natural progression from the growing sense of independence that emerges as one presents at conferences, completes a dissertation, enters the job market, and continually moves forward toward the new professional identity. The early years on the tenure track are marked by similar demands to establish (continually) a professional profile in our fields and within our institutions. This is my case presently, as it was Paul's when I was his advisee (see Matsuda, this volume).

I feel fortunate that I was able to work and observe Paul during his early years in this profession, watching him navigate much of the tenure-track terrain that I now find myself on. At the time, I didn't always understand what I was seeing: the balancing act between defining one's own career and helping move students forward, negotiations and programmatic choices that were made at the department level, or the decisions to take on certain difficult discussions (e.g., studio courses for basic writers) and professional roles (e.g., program administration) within one's institutions, but not others. I also learned the importance of timing. I observed how Paul engaged in certain contentious conversations by turning to allies who were tenured and more fully aware of the larger conversations in a department or across a campus. Furthermore, he taught me to be open to the reality that the timing of a proposed initiative may not be right and that often one needs to do more foundational work by building a network of stakeholders and a sense of exigency within an institution. Paul, often over coffee, would frequently ask me where I wanted to be five years from that moment. To be truthful, I sometimes didn't have an answer to that question or perhaps more accurately, I had competing answers and scenarios (it is a difficult question!). But Paul helped me to understand how one might think beyond the day-to-day goals of the semester—the seminar paper, the annual faculty report, the administrative role, and the CV—in order to set a course for larger goals and initiatives. As an advisee, I appreciated Paul's willingness to make transparent many of his own goals and decision-making processes. And even when he was more evasive, I learned to listen and watch, thinking about how certain choices he made led him to new opportunities or propelled him in new directions.

I also learned a great deal from just listening and learning from other mentors and professionals, many from the second language writing community and my home institution. From talks in the corridors of conference venues and sometime continued over email, I gained insights into decisions on committee work, professional ways of working with fellow faculty and administrators, and handling frustration and setbacks, and other tales from the tenure track. For example, Dana Ferris gave a brilliant—and wonderfully direct—presentation at one Symposium that explicitly showed how her research and publications unfolded alongside her teaching and personal life (see Ferris, 2005). Others, like Deborah Crusan and Sarah Hudelson, graciously shared insights into their own department dynamics, their campus initiatives, the tenure process, and their work with publishers. I have learned so much from the candor and examples set forth by the women in my field. Those conversations and observations have helped me, in recent years, to think strategically about my own choices and pathways in the field and at my institution.

Doctoral students should not limit these kinds of questions and conversations only to their formal advisors. It is important to seek out other mentors, as well, and listen to their perspectives. Mentors can exist in array of capacities, inside one's program and also through various other organizational structures. Over the years, I've listened and learned from stories told by other compositionists and L2 writing scholars as they shared how they have navigated through decisions at their home institutions, regarding administrative work, departmental politics, tenure, and teaching. I read books like *ESL Composition Tales: Reflections on Teaching* (Blanton & Kroll, 2002). I wondered, and sometimes asked, from where did these scholars derive their sense of achievement and accomplishment? There is no doubt that students, listening and asking such questions, will hear about different strategies in different settings. This is important and valuable, because there are an array of professional and academic decisions that will arise over the course of a career. I also listened to colleagues as they shared the outcomes of the decisions they had made. What might they have done differently? What other choices existed? How did they define success?

I continue to listen and learn from my mentors as I navigate new pathways and decisions. Over the years, I've come to realize that there isn't just one way to have success in the academic world. Listening to a multitude of perspectives has given me insights into the opportunities and the choices that exist.

Lesson 4: Become Aware of the Importance of Community and Invest in the Communities That Surround You

Individual perseverance is a part of the commitment to a doctoral education, but I'm not sure that any of us make it through as pure soloists. The best experiences are never complete solo ventures. Wenger (1998) in his work on community of practices (CoP), defines the roles and competencies of members within CoPs, noting that

> members build their community through mutual engagement. They interact with one another, establishing norms and relationships of mutuality that reflect these interactions. To be competent is to be able to engage with the community and be trusted as a partner in these interactions. [...] Communities of practices have produced a shared repertoire of communal resources—language, routines, sensibilities, artifacts, tools, stories, styles, etc. To be competent is to have access to this repertoire and be able to use it appropriately. (p. 229)

Wenger's theory of CoP is often drawn upon in discussions on doctoral education, particularly when scholars consider how students enter and begin to engage with the academic discussions in their disciplines. Advisors encourage students to learn the discourse and norms of the disciplinary communities that they are entering. These are important endeavors. But I encourage doctoral students and their advisors to consider their communities more broadly and to work to establish an awareness of CoPs on multiple fronts. In short, I suggest that we expand our vision of disciplinary CoPs to include some of the smaller communities that graduate students encounter during their programs. The importance of nurturing these smaller communities for doctoral students cannot be overstated.

When I attended my first Symposium in 2002, I knew very few people in this field. But over the course of that conference, I met students from a number of other doctoral programs. It was exhilarating to be among peers who held a similar passion for this work. Over the years, these individuals who were graduate students when we first met have become important collaborators, strategic advisors, and skillful partners in creating organizational/institutional change. We've done workshops at CCCC and NCTE, advocated for the foundation of the SLW-IS, and introduced one another to other colleagues, other scholars, and advisors. Along the way, some of us even shared hotel rooms on shoestring budgets, found the best sushi at conference sites, shared in the trials of the tenure-track, and celebrated one another's successes. As we continue on the tenure track, we often contact one another to work in leadership roles, write position statements, visit one another's institutions as guest speakers, and sit on committees.

These types of relationships often grow from attending smaller, more intimate conferences, like the Symposium on Second Language Writing. I recommend to my own graduate students that they keep an eye out for smaller conferences and submit proposals to share their work at these venues as well. Students should seek out and become involved in the smaller work groups and communities that exist at the larger conferences like TESOL, AAAL, AERA, and CCCC. Students shouldn't be reluctant to reach across campus borders to meet and befriend graduate students from other programs with similar interests. These fellow students will be future colleagues.

In the same vein, it is also important to build circles of community among graduate student at our home institutions and programs. I was fortunate to be part of UNH's graduate student community with its long tradition of collaboration, support, and camaraderie. Alumni regularly mentor new students; we have regular potlucks; and graduate students often work together to write proposals, submit articles, organize workshops, and present at conferences. When I was a student in the program, my own cohort formed study groups early on to discuss readings and prepare for exams. During our dissertation years, we formed a writing group that met regularly at a local restaurant, staying late into the night fueled by multiple cups of coffee, good humor, an encouraging wait staff, and chocolate cake. We help set writing assignments and goals for one another. Sometimes, we shared freewrites, working arguments, and rather clunky chapters. Other times, we simply met, took out our laptops, and wrote side-by-side. That group met for years and regularly invited other doctoral students, who were at earlier stages in program, to join in so that they could learn more about the next steps.

Aside from the intrinsic value of the friendships I gained, these meetings aided my development as a scholar and influenced my work today as a doctoral advisor. Through ongoing conversations about my peers' work and interest areas, I became more familiar with a range of discussions in college composition, workplace literacies, archival methods, feminist theories, race theories, and more. Second, we all learned to be more astute readers and responders of one another's scholarship and research methods. To this day, that trusted group of individuals remains some of my first readers and responders when I approach a new project or challenge. Those experiences also helped to train us for the responsibilities of serving as editors and reviewers that would be forthcoming. My community of peers also prepared me for my own eventual work with graduate students. We all had different backgrounds, work experiences, personal circumstances, and various passions in the field, all of which drove and inspired us in an array of ways. As friendships grew, we candidly shared with one another our individual and differing concerns, needs, and strategies for venturing through graduate coursework, teaching, and the dissertation process. We shared advice, became one another's sounding boards, encouraged one another's writing, and provided support when needed. These days, we've all moved on to various new positions along the tenure track, but I continue to draw upon the memories, wisdom, humor, and varied insights of my peers whenever I sit in my office and find myself advising the doctoral students in our program.

Some Thoughts on Deliberate Choices

The pursuit of a doctoral degree is not always a direct path, nor are there cookie-cutter approaches to success and completion. Writing this chapter has given me an opportunity to reflect upon my years as a doctoral student and my decisions in recent years along the tenure track. As I noted earlier, I never would have characterized steps in my journey into this field as well-defined, deliberate, or calculated. But I do admit that there have been certain ideals that I have tried to stay true to, and those have, in turn, guided many of my choices.

First, my professional choices continue to be guided by my concerns for young multilingual students. Pictures of my former middle school students still hang by my desk, and I regularly think about those that made it onto higher education and those that did not. On the job search, I purposefully sought out institutions with substantial roots and collaborative opportunities in literacy studies and K-12 teacher education. My work as a graduate advisor in these kinds of programs means that I have the opportunity to work with master's candidates who will work in K-12 schools, as well as, doctoral students who will work in higher education, often as future teacher educators or writing program administrators.

Second, at my institution and in composition-rhetoric circles, I have made a conscious decision to define myself as a second language writing specialist. I regularly teach a second language writing course which is now, with the support of my colleagues in composition and linguistics, a fixture for our graduate students, as well as our undergraduate teaching majors. This summer, I developed new L2 writing courses including a summer hybrid course directly tailored for teachers working with immigrant students in public schools. I am developing a new seminar on globalization and cross-cultural rhetoric that I'll offer next year. L2 writing scholarship seeps into every course I teach, and it is a regular part of all my students' reading lists.

Third, I make deliberate choices about the work I pursue. To date, I have always tried to intertwine my passions with the research that I pursue. I draw upon the very real concerns that I see and hear from students and teachers in order to shape the inquiry questions that drive my projects. I have purposefully pursued work that crosses traditional disciplinary borders in writing scholarship, whether they be the borders between secondary school and college, or the borders between L1 composition and L2 writing. In practice, this has meant publishing in college-level composition and L2 writing journals, as well as, education and more teacher-focused journals. It has also meant attending and presenting at a range of conferences—from TESOL to CCCC to NCTE—often bringing colleagues from other areas with me in order to extend the conversations across these borders.

Finally and this is probably the most personal of my choices, I have deliberatively tried to pursue a whole-self perspective, not putting certain aspects of my life on hold while pursuing others. I have three children—ages 3, 8, and 11. The first was born when I began my doctoral program; the second was born after I took my comprehensive exams; my youngest son arrived while I was on the tenure-track. I am not the only student or faculty member to make such choices (see Coiner & George, 1998; Slaughter, 2012). My personal and professional aspirations have often intertwined in ways that others may find contradictory, or at the very least, ill-advised. But as a doctoral student, I was fortunate to have professors who were very supportive. If Paul, as my advisor, had concerns about how my personal responsibilities might have impacted my drive or my work ethic, he never voiced them. He never questioned my abilities. At the same time, he respected the choices that I sometimes had to make in regards to a one-year leave of absence after my second son, scheduling meetings during babysitter's hours, and sometimes having to forego a conference.

Today, like many working mothers and fathers, I live in a rather busy world. My minivan is regularly piled high with soccer gear, car seats, and Goldfish snacks. I start my days at 5am in order to fit it all in, but I treasure the insights and experiences that my children—and my family, more broadly—bring into my world. The balancing act is not an easy one. I continually find myself recalibrating my responsibilities, my schedule, my communication skills, and more. I don't always get it right, but I keep trying and I have an incredibly supportive spouse. My family and children remind me that life is short, and that I am not solely defined by my CV. Currently, none of my graduate students have children, but they do have other life responsibilities—taking care of ailing grandparents, balancing the work of spouses, financial concerns, volunteer work with veterans, etc. As an advisor, I am open with them about the need to find some balance in their professional and personal lives. I encourage them to pursue success in their academic lives and careers, but I also encourage them to pursue satisfaction and joy in the other areas of their lives as well.

Paying It Forward

Nowadays, as a faculty member, I've come to understand that the experience of teaching graduate students shapes advisors, as much as advisors shape their students. As an advisor, I am (and suspect I will remain) a work in progress. From my work with my students, I continually learn and develop in my role as their teacher and advisor. Working with them acts as a catalyst for me. They ask questions that I have yet to consider and drive me to think more critically and more attentively to questions from the field and in the classroom. My students continually fuel my energy and my passion for the field, for student writers, for schools, and for writing. I also realize that I was fortunate in my own doctoral education. I had a supportive advisor with a sense of transparency that let me know what I needed to do and how I might do it. I had loyal and caring peers. I also had passionate, encouraging professors in my graduate program and welcoming scholars from the field, who formally and informally, became my extended group of mentors. The generosity and shared experiences of those individuals have been instrumental and inspirational on so many fronts. Now, I find myself in a unique position to give back what I've been given—to pay it forward. To the best of my ability, I intend to do just that.

Acknowledgments

Conversations with Tanita Saekham and Paul Kei Matsuda about graduate education in the field of second language writing greatly advanced my own reflections as I composed this piece. I thank them for their insights and for the wonderful discussions along the way. In addition, I thank Michelle Cox for her useful comments on earlier drafts of this chapter.

References

Atwell, N. (1987). *In the middle: New understandings about writing, reading, and learning.* Portsmouth, NH: Heinemann.

Blanton, L.L., & Kroll, B. (2002). ESL Composition Tales: Reflections on Teaching. Ann Arbor: University of Michigan Press.

Blanton, L. L. (2005) Mucking around in the lives of others: Reflections on qualitative research. In T. Silva & P.K. Matsuda (Eds.), *Second language writing research* (pp. 147-156). New York: Erlbaum.

Calkins, L. M. (1994). *The art of teaching writing.* Portsmouth, NH: Heinemann.

Casanave, C. P. (2008). Learning participatory practices in graduate school: Some perspective-taking by a mainstream educator. In C.P. Casanave & X. Li (Eds.), *Learning the literacy practices of graduate school: Insiders' reflections on academic enculturation,* (pp. 14-31). Ann Arbor: University of Michigan Press.

Casanave, S.P., & Li, X. (2008). *Learning the literacy practices of graduate school: Insiders' reflections on academic enculturation.* Ann Arbor: University of Michigan Press.

Coiner, C., & George, D. H. (1998). *The family track: Keeping your faculties while you mentor, nurture, teach, and serve.* Urbana: University of Illinois Press.

Edelsky, C. (1986). *Writing in a bilingual program: Habia un vez.* New York: Praeger.

Ferris, D. (2005). Tricks of the trade: The nuts and bolts of L2 writing research. In T. Silva & P. K. Matsuda (Eds.), *Second language writing research* (pp. 219-230). Lawrence Erlbaum.

Hudelson, S. (1989). *Write on: Children writing in ESL.* New York: Prentice Hall.

Tardy, C. M. (2010). Cleaning up the mess: Perspectives from a novice theory builder. In T. Silva & P. K. Matsuda (Eds.), *Practicing theory in second language writing* (pp. 112-125). West Lafayette, IN: Parlor Press.

Lave, J., & Wenger, E. (1991). *Situated learning: Legitimate peripheral participation.* London: Cambridge University Press.

Leki, I. (1992). *Understanding ESL writers.* Portsmouth, NH: Heinemann.

Kroll, B. (1990). Second language writing: Research insights for the classroom. Cambridge University Press.

Murray, D. (1995). *The craft of revision, second edition.* Harcourt Brace College Publishers.

Reid, J. (1993). *Teaching ESL writing.* New York: Pearson ESL.

Santos, T., Atkinson, D., Erickson, M., Matsuda, P. K., and Silva, T. (2000). On the future of second language writing: A colloquium. *Journal of Second Language Writing 9,* 1-20.

Simpson, S. & Matsuda P. K. (2008). Mentoring as a long-term relationship: Situated learning in a doctoral program. In C.P. Casanave & X. Li (Eds.) *Learning the literacy practices of graduate school: Insiders' reflections on academic enculturation,* (pp. 90-104). Ann Arbor: University of Michigan Press.

Slaughter, A. M. (July/August 2012). Why women still can't have it all. *The Atlantic Magazine.* Retrieved from: http://www.theatlantic.com/magazine/archive/2012/07/why-women-still-cant-have-it-all/309020/

Vandrick, S. (2006). Shifting sites, shifting identities: A thirty-year perspective. In P. K. Matsuda, C. Ortmeier-Hooper, & X. You (Eds.), *The politics of second language writing: In search of the promised land* (pp. 280-294). West Lafayette, IN: Parlor Press.

Wenger, E. (2000). Communities of practice and social learning systems. *Organization, 7*(2), 225-246.

9 The PhD Process as Activity

Wei Zhu

Efforts to describe the PhD process and offer guidance for doctoral students have not been missing in academia, as reflected by books dedicated to describing both the various stages of the PhD process and the skills, personal attributes, and support doctoral students need in order to successfully complete the PhD degree (e.g., Hawley, 2003; Phillips & Pugh, 2005). However, it may be argued that reflection on and investigation of the PhD process as an object of scholarly inquiry is a contribution of applied linguistics, particularly the field of second language writing. Second language writing research addressing advanced academic literacy development has provided significant insights into various aspects of the PhD process, including student learning and development of rhetorical knowledge (e.g., Tardy, 2005) and student-advisor relationships in academic literacy development (e.g., Belcher, 1994). Recently, an edited volume by Casanave and Li (2008) is dedicated to the discussion of learning and developing literacy practices in graduate school, particularly by doctoral students. This body of scholarship has revealed the complex and multifaceted nature of the PhD process, influenced by a wide array of factors.

The call for a collective reflection on the PhD process as situated in specific institutional contexts is a timely one as such reflection can afford a better understanding of the PhD process. In this chapter, I share my reflection of Iona's PhD process. In the next chapter, Iona reflects on her PhD process (see Sarieva, this volume) from the discourse community perspective. My reflection is guided by activity theory, which emphasizes the mediated and transformative nature of human activity (Leont'ev, 1978, 1981; Engestrom, 1990, 1999). Thus, my account reinterprets some of Iona's experiences and offers my conceptualization of her PhD process from an activity theory perspective. Because most of my interactions with Iona occurred during the dissertation phase of her doctoral studies, I will focus more on the dissertation activity in my discussion. First, I provide a brief discussion of key activity theory constructs as relevant to the present discussion.

ACTIVITY THEORY PERSPECTIVE

Seen from the perspective of activity theory, human activity is mediated, and is social, cultural, and historical in nature. Engestrom's (1990, 1999) "activity system" depicts human activity as comprising six essential components: subject, referring to the actor of the activity; object, referring to the "problem space" toward which the activity is directed; mediating tools, referring to physical and/or symbolic instruments, artifacts or signs that mediate the activity; community, referring to groups of people with a shared object; rules, referring to regulations and norms that afford or constrain "actions and interactions within the activity system" (Engestrom, 1990, p. 79), and division of labor, referring to division of task roles and responsibilities, and power status of members of the community. According to Engestrom (1990; 1999), human activity is a process of transforming the object into outcomes, and this process of transformation is mediated by tools and influenced by rules, community, and division of labor. Another construct important to understanding human activity is motive, which offers an explanation concerning why people participate in an activity (Leont'ev, 1978, 1981).

Viewed from an activity theory perspective, Iona's PhD process comprised an intricate web of activity systems (e.g., research, teaching and family). The central activity, however, was oriented toward learning to do research in the local activity system of the program. I will focus on this central activity and refer to it as the PhD activity, of which Iona was the subject. The PhD activity was evolving and carried out in two main cycles: the initial learning cycle and the dissertation cycle, each with its own object and mediating tools, and pertinent community, division of labor and rules.

The Initial Cycle of the Phd Activity

The initial cycle of Iona's PhD activity occurred during the coursework phase when Iona was introduced to the local activity system and research areas related to the goals of the program: Second Language Acquisition (SLA) and Instructional Technology (IT). This cycle of the PhD activity was directed toward the object—problem space—of gaining knowledge of the goals and various aspects of the local activity system and developing an understanding of SLA and IT. A key mediating tool for this cycle of activity was the curriculum, and factors related to the local activity system, especially the community, influenced this process. The initial cycle of Iona's PhD activity, as I see it from Engestrom's activity theory perspective, is depicted in Figure 1.

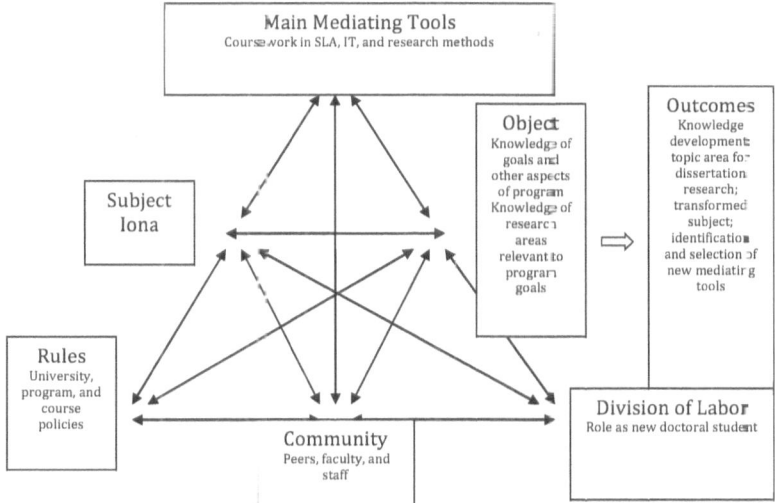

Figure 1. Initial Cycle of PhD Activity

When Iona entered the interdisciplinary PhD program in Second Language Acquisition and Instructional Technology (SLAIT), the curriculum consisted of four components: SLA, an important part of which was the SLA lab series designed to introduce students to various aspects of the program and SLA research, instructional technology, research methods, and electives in second language acquisition, instructional technology, and education. The second language writing course that I taught was an elective, and it was in this course that I began to work with Iona. The writing course was designed to introduce students to various issues and topics related to second language writing, as well as to theories and relevant constructs underpinning second language writing research. In her reflection (see Sarieva, this volume), Iona comments on how coursework helped her better understand the goals of the program and research principles of SLA and acquire a new view of writing. In this initial cycle of Iona's PhD activity, I, like other faculty members in the program, mediated Iona's learning through my role as a course instructor.

Mediated by the curriculum and supported through interactions with faculty and peers of the local activity system, Iona developed a keen understanding of program goals and topic areas pertinent to the program: second language learning and teaching, including second language writing; quantitative and qualitative research methods; and instructional technology, including specific tools available to learning and teaching as well as theories and research underpinning the integration of technology into education. Iona successfully transformed the object into the intended outcome of knowledge development. In my view, the outcome of knowledge development entailed three interrelated specific outcomes, all of which were essential for the next cycle of her PhD activity.

First, the construction of a problem space for the dissertation study. As Iona learned more about the field of second language writing, she became increasingly drawn to the notion of writing process and a social view of writing and writing development. At the same time, Iona was attracted to the view that technology, particularly computer-mediated communication, serves as a tool for forming social communities. Iona integrated these views, and this integration enabled her to construct a specific and novel problem/research space—computer-mediated student collaboration during the pre-writing phase of the writing process—as the topic area for her dissertation.

Second, the transformation of the subject of the activity. As Iona mentions in her reflection (see Sarievea, this volume), she entered the SLA/IT PhD program because she wanted to secure a language teaching position at the university level after graduation. Her learning was initially driven by a motive shaped by her interest in and extensive experience with language teaching as well as her knowledge of the field then. As Iona gradually developed an understanding of the goals of the program and of the field of second language acquisition, her motive for pursuing a PhD changed, and her learning began to be driven by a motive that was oriented more toward research. This reshaped motive would drive Iona's dissertation activity.

In addition, as Iona was learning more about the field of second language writing, her views and beliefs of the nature and importance of writing began to change. She began to see writing more and more as a process that occurs in specific social contexts, rather than merely as a product. She also began to see the instructional value of the conception of writing as a process and the benefits this view of writing could bring to the students. Further, with more knowledge and experience, Iona changed the "silent and observant" (Sarieva, this volume) role she assumed as a new doctoral student to become a more confident participant in her interactions with community members in the local activity system and in her writing. Thus, towards the end of the initial cycle of the PhD activity, a transformed Iona emerged, who would be the subject of the ensuing dissertation activity.

Last but not least, learning during the initial cycle of the PhD activity allowed Iona to identify, select, and create new tools and means that would mediate her dissertation activity. For example, when Iona was in the program, students formed their dissertation supervisory committees towards the end of the coursework phase, after having taken courses with various faculty members in the program. Based on her interests and goals developed during the initial cycle of her PhD activity, Iona formed a dissertation committee, and, by doing so, created an important mediating tool for her dissertation activity.

Dissertation Cycle of the Phd Activity

The second cycle of Iona's PhD activity was oriented toward the dissertation study. The object—problem space—of the dissertation activity was the dissertation project, with the initial problem space being the dissertation problem/topic. Iona, or more precisely, the transformed Iona, was the subject of the dissertation activity, which was mediated by a broad range of sociocultural and sociohistorical tools/instruments, such as relevant theories/constructs, frameworks of data analysis and interpretation, relevant research literature, computers and software, and language. As a co-major professor of Iona's dissertation committee, I, along with other committee members, served as mediators of Iona's dissertation activity. The dissertation cycle of activity, as I see it from Engestrom's activity perspective, is depicted in Figure 2.

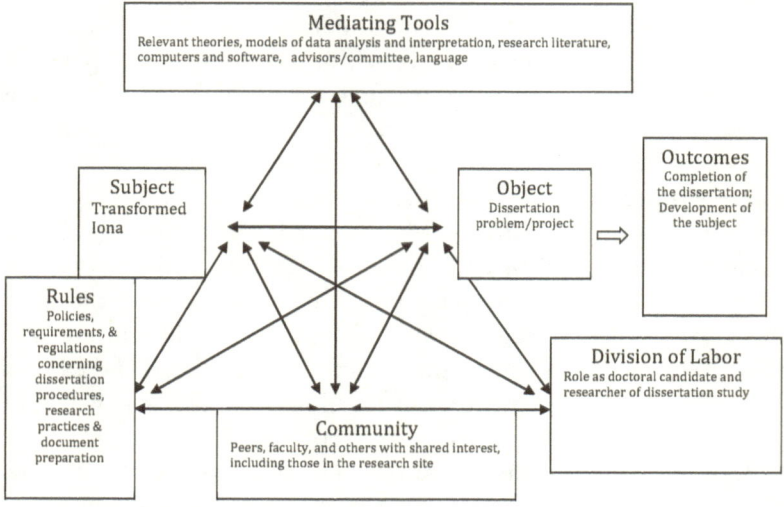

Figure 2. Dissertation Cycle of PhD Activity

Iona's dissertation activity aimed at transforming the dissertation problem into intended outcomes: a completed dissertation and development of Iona as a researcher. This transformation was a gradual and mediated process, and was influenced by rules, community, and division of labor pertinent to the dissertation activity. The transformation was also a dynamic process entailing exercising agency on the part of the subject, and, as will be discussed later in this section, resolving various contradictions arising within the dissertation activity.

Mediation and Agency of Subject

As an important mediating means for Iona's dissertation activity, the dissertation committee mediated many aspects of the dissertation study, from designing the study, to collecting data, to creating the final dissertation product. A specific means of mediation used by the committee was feedback, both oral feedback as provided in feedback sessions and written feedback as provided on students' written work. In my role as a co-major professor of Iona's dissertation committee, I tried to provide feedback that would stimulate thinking and scaffold revision. In my feedback, I tried to focus on more global issues such as connections between theoretical frameworks and analytical methods, between claims made and evidence provided, and between writer assumptions and reader expectations/needs. Feedback itself, however, does not automatically lead to rethinking or revision. For feedback to function as a mediating tool, it needs to be negotiated, understood, and acted upon.

The terms "advisor" and "advisee" reflect an institutionalized division of labor (that is, the advisor gives advice and the student/advisee receives advice); therefore, negotiation of feedback reflects the negotiation of a structure of relationship and opens up a communication space in which shared understanding may be achieved. Iona, as the subject of her dissertation activity, contributed a great deal to this negotiation through exercising agency, and hence, allowing mediation to occur. I provide a few examples below to illustrate this.

Throughout her dissertation process, Iona actively sought confirmation of her understanding of the feedback provided on her work. She prepared summaries of the feedback provided during feedback sessions and sent the summaries to her professors to achieve a shared understanding of what had been discussed. For example, after a feedback session on her dissertation proposal, she sent me an email along with a summary of our discussion. The first part of the email read:

> Dr. Zhu,
>
> *Thank you for your time and the thoughtful suggestions you gave me today. I synthesized your suggestions in a word document which is attached to this email. I hope that I have not missed or misinterpreted anything; but if I did, I would really appreciate your feedback and corrections.* (personal communication, August 3, 2005)

In addition to checking her understanding of the feedback provided, Iona also actively asked for clarifications of the comments made by her professors. After her proposal defense, I sent Iona a summary of the questions and comments from the committee that included a question from a committee member regarding the difference of the possible impact two different modes of computer-mediated communication could make on student discussion and writing. She responded to the question by requesting clarifications (the bolded part is Iona's response).

> *How sure is the researcher to get a difference between the Asynchronous and Synchronous mode?—I don't understand this question. Is it about how sure I am about detecting the difference between the writing when it is supported by ACMC and SCMC? <u>This is the goal of the research and this question will be addressed in the discussion of the findings.</u> If it is about the difference of the two modes of communication, <u>this is stated in the lit review: p. 75-77.</u>*

This type of negotiation, however, is not without potential difficulties. As Iona indicates in her reflection (see Sarieva, this volume), her ways of negotiating meaning were influenced by various aspects of her dissertation activity, and such negotiations were not necessarily effortless or simple.

Throughout my experience working with Iona, I learned to appreciate her efforts to mediate her own activity by planning and managing her progress and communicating her plans and progress to the committee. Iona initiated and maintained communication with me and her committee members on the progress of her work using "progress reports." At the beginning of the Fall 2005 semester, for example, she sent her committee an email with the subject line "Proposal Progress Report." Iona provided a summary of her progress with 6 bullet points outlining what she had accomplished during the summer. The first part of the email read:

> *Dear (Names of committee members)*
>
> *I hope you enjoyed your summer and were able to relax and gain plenty of energy to teach and guide your students during the fall semester.*
>
> *With this email I would like to update you with the progress of my dissertation:* (personal communication, August 25, 2005)

This type of report was not required nor suggested by the committee; it was completely Iona's initiative. As shown in this example, Iona created and used her own tools/artifacts to mediate her dissertation activity. She also created timelines and charts that laid out the planned phases of her dissertation work, sometimes with general timelines, and sometimes with rather specific dates. In the same email she sent to the committee on August 25, 2005, for example, she included a general timeline:

At this point, I have the following rough timeline:

- Fall 2005—Data collection
- Spring 2006—data coding, writing chapters 4 & 5, submitting chapters 4 & 5 to the committee for feedback.
- Summer 2006—incorporating committee's feedback.
- Fall 2006—dissertation defense.

These efforts to create tools to mediate her activity demonstrated Iona's agency as subject of the dissertation activity.

Resolution of Contradictions and Development

According to activity theory (Engestrom, 1990), activity systems are fraught with contradictions, tensions, disruptions, and conflicts. Contradictions can cause problems to the activity, but resolution of contradictions constitutes a powerful source for learning and development. Although contradictions existed during the initial cycle of Iona's PhD activity (for example, Iona's early frustrations in the SLA/IT program as described in her reflection indicated contradictions between her previous activities and her new activity in her PhD program), their presence seemed to be more marked for the dissertation activity, perhaps due to the complex nature of the work that needed to be carried out. Contradictions could exist within an activity system (i.e., inner contradictions) or between activities (Engestrom, 1990). I will focus on the inner contradictions below.

Inner contradictions may exist within a component of the activity system or between components of an activity system (Engestrom, 1990). Due to the various roles the doctoral student assumes during the dissertation activity, contradictions often exist within the subject component of the activity. On the one hand, for example, the doctoral candidate has institutionalized roles of student and advisee, as a novice being guided; on the other hand, the doctoral candidate is expected to demonstrate expertise on the research topic and to assume the role of an emerging expert. These dual roles may create tension within the subject component of the dissertation activity, and, if not resolved, may affect student interactions with others (e.g., the dissertation committee) and the voice and construction of "textual identity" (Ivanic, 1998) in the dissertation document.

Iona balanced these roles well; she was able to stand by her ideas and take ownership of her texts, but at the same time she was open and responsive to suggestions and different opinions. She was also able to balance other roles she assumed as the subject of the dissertation activity. As indicated in Iona's reflection (see Sarieva, this volume), one of the obstacles she had to deal with was the need to switch among the multiple roles of being an observer, a communicator, and a writer. Each role entailed specific tasks, required different skills, and needed to be enacted at the right time and in the right setting. Dealing with the multiple roles associated with the dissertation activity was not easy but being able to do so was essential for the success of Iona's dissertation activity.

Contradictions also existed between components of Iona's dissertation activity system. The SLA/IT program integrated instructional technology and second language acquisition, and this interdisciplinarity was often reflected in the "problem space" of the students' dissertations. Integration of SLA and IT allowed students to carve out new problem spaces for their work, thus offering opportunities for innovation. At the same time, it might introduce potential contradictions into the dissertation activity system, for example, between the "novel object" and the lack of existing mediating tools (Engestrom, 1990).

Iona's dissertation study focused on the pre-writing stage of the writing process and examined the impact of a computer-mediated pre-writing discussion task on the drafts written by a group of adult ESL students at an intermediate level of English language proficiency. The study utilized a mixed-methods design, with the qualitative part of the dissertation study consisting of case studies. Iona selected eight case study students and aimed to examine 1) how the students established intertextual connections between the pre-writing discussion and their drafts, and 2) how the different modes of computer-mediated communication (i.e., the asynchronous vs. synchronous modes communication) influenced the intertextual connections that students built.

In order to achieve her research goal, Iona needed an analytical tool that would allow her to conceptualize and identify connections between the students' computer-mediated collaborative discourse and drafts that the students composed following the computer-mediated pre-writing discussion. The extant literature on intertextuality did not offer available tools for analysis as research had rarely dealt with intertextual connections in the computer-mediated context. Inspired by a model of text construction presented by Grabe and Kaplan in their book *Theory and Practice of Writing (1996)*, Iona created an analytical procedure that allowed her to compare the CMC discourse line by line with students' drafts and to examine the connections between the computer-mediated peer collaborative discourse and students' drafts at three levels: organizational, lexical, and textual. The analytical procedure also captured different strengths of intertextual connections as well as the strategies used by the participants to establish such connections (e.g., paraphrase and repetition). From my perspective, this resolution of the contradiction between the object and mediating tools was essential for the dissertation activity and reflected learning and development on Iona's part as a researcher.

Transformative Nature of the PhD Activity

Iona's PhD activity was transformative in nature. Transformation of the objects of different cycles of the PhD activity led not only to a concrete outcome in the form of a completed dissertation, but also to learning and development on the part of the subject. In other words, the transformation of the object had intertwined with that of the subject of the activity system. As we have seen in this case, Iona was transformed, and the transformation encompassed her changed motive for PhD studies and reshaped views and beliefs about writing. It also included her improved knowledge of and skills in using mediating tools for participating in disciplinary practices as demonstrated in the dissertation study. In Iona's case, the transformation through the PhD activity also provided the foundation for her transformation into a professional: an educator who is actively involved in teacher development nationally and internationally, and a scholar who is a frequent presenter at professional conferences, as well as a participant in multinational research projects. What has been transformed, however, is not confined to the subject and object of the PhD activity. Other components of the PhD activity have also been transformed.

Take myself for an example. Through working with Iona and other students on their dissertation projects and interactions with dissertation committee members with expertise in various areas, I have developed a better understanding of instructional technology as a field and of the roles that technology could play in second language writing research and instruction. I have also developed a deepened understanding of various research methods and their possible uses in second language writing research. My interactions and collaborations with students have introduced me to new mediating instruments and new activity systems (e.g., my students introduced me to activity theory). As a mediating tool in Iona's and other students' PhD activities, I have undergone transformation.

CONCLUSION

As illustrated by Iona's example, the PhD activity, when viewed from the activity system perspective, is carried out in interconnected cycles, each of which has its own (albeit related) specific object. Each cycle of activity is transformative, transforming not only the object but also the subject and other elements of the activity system, with outcomes of the earlier cycle of activity becoming important components of the subsequent cycle of activity. Each cycle is mediated by a variety of mediating tools and instruments, including the dissertation committee and advisors, and influenced by pertinent rules, community, and division of labor of the local activity system. Further, agency on the part of the subject has an important impact on the activity. The PhD activity is not without contradictions that, when resolved, provide opportunities for learning and development.

REFERENCES

Belcher, D. (1994). The apprenticeship approach to advanced academic literacy: Graduate students and their mentors. *English for Specific Purposes*, 13, 23-34.

Casanave, C. P., & Li, X .M. (Eds.) 2008. *Learning the literacy practices of graduate school*. Ann Arbor, MI: The University of Michigan Press.

Engestrom, Y. (1990). *Learning, working, and imagining: Twelve studies in activity theory*. Helsinki: Orienta-Konsultit.

Engestrom, Y. (1999). Activity theory and individual and social transformation. In Y. Engestrom, R. Miettinen, & R. L. Punamaki, (Eds), *Perspectives on activity theory* (pp. 19-38). Cambridge: Cambridge University Press.

Grabe W., & Kaplan R. B. (1996). *Theory and practice of writing*. London and New York: Longman.

Hawley, P. (2003). *Being bright is not enough: The unwritten rules of doctoral study*. Springfield, IL: Charles C. Thomas Publisher, Ltd.

Ivanic, R. (1998). *Writing and identity*. Amsterdam/Philadelphia: John Benjamins Publishing Company.

Leont'ev, A. N. (1978). *Activity, consciousness, and personality*. Englewood Cliffs, NJ: Prentice Hall.

Leont'ev, A. N. (1981). *Problems of the development of the mind*. Moscow: Progress.

Phillips, E. M., Pugh, D. (2005). *How to get a PhD: A handbook for students and their supervisors*. 4th edition. Open University Press.

Tardy, C. (2005)."It's like a story": Rhetorical knowledge development in advanced academic literacy. *Journal of English for Academic Purposes, 4*, 325-338.

10 The PhD Process as Growing in a Community

Iona Sarieva

The Framework Of Discourse Communities

Our life experiences are usually stored in our memories; they often stay dormant or trigger emotional responses and motivate us for specific actions in our later life. The transformation of the tacit knowledge we gain through our involvement in certain processes into concrete, articulated, and reflective narrative is not always an easy task. It requires concentration, time, and effort to reflect and analyze; choosing a framework that would structure this narrative would allow me to reach a deeper understanding of personal and professional growth. The same process can be conceptualized within different frameworks. In the previous chapter, my major professor, Dr. Wei Zhu, interpreted her observations of my engagement in the PhD process from the standpoint of Activity Theory (Leont'ev, 1978), which accounts for the dynamics and driving forces of the activity system. In my own reflection on my PhD experiences as a growing second language writer and a professional, I chose the framework of discourse communities. Adopting this framework allowed me to capture, conceptualize, and present my experiences and growth as a doctoral student, second language dissertation writer, and a professional.

Initially, I planned to address specifically how I engaged in the process of dissertation writing. However, I found this approach to the preparation of doctoral students for academia to be limited to only one step of a process that is much longer and more complex. When thinking about my own experience, I have always perceived the coursework and the dissertation writing as parts of the same continuum that I would interpret as joining a specific community—that of educators and researchers in the field of second language acquisition and language education. I would define this community as a discourse community in which writing is perceived as a process embedded in social-rhetorical situations in a manner that naturally includes writers, readers, texts, and social contexts (Grabe & Kaplan, 1996). My understanding of discourse community was guided by the following criteria outlined by Swales in his 1990 book *Genre Analysis*. These criteria allowed me to interpret my own perception of the process of becoming a researcher:

- The members of a discourse community share common public goals;
- Discourse communities provide a forum for discussion for their members;
- Discourse communities allow for member participation and provide mechanisms for such participation;
- Discourse communities have discourse expectations for genres, terminology, and specialized vocabulary;
- Discourse communities are large enough to address matters that are of importance to a broader group of people (Swales, 1990, pp. 23-27).

However, when looking back at my personal experiences in the context of these criteria, it is quite clear to me that the process of my "initiation" into the community was not that straightforward.

FINDING MY DISCOURSE COMMUNITY

I came into the Second Language Acquisition and Instructional Technology (SLA/IT) doctoral program at the University of South Florida (USF) with a lot of foreign language teaching experience and very little (it may actually be correct to say almost zero) experience in second language acquisition (SLA) research. This of course shaped my initial understanding of the program; even more so, it shaped my initial limited awareness of community practices and goals that were set in the program.

I came to the United States as part of the Diversity Visa Program, and my personal and professional goals were to find an interesting and stable job in the field of language teaching, preferably at the tertiary level where I had the most experience. Soon enough I realized that my choices were quite limited, and it would be difficult to find a teaching position without continuing my education. Thus, the motivation that initially drove my search for a professional community was rather extrinsic and instrumental. In this search for a community, I was not driven by the specifics, priorities, and the communication within the targeted community but rather by the professional goals I set for myself. Today, I interpret this entry process as one guided by some false expectations and incomplete knowledge about the specifics of the target community. While being well-prepared in the field of theoretical linguistics and aware of the main current trends in foreign language teaching methodology, my understanding of SLA research, both in terms of carrying it out and how it connects theory and practice, was rather limited. This of course shaped in a certain way my initial steps in the community. I was limited in my understanding of what the overall goals of the program were and, due to these limitations, initially felt frustrated and stressed. Today looking back, I would say that during the first semester of my studies, I could have been described as a student at risk.

In order to gain membership in the community, I needed to work on certain approaches to my teaching (due to my teaching assistantship responsibilities); I also needed to build a deeper understanding of the principles related to SLA and more specifically to writing. In my previous training, the nature of writing had never been discussed explicitly, let alone presented in a systematic way in historical context and supported with research outcomes. This is why for me, as a learner and educator, the introduction to the concept of writing-as-a-process and the related practices was quite revealing. This new view on writing significantly changed my beliefs about the nature of writing, the role of feedback, and the place of writing in the curriculum.

Entering the community was a process that formed the basis for my dissertation writing, becoming an important phase in my development as an educator and researcher. If we draw a parallel between this phase and the phases in the writing process model, this was a pre-writing stage I needed to engage in to prepare myself for the other phases of the dissertation writing process and professional development. I feel that sharing my awareness of the complexity of the process of finding and interpreting a discourse community may provide support to other graduate students, especially to those who come from academic cultures different from the Western-oriented tradition.

There were a number of factors that shaped the way I understood my participation in the discourse community. To identify these factors in the context of my development, I looked not only at the specific rhetorical situations of the target discourse community but also at the broader social network in which I participated while gaining access to this community. To a great extent, I was (and still am) influenced by Cooper's ecological model of writing (Cooper, 1986). This view on the writer as a subject of influence and a participant in various social processes and contexts motivated me to define the specific boundaries of my discourse community as they were evident in the process of my entry into it.

Of course, in the core of the discourse community were the experts and the extended community of professionals; however, this community, in my case, also embraced the peers and the extended membership of research participants, family, and friends. This extension of the community is supported by my belief that the interpretation of my development as a writer would be limited if a broader social context is not taken into account. Considering this broader context prompted my inclusion of these seemingly marginal members. This expansion will be clearer if viewed within the context of my experience as a novice discourse community member.

At the Doorstep of the Discourse Community: Listening to the Experts

Through the course of my dissertation studies, my communication with experts in the field and with the extended professional community was accomplished through texts and interactions in learning and professional environments. It is important to note that this communication was not at the same level of interactivity. Scholars such as Cooper (1989) and Bizzell (1993), among other researchers who view the process of writing through the critical discourse paradigm, raise their concern that the initiation of novice writers into a discourse community can actually have a limiting instead of an empowering effect. They warn about the potential danger of posing limits to the novice writers' voice, ideas, and values. In my case, however, I perceive this limiting effect to be part of the development curve (it might well be the case with the majority of graduate-level writers as well). When going through the course sequence during my doctoral studies and preparing for dissertation writing, I progressed through different stages in terms of comfort of participation and preferred manner of participation in the discourse community. In the beginning, I preferred to be "the fly on the wall"—silent and observant. This was a behavior evident not only in face-to-face communication, but in my writing as well. This was the period when as a writer who develops within a particular community, I tuned myself into the ideas of this community, its values and language; in the center of my agenda was the development of skills of listening and reading for writing.

Going back to this stage of my professional development, I recognize that indeed there were limitations in terms of expressing my values and voicing my ideas. These limitations were to a great extent self-initiated and, in my opinion, they helped me get insight and a better understanding of the community, of the central aims as well as of the specifics of the dialogue development within the community. I recognize this stage as a stage of relative alienation from the community as well. The further integration was a process that required a lot of effort and work on my part; I realize that without the support I received from the expert community members I would not gain full entry and would not be able to successfully progress to the dissertation writing stage of my development.

Support From The Extended Community

My belief is that without adequate support from the nearest members of the community, there is a great danger for a novice to remain in the passive stage of participation or, when engaged in more active communication, to be limited in the ability and power to develop one's own voice, ideas, and values. This is especially true of second language writers, who bring into the community their culture and values, as well as previous professional and academic experiences. In this respect the SLA/IT doctoral program laid the groundwork for developing a constructive dialogue between expert and novice and between novice and novice.

The program faculty, who were our guiding experts, engaged in interactive student-centered instruction in which we, the learners, could voice our opinions in discussions, test ideas, and experiment with writing and research designs. This was a valuable opportunity for us to engage in active forums and develop a language that can be heard and valued by the members of the extended discourse community. These initial steps of active engagement in the community were made in a safe environment, which I perceive not only as an opportunity to adopt the target genre expectations but also as an empowering experience. Although nearly all courses offered in the program curriculum supported this development of active engagement, I would like to mention two that were extremely important for my own evolution within the context of the discourse community of researchers in the field of SLA: the research laboratories and the Second Language Writing course. While these courses were addressed in the context of the SLA/IT doctoral program curriculum by my major professor in the previous chapter (see Zhu, this volume), I would like to highlight the aspects of these courses that facilitated my community engagement and growth.

The research labs were a sequence of courses that served as a sandbox where we, as novice researchers, could play with connecting research theories introduced in other program courses with our own research practices, and then present the outcomes to the broader public. We designed, conducted, and wrote up our projects and prepared them for conference presentation and/or publication. This experience would not have been complete without the course in second language writing that provided me with the opportunity to gain insights into theoretical views on writing and to interpret these theoretical views in the context of second language development. These learning experiences were empowering in my progression from a novice to a more active discourse community member and set the ground for building a more confident participation in the dialogue within the immediate community of peers and the broader community of experts in the field.

The SLA/IT program had another feature that I find to be an important element supporting my growth as a writer. The course sequence of the program, while being to some extent flexible, was set in a way that allowed the formation of cohorts, groups of peers who would go through their doctoral study following similar sequences of courses and engaging in similar activities. This allowed us, the doctoral students, to engage in more informal community interactions in which we contributed to each other's ideas, shared our growing expertise, and further expanded our understanding of how academic communities build knowledge within a certain field.

In this respect, student-initiated informal groups for research project brainstorming, discussion, and reviews had a significant impact on my development as a researcher and a writer. The informal nature of these groups allowed for a community engagement within my comfort zone: progressing from being a novice member mentored by more advanced peers to being a mentor myself, from relying on peer expertise to offering advice to peers. The peer efforts for building a community within the program were supported by the program structures and faculty in another way as well: we were encouraged and supported in establishing a doctoral student organization that aimed at providing opportunities for doctoral students from our smaller community to step out into the larger community of researchers through various activities such as invitation of experts to speak, funding conference attendance for the members of the organization, and informing each other about publications and attended conferences. The program also supported our development as strong community members through providing various work opportunities within the field and assuring our exposure to different experiences consistent with our theoretical and practical knowledge. Last but not least, the program supported us as individuals who have families providing opportunities to gather as a larger community.

The recognition of the role of families might seem a marginal aspect that is unrelated to the process of gaining entry in a discourse community. However, according to the Census Bureau Report (2010), today few doctoral students have the opportunity to fully immerse into their studies because they have to handle family responsibilities during graduate school. Inevitably, our experiences of growth and gaining entry into target discourse communities cross paths with our experiences as participants in other communities including the most important one: the family. In my case, the support that I received from my family while being a doctoral student played a key role in my development. My then very young daughter and my husband supported me emotionally; the willingness of my husband to listen and talk with me about my research helped me in clarifying and developing my ideas.

He took the time to brainstorm with me, which helped me step aside and take an outsider's view of the dissertation project.

The Actual Dissertation Writing Process

The process of gaining access to a particular discourse community was vigorous and challenging during the course-taking phase of my doctoral studies. It was supported by the members of my immediate community of faculty and peers, as well as by family. When I reached the stage of dissertation writing, my self-confidence within the target discourse community of scholars was established to the extent that I could have ownership of my ideas and writing. While I still felt to a certain degree a novice, I was able not only to formulate my own research goals and ideas but also stand by them. I feel that this confidence supported my ability to effectively communicate with my committee members and especially supported the ongoing dialogue with my major professors. In my case, I had two major professors, whom I chose based on their extensive expertise in the two main aspects my dissertation study: addressing second language writing and working with ESL writers in the context of intensive English language programs. At the stage of dissertation writing, they were the ones to provide the major guidance and support.

As my confidence as a writer and community member grew and I developed an ownership of my writing project, I felt more comfortable engaging in a dialogue with the immediate community of experts: that of my dissertation committee and the major professors. Wei Zhu provided several examples of my attempts to extend the dialogue beyond the feedback meetings through written follow-up comments, summaries, interpretations of suggested changes, and projections of further dissertation development steps. I felt this extension of our dialogue to be necessary in order to verify my understanding of the feedback and provide my interpretation within the broader context of the dissertation process. In a way it was a newly gained freedom, responsibility, and expertise that I appreciated but also found challenging; while being part of the program prepared me for engaging in such dialogue, the scope and the high-stakes nature of the dissertation project shaped the way I engaged in the process of negotiating meaning, making it somehow more strenuous, complex, and even tenser for me.

Support from peers, faculty, and the program was available; however, the nature of dissertation writing called for much more focused expert support. The scope of a dissertation, the variability of tasks and activities that need to be designed, planned, and conducted as well as the volume of writing requires constant engagement both on the part of the writer and on the side of the support group. This intensity of the process resulted in the reduction of community members actively engaged in it. In many cases it is unrealistic for an outsider to embrace the whole dissertation project and provide insightful and extensive feedback. In my case, it was evident as well: we, as peers, still engaged in support groups, brainstormed ideas, and shared research design approaches; however, the main support I received was from my major professors. In a way this more advanced stage of entering the discourse community was a lonelier experience as compared to the initiation stage addressed earlier. This, in my opinion, was the appropriate developmental progression of gaining self-reliance and independence as a discourse community member.

Today, going back to this stage, I view my major professors' guidance as significant yet unobtrusive. In our research design and conceptualization discussion sessions, they helped me to make my objectives more focused and refine the research goals. I truly value their wisdom to ask the right questions about my first drafts of the dissertation proposal, rather than directly giving me the solutions. This motivated me to search for answers in the literature and experiment with research design ideas.

Dissertation writers are usually new to the dissertation genre. Reading research and dissertations in the field is helpful; however, interpreting somebody else's research project is not the same as writing one's own. Even if the dissertation writer has experience in conducting research and writing about it, this is often a recently acquired experience, as it was in my case. Thus, my limited expertise and my perception of the dissertation as a research and writing project that requires an excessive complexity and volume led me initially to design a project that was too broad and grandiose. My major professors were the ones who helped me define the scope of the project and turn it into manageable, yet complex and rigorous research. Later in my teaching career, when advising graduate students in the process of their thesis and dissertation writing, I saw that refining the scope of a project is a common problem for novice dissertation writers; moreover, it is a key step that needs to be taken early in the process in order to achieve the successful completion of the project.

One of the most helpful activities during the feedback sessions with my major professors was the discussion of my first dissertation proposal drafts. This guided shifting between the written text and oral discourse helped refining ideas, building a better understanding of the caveats, and defining effective solutions to identified issues. Going back and forth between oral and written discourse in the process of our communication also helped me with a problem that I had with my writing: my sentences tended to be long and frequently convoluted, and the logic was sometimes lacking in the structure of my text. Refining the text was a valuable learning experience that would not have been possible without the additional face-to-face communication.

When I worked on my chapter drafts, I noticed that even at later stages I appreciated to a greater extent the written feedback given by my major professors and the committee members when it concerned design ideas and particular steps in data presentation, analysis, and interpretation. I perceived the feedback, which focused on grammar and form, as not timely because I was still in a stage that required interpretation of data and making meaning of the outcomes of the research. Now I realize that I prolonged this stage of my work—it was much more comfortable for me to remain in the research stage of the dissertation project. Today, I interpret this procrastination in moving to the final editing stage as a fear of concluding the study, presenting it to the committee, and subsequently defending it in front of peers and other members of the community. This suggests that, for me, the confidence of a discourse community member was not fully established at this very late stage, and I perceived the actual dissertation defense to be the major step that I needed to take in order to be fully recognized as a member of that community.

Dealing With Obstacles

The process of writing a dissertation is complex and extensive both in terms of time and invested effort; it requires consistency and the ability to deal with various obstacles down the road. This is especially true for projects that entail longitudinal entry into particular settings for qualitative data collection. There are various obstacles that a researcher needs to deal with in order to successfully complete a research project, especially a research project of the magnitude of a dissertation study.

An obstacle that I needed to find a way to handle was the various roles I had to assume in the process of my dissertation writing. I was teaching full-time in settings different from the ones I was researching, I had family, and was engaged actively with the participants of my study—more than 90 international students and their teachers.

Longitudinal studies with a major qualitative component require constantly switching roles between an observer, communicator, and a writer. In this respect, I found that the key issues for me were psychological flexibility, time management, organization skills, and keeping clear focus. While it is impossible to define a formula for overcoming these obstacles, my solution was seeing all the elements of the process as a whole and making connections on different levels between the different scenes and roles.

Making meaningful connections between the different facets of the process of conducting and writing up research also supported my ability to establish effective collaboration with the research participants and gain their trust. It supported the further development of my interpersonal communication skills: working with people from different cultures going through the process of cultural adaptation, adjustment to their new cultural experiences, and the new language of communication that required refined communication skills, sensitivity, and perspective. One of the most important aspects of conducting longitudinal research with people was the realization that my priorities related to the project in many cases were only my priorities and that the participants and collaborators had their own set of objectives. Realizing this was surprisingly hurtful; however, these insights and the interpersonal skills gained in the process supported my understanding of the collected data and allowed for more in-depth interpretation.

Connecting Communities

Engaging in the process of dissertation research while taking into consideration the role and interplay of different discourse community members helped me to better understand the diversity of the socially embedded systems and activities in which I participated as a writer; it supported my professional development and ensured full entry into the discourse community of researchers in the field of second language acquisition and education. I believe that the insights I gained in the process allowed me to contribute to the community through active involvement in research and education and to reach beyond the boundaries of my original discourse community. I also believe that these insights helped me to engage actively in building international connections between similar discourse communities situated in different cultural contexts through international teaching assignments, conference presentations, and engagement in multinational research projects.

REFERENCES

Bizzell, P. (1986). Composing processes: An overview. In A. Petrosky & D. Bartolomae (Eds.), *The teaching of writing* (pp. 49-70). Chicago: University of Chicago Press.

Census Bureau Report (2010). Statistical Abstract for the United States Retrieved December 10, 2012, from http://www.census.gov/compendia/statab/2012/tables/12s0231.pdf.

Cooper, M. (1936). The ecology of writing. *College English, 48*, 364-75.

Engestrom, Y. (1990). *Learning, working, and imagining*. Twelve studies in activity theory. Helsinki: Orienta-Konsultit.

Grabe W., & Kaplan R. B. (1996). *Theory and practice of writing*. London and New York: Longman.

Leont'ev, A. N (1978). *Activity, consciousness, and personality*. Englewood Cliffs, NJ: Prentice Hall.

Swales, J. M. (1990). *Genre analysis: English in academic and research settings*. Cambridge: Cambridge University Press.

11 Knowledge Consumer to Knowledge Producer: Preliminary Exams and the Prospectus (A Dialogue)

Tony Cimasko and Tony Silva

Introduction And Overview

Silva

I'm Tony Silva. Currently, I am a Professor of English and the Director of the Graduate Program in Second Language Studies/ESL at Purdue University. I have an AA in Liberal Arts from Northampton County Area Community College (1975), a BA in Spanish from the world-renowned Kutztown State College (1977)—the Golden Bears—an MA in Teaching English as a Second Language from the University of Illinois at Urbana-Champaign (1981), and a PhD in Rhetoric and Composition and Linguistics from Purdue University (1990). I have taught at the University of Illinois, Harvard University, the University of Florida, Auburn University, and at Purdue for the last twenty-four years. Perhaps most germane to our story, I have (at the time of publication) had the opportunity to serve on a total of 154 MA and PhD committees. Most relevant here are the PhD committees: I have chaired 38, co-chaired ten, and served as a member of 67 more.

Cimasko

I am Tony Cimasko. I work at Miami University of Ohio, where I am the head of ESL Composition in the university's English department. Immediately before that, I earned my PhD in second language writing at Purdue University in 2009, under Silva's generous, wise, and calm advising. My path to second language writing has been elliptical. My bachelor's degree is in economics from Rutgers University in New Jersey, but I eventually found an opportunity to teach English in Korea—and with that I almost instantly decided that L2 studies would be my career focus. After returning to the States, I earned my MEd in Bilingual, ESL, and Multicultural Studies at the University of Massachusetts at Amherst, and then came to Purdue for doctoral work. At Miami, I have been building an ESL writing program for a very rapidly growing international student population.

Purpose

What we want to do here is talk about how doctoral students need to inhabit two worlds simultaneously: on the one hand, absorbing and satisfactorily representing all the relevant literature of her or his work, and on the other hand, going beyond that knowledge and *demonstrating that they can add something new to it.* Of course, this is never an equal balance—pre-ABD doctoral students are very clearly weighted toward the quote-unquote consumer side, only to shift more fully to the producer side for the dissertation. For someone pursuing a PhD, there is a *space in between*, a transitional space between the status of traditional "knowledge consuming" student and being a knowledge producer. Preliminary exams mark the start of that transition. Writing the prospectus and having it accepted marks its end. Understanding that transitional space in between is necessary for all of us to do our work better, whether we are advising students or we are students being advised. We will share our experience with that time in between. But we need a little background first, and Silva will start us off.

Silva

At this point, I'd like to put our story in context—that context being Purdue University.

Contexts

University

Purdue University, one of Indiana's two flagship state universities, was founded in 1869 as a land-grant university when the Indiana General Assembly, taking advantage of the Morrill Act, accepted a donation of money and land from Lafayette businessman John Purdue to establish a college of science, technology, and agriculture in his name.

Since then Purdue has become a full service university with roughly 40,000 students (including over 9,000 international students) that offers both undergraduate and graduate programs in over 210 major areas of study, and is well known for its programs in engineering, avionics, and astronautics.

College Of Liberal Arts

The College of Liberal Arts is made up of 9 academic departments including, of course, the English department.

Department Of English

The English department comprises approximately 60 faculty members and 200 graduate students. Departmental Programs currently include Creative Writing, English Education, English Language and Linguistics, Literary Studies, Professional Writing, Rhetoric and Composition, Theory and Cultural Studies, and, of course, Second Language Studies/ESL.

Graduate Program In Second Language Studies/ESL

The year Cimasko entered the program it was actually a part of the Graduate Program in English Language and Linguistics. The following year it became the Graduate Program in ESL, and more recently the Graduate Program in Second Language Studies/ESL. The graduate program currently has four faculty members (all tenured), roughly 40 PhD students, and a handful of MA and Certificate Students.

PhD students in the program usually complete their studies within five years. Students work toward their PhD in several stages that they complete with the advice and assistance of their major professor and the members of their advisory committee. The stages (in chronological order) include:

- Completing course work (typically during their first two years), specifically a prerequisite course on inquiry in second language studies, four core courses—theory, curriculum, quantitative research, and qualitative research, two language studies/linguistics courses, two seminars, and four courses in a secondary area.
- Developing a plan of study in their third semester
- Meeting the foreign language requirement
- Taking the preliminary exam
- Preparing the dissertation prospectus
- Defending the dissertation prospectus in an oral exam
- Conducting research for the dissertation
- Writing the dissertation
- Defending the dissertation in an oral exam
- Depositing the dissertation

As mentioned, we will be focusing on the preliminary examination and the prospectus.

CHOOSING THE PROGRAM, COURSEWORK, AND REFLECTIONS LEADING UP TO THE PRELIMS

Cimasko

Silva has given you an overview of what awaited me at Purdue, but as a potential doctoral student fussing over where to go, I saw only a sliver of this. In my mind, the factors that loomed largest were these. First, Doctor Tony Silva and the *Journal of Second Language Writing*. As a master's student, I quickly began to focus my interests in ESL onto second language writing specifically—and time and again I came into contact with the *Journal*, and with Tony Silva's work. Secondly, beyond Silva and the *Journal*, what I was hoping for was a program that was closely tied to a mainstream rhetoric and composition program. Purdue's ESL program was exactly that, and it was housed in an English department. My goal—one of the very few specific goals I had in mind at that point—of drawing on L1 writing and potentially contributing to L1 writing from an L2 perspective seemed achievable.

Thirdly and finally, the program had very diverse course requirements, covering rhet-comp, cultural theory, L2 education and theory, linguistics, and sociolinguistics. To me, this was a guarantee that the program was open to diverse agendas, and a little bit of uncertainty on the part of an applicant at the beginning of his PhD work. So, the choice became clear.

CHOOSING THE APPLICANT

Silva

What we (the admissions committee) saw in Cimasko's application were impressive credentials: GRE verbal score in the 90th percentile, excellent hypertext writing sample—*The field of composition in three dimensions*, all A's in his relevant Master's courses at Amherst, Korean as a second language, nearly ten years of teaching experience—with kids in a bilingual school, university students and adults in Korea, adult Education students in Massachusetts—experience in the American Culture and Language Program at Amherst, online international teaching experience, and a secondary area interest in rhetoric and composition. The decision was easy. We offered him admission with a teaching assistantship and promised him the staggering sum of $11,600 a year along with a cheesy health plan (we do better now). He graciously accepted.

What Cimasko didn't know was that he was entering a brand new graduate program. Previously, graduate study in ESL was done under the aegis of the graduate program in English Language and Linguistics or ELL. In fact, Cimasko—I don't know if he remembers it or not—actually applied for admission to and was accepted by the ELL program. What was going on here? Well, for several years before this, the percentage of students focusing on ESL in the ELL program had been increasing while the number of students focusing on linguistics had been decreasing. By 2004, nearly 90% of the students in ELL were actually interested in working in ESL. It seemed a good time to make a break, especially since the courses required by the ELL program included more linguistics courses than ESL courses and the linguistics faculty resisted any change in the status quo.

Breaking away would not be easy, however. In addition to resistance from the ELL program, the English department as a whole was not exactly overjoyed at the prospect of creating a new program. This was a time of turf warfare in the English department—many faculty members, including most of the department's administrators, had a zero-sum game attitude—any gain for someone else was a loss for you. And exacerbating this situation, we had a dean at the time who was intent on shrinking the graduate program in the English department—in diametrical opposition to the provost's desire to grow the university's graduate programs. The dean was soon let go, I'm happy to say.

However, after a fairly acrimonious, bruising, and protracted struggle, the ESL graduate program's secession succeeded, barely. When our proposal for emancipation came to a vote at a faculty meeting in the spring of 2004, the vote was 21 for, 20 against. But a win is a win.

So when Cimasko came to Purdue in 2004, he was a member of the first student cohort in the newly minted ESL graduate program. Actually he represented half of that cohort. That's right—we were only given two slots to fill.

Over the years, the departmental climate has become much more hospitable for the ESL graduate program, recently renamed the Graduate Program in Second Language Studies/ESL to signify that we are interested in the learning and instruction of any second or foreign language, though we specialize in English.

In fact, in my estimation, we are now seen by the majority of the English faculty as a legitimate, successful, and even valuable, part of the department. Now everybody loves us and we are well on the way to living happily ever after. Well, maybe that's going a little too far.

Cimasko

So, into this context I went. However, it wasn't until my second semester and an independent study course under Silva's supervision that really pointed the way forward. In my earlier readings, I had found genre to be one of the few places where L1 and L2 scholars were able to have more of a two-way relationship, rather than just the traditional unidirectional flow from L1 to L2, and made it the subject of my independent study. During that semester, I eventually narrowed my focus, reflected on and discussed several options, then shared with Silva the direction I wanted to take: the idea that genre could help L2 writers *resist* existing native writing patterns and do something different, something new. It was vague enough at that point to be uncontroversial, yet interesting and substantive enough to help me consider the details of my plan of study. For the following year or so, the idea stayed on the back burner as I finished my courses in the core areas and fulfilled the foreign language requirement, as Silva described earlier. The last course credit was finally recorded, and then I was ready to begin the prelims, and start proving that I had been paying attention once in a while during those two years.

Preliminary Exams: Consuming It All, Again

Silva

Cimasko had, indeed, been paying attention and was ready to go, but a couple of options awaited him.

Options

Once SLS/ESL doctoral students are eligible to take the Preliminary Exam, they can choose between two forms of the exam: a two-part, take-home exam (the 24/7 option) or a set of three papers (the Papers option).

The 24/7 Option.

The 24/7 option involves completing a two-part examination. In the first part, examinees are given twenty-four hours to respond to four questions, one in each of the PhD core areas. In the second part, examinees are given one week to write an essay on a more specialized topic or issue within the examination area.

Before the beginning of the semester in which a student plans to take the 24/7 examination, she or he needs to consult with her or his advisor about examination procedures and discuss potential questions/prompts for the seven-day essay. Questions for the 24- hour examination are submitted by the faculty without consulting the student. Both parts of the examination are scored on a pass/fail basis by the examination committee. Success on the exam requires a passing grade on both parts of the exam.

Let me digress a bit here to deliver a short rant on traditional sit-down prelims.

What I offer is just my opinion—though it is an opinion informed by much experience. And one important experience was taking my prelims at Purdue in the late 1980's. At that time, I needed to take two four-hour sit-down prelims: one in my primary area and one in my secondary area. The customary way to prepare for these prelims was to take a semester or a summer studying for each one, reviewing class notes, doing some additional reading/rereading, working with others in study groups, practicing writing answers to questions that had been used previously, and so on. While I knew more or less the *general areas* I'd be tested on (in my case, invention, audience, style, and empirical research for Rhetoric and Composition; and phonology, syntax, semantics, and historical linguistics for Linguistics), I really didn't know the specific questions that would be asked. Would I have to explicate Cicero's view on invention? Would I have to provide a discussion and analysis of the Great Vowel Shift? That is, I had to try to read the minds of the people dreaming up the questions. This, of course, resulted in a great deal of anxiety and of time spent memorizing large amounts of information of dubious value, much of which I would forget almost immediately after finishing the exam.

I spent a total of eight months studying for these prelims. Eight months that I could have used to do much more interesting, useful, and productive things, eight months that I will never get back. A line from 60's poet Richard Brautigan sums up my feelings on this very well. The line is from a poem called "The Memoirs of Jesse James" in a collection called *Rommel Drives on Deep into Egypt*. Brautigan writes: *"My teachers could easily have ridden with Jesse James for all the time they stole from me."*

Now some people (even some students) will defend these types of examinations, saying "they helped me pull together everything I learned in my classes," "I made connections between topics and ideas that I hadn't seen before," "they helped me build a strong foundation for my future work," "I developed a real sense of camaraderie working with other students in my study group" and so on. And if this is how you feel, more power to you. What I got from the prelims (which I passed, as did all the other people taking them that year) was lifelong resentment for this form of academic hazing and a great deal of enmity for the departmental power structure that either championed or just went along with subjecting their students to this process. To add insult to injury one of my examiners claimed he couldn't read my handwriting—one's handwriting suffers a bit when writing continuously for hours—and I was instructed to type up my answers. But it's not like I'm bitter or anything.

But this is not just about me (or at least not completely about me). Consider this: One of the reasons that people are PhD students is that they have always been good students and successful test takers: in their classes from first to twelfth grade; on standardized tests like the ACT and SAT to get into college; on examinations in their undergraduate college courses; on more standardized tests, like the GRE and TOEFL, to get into Master's and PhD programs; and on examinations in their graduate courses. Why, after all of this, do we want to test them again? All of a sudden they've become bad students or poor test takers?

So what's behind this, in my view, questionable requirement? Tradition:

- We've always done it this way?
- A no-pain, no gain view of learning?
- An I-had-to-do-this-so-you-will-too orientation?
- Minimizing faculty work?—writing a question and grading the answer takes very little time and effort.

Is this sort of test valid? Does regurgitating memorized information for four hours or twenty four hours or one week in any way reflect what scholars do? What exactly is the test supposed to test? How well can one guess what the examiners will ask? How well can someone memorize large amounts of information? How well can one write under time pressure?

Is this sort of test reliable? Could the test taker perform similarly on the test, a month, a semester, or a year later (without studying intensively for it again)? I don't think so.

Furthermore, we faculty spend a whole lot of time on our doctoral students: closely reading their applications, making hard decisions about admission, teaching them, advising them, supporting them intellectually and emotionally. So, at roughly the mid-point of their doctoral studies, we want to give them the opportunity to fail a timed test and flunk them out?

For me the burden of proof for the usefulness and appropriateness of a timed sit down exam falls upon those who advocate and impose it. When someone fails such a test, it is possible that the problem is in the test and not with the student.

That said, the 24/7 is an option sanctioned, enshrined, reified, and required by the department. And since I believe in providing options, if my advisees choose to take the 24/7, I do not try to dissuade them.

Okay. I feel better now.

The Papers Option.

Consequently, when I became a faculty member I was determined to give our graduate students another option. This option was not a new idea—other departments and programs at Purdue and elsewhere had been using it for years—we called it the papers option. At the time Cimasko took it, it involved writing four 20-page papers, one in each of our four core areas: theoretical foundations, curriculum, qualitative research, and quantitative research. Ideally, the papers would build on work done in the SLS/ESL core courses and serve as a bridge to the prospectus and, ultimately, the dissertation. Examinees had one calendar year to successfully complete their papers.

However, there was a serious problem with this year-long papers prelim, which I should have seen coming: some students spent too much time worrying and reading and not enough time writing. A year sounds like a long time, and some people tended to procrastinate and wait until time was short and they were forced to produce. Thus, they wound up using the last few months to actually get down to serious writing, generating a great deal of anxiety for themselves and putting their readers (the faculty members charged with evaluating their papers) in a tough spot. This process was flawed.

So in recent years we've made some changes. We decreased the number of papers required from four to three, asked students to choose three of the four core areas in which to write, and provided better guidelines and instructions for both the writers and their faculty readers. This iteration of the papers prelim seems to be working better than the original, but it is not problem-free. There is no panacea for this process.

Thanks again for your indulgence. Now back to Cimasko's story.

Cimasko

I share more than a few of Silva's feelings on the prelims, but if you cannot escape the process, you need to endure it as best you can, and from this point forward, I would like to frame my experience in terms of "morals," lessons about doctoral work and scholarship beyond the content that I learned during this process. The first "moral" or guiding principle is this:

1. Get maximum value out of everything.

No matter the institution, the prelim is already very much about satisfying members of your program that you have actually learned the content and that you can think about it coherently. It's very much about satisfying your immediate disciplinary community, about meeting their needs. Given that, a student should think about finding any and all available options within that system that benefit his or her own work, as well. With a short, timed prelim, it may be harder to find that value, but negotiating with your advisors ahead of time will move things in your direction.

Luckily, as Silva said, I had two options in front of me: the "24/7" option or the yearlong papers option. A couple of important facts floated to the top as I considered which one to take:

- First, I am a slow writer. Years of studying and teaching process writing forces one to understand one's own writing processes, for better or for worse. I had to admit that generating lengthier and well-reasoned academic discourse in one day or one week, at the same time that I was attending to my other responsibilities, was not realistic. And secondly,
- I wanted to be able to use my writing later. In other words, I was focused enough and specific enough about my dissertation ideas at the time that I wanted the prelim experience to be directly useful for the dissertation. It had to be more than a "classroom genre" that lost all value once the "pass" grade was recorded, forcing me to start from scratch once it was over.

So I chose the papers option. In addition to Silva, I worked with other faculty at Purdue who were equally open to my ideas, and in negotiating my topics, they really needed to be sure of only two things: was the topic broad enough but still focused enough for a 20-page paper, and collectively were they doable in one year? On three of the four papers, the challenge was to *scale it back*, cut my gargantuan ideas down to size. Here's an example I dug out of my archives of the process I went through with Silva on my theoretical foundations paper, an example of my need to scale down, to focus, focus, focus:

Genre dynamics

Genre dynamics in a single field

Genre dynamics in a single field as a dialogic process

Genre dynamics in a single field as a dialogic process between the genre in question and one or more other varieties of discourse

On the fourth paper, I had quite the opposite problem: not really knowing how the core area fit into my topic in the first place! After a few weeks of concocting and trashing ideas for not connecting adequately with my dissertation plans, I had to concede that only a quarter of that paper would really be relevant, and the rest would have to be useful only for the exam. So be it. Now, I had two more "morals" to add to the list:

2. If you have a clear idea that you are confident about, cut it in half, and then cut it in half again, and repeat as needed (the mind is always too big for the Microsoft Word page).

3. Good writers—and good scholars—know a lot more than their own particular research interests. Imagine how narrow and limited someone's scholarly career would be if they didn't.

Earlier, I talked about how the prelims existed in a "space in between" being a student and a researcher, a consumer and a producer. And like any successful prelim writer, whether it's trying to do it "24/7" or over twelve months, I consumed and re-consumed literature, took notes, and showed how well I had consumed it in my papers. But in writing papers for a year, I was already in transition, shifting toward the producer end of the continuum, at least in terms of learning more about writing scholarship on a longer-term basis. Over those twelve months, several more "morals" emerged on the way to knowledge production:

4. Know when to stop reading.

Even when it appears that your task is to represent absolutely all the scholarship on a topic, it isn't. Nothing so completely comprehensive is going to be more interesting than a list. Talk with your advisors if you're a student, and talk to your students if you are an advisor, about how much you need to read, who the biggest scholars are (although who is "big" and who isn't is stretched a bit when taking an exam), and what the important sub-categories of the subject are. Students have to fill in most of the details themselves, of course, but as Silva said earlier, it is so easy to get caught up in reading, moving closer to the end of it but never quite finding it. But most important is to designate a date or time to just stop reading, no matter what. Whether it's a 24/7 timed exam or a yearlong process, the clock is ticking, and no matter how good your process, it's the written product at the end that counts. Once a time is set, both the student and the advisor should decide together on a "red line" and stick with it.

Silva

I think it's crucial that advisors help their student circumscribe their topics so as to make reasonable coverage possible in the time allotted. It's impossible to read everything that is germane to one's topic; what is necessary—and viable—is to read relatively current and reputable scholarship that will adequately contextualize, motivate, and support your paper. Strategically, staying on task, working slowly but steadily, setting realistic deadlines, and checking in when you need help seem to do the job. Moving from coursework to the preliminary exam is a big change. In coursework your time is more or less structured for you; in the prelim you need to structure it yourself.

Cimasko

5. Don't hesitate to communicate.

Even prelim exams aren't that kind of exam—talking is permitted. On a 24/7 exam, there isn't much time once the clock has started, but the preparation phase provides ample opportunities. At that point in my doctoral work, theory was arguably the one area where I felt least confident, and I can only imagine that Silva was getting rather sick of my emails clogging his inbox by the end of the first quarter. Nevertheless, advice always arrived from him, without complaint.

6. Trust your plan, but only to a point.

Stay focused, but if you have time to change your plan, and the evidence against your plan is becoming increasingly insurmountable, then do so. Nothing slows down writing and makes it irritating like doing something that should not be done. A good advisor will catch something quickly, before it goes too far—if you are sharing you work with your advisor, that is. At the six-month mark, I trashed my own work on one paper and started fresh. It was painful, but it was one of the most beneficial things to happen to me during that year.

THE PROSPECTUS: PROVING THAT YOU *MIGHT* ADD SOMETHING TO THE FIELD

Silva

In our context, this is what a prospectus is, and how it is to be done is well specified at both the departmental and program levels.

The Process

After doctoral students finish their course work in their primary and secondary areas, meet the departmental foreign language requirement, and successfully complete their preliminary exams, they can begin work on their prospectus.

Students must complete and defend their prospectus no later than ten months after they finish their preliminary exams. By the end of four months, students need to form an advisory committee comprised of at least three faculty members. By the end of the seventh month, students must submit a prospectus draft of approximately five thousand words to the chair of their advisory committee. By the end of tenth month, students must complete and defend their prospectus. If students do not meet this ten-month deadline, they are not allowed to register for teaching or course work for the following semester.

The reason for imposing this rather rigid departmental process was basically to keep people on task. Prior to the formulation of these rules, there was a perception, which I believe was accurate, that a substantial number of students in the English department lost their way after completing and passing their preliminary examinations. Perhaps it was the loss of structure imposed by the course work or the prelims, perhaps it was an irrational or rational fear that they weren't up to doing a prospectus, perhaps it was the unwillingness to commit to a plan for their dissertation. In any case, I believe this policy has been quite successful.

I urge my students not to spend ten months on their prospectus. I suggest that they not devote more than a semester to the prospectus. This assumes, of course, that students have already thought seriously about the focus of their dissertation. In my experience, they typically have. I advise them to take a week or two off after completing their prelims but not to lose the momentum they built up in preparing for their prelims. I do this because (1) my students typically can produce a good prospectus in this time frame, and (2) putting off work on the prospectus for some students makes the process seem more foreboding and insurmountable than it needs to be.

Document Specification

Our department and program specify that the prospectus, a proposal for the student's dissertation project, should be approximately five thousand words long (plus bibliography), and be written in consultation with the major professor and other members of the advisory committee. In our program, the writer typically works in consultation with only the major professor in drafting the prospectus.

The elements of the prospectus are also specified. They include:

- A problem statement
- A theoretical framework
- A literature review
- A description of the methodology to be used to explore the problem [whether hermeneutic or empirical]
- A discussion of expected results and potential contribution of the study
- A tentative chapter outline for the dissertation
- A bibliography

Knowledge Consumer to Knowledge Producer   185

- A tentative time table for conducting the research and writing the dissertation, and
- A projected date for the oral defense of the dissertation

This process culminates in the oral defense of the prospectus. The objective of the prospectus defense is to ensure that the study will go smoothly and will obtain meaningful results. Often, the outcome of the discussion is a modification of the project to some extent. The student and the committee may decide, for example, to limit the project in size and scope, to adjust the timeline, or to further develop the theoretical framework.

A successful defense formally admits the student to candidacy for the PhD, known informally as "ABD" (all but dissertation) status, and work on the dissertation project can begin. If the members of the student's advisory committee are asked to continue to advise the student, they then become members of the student's dissertation committee.

As you might imagine, I like the prospectus much more than I like the preliminary exam. The prospectus is a well specified, purposeful, goal-oriented task. It is not cloaked in mystery and requires much less guesswork. It is more a project than a test, more formative than summative, more affirming, more interactive, more cooperative, and much more representative of what scholars do. It is also more productive in that it literally lays the foundation for the dissertation. A successful prospectus is a flexible blueprint for a viable dissertation that represents an advancement of knowledge in the field.

Back to Cimasko's story.

Cimasko

The prelim clock stopped, and now the prospectus clock started. From the very nature of the switch from prelim to prospectus, from consuming to producing, and with some of the literature work already in place, my seventh moral was realized:

7. *Work from the inside out—think about your own research plan first, then compare it with the literature.*

Of course any researcher has to account for prior literature, and build on it—no researcher works in a scholarly vacuum. However, trying to account for the literature at the same time that you are planning your own research topic can be a little disorienting, and it can squelch the unique insights that you might bring. My own topic development in the prospectus followed that pattern: come up with the idea first, and then see how it fits with the literature later. Over the course of weeks, my topic would transform into this, the eventual title of my dissertation: *Genre Core and Periphery: Opportunities for L1-L2 Hybridity in the Empirical Research Reports of Second Language Writers*.

This was the end of the process. However, at the start of the process, after trying out titles and ideas for real during the first week or so after finishing the prelims, I had nothing substantial. *Bubpkis*! Not surprisingly, I think I had spent so much time accounting for the work of others that I hadn't gotten around to developing my research plan into something more concrete. Reflecting on it, I think the initial problem lay in this part of the title: HYBRIDITY. At this stage, the term I was using was RESISTANCE. What does *resistance* look like, in all its possible manifestations? It was a word I had encountered frequently in rhet-comp, and I was eager to see how it might be possible in a field in which pedagogy and research were mostly predicated on students NOT resisting norms, doing everything they could to align with them. I had to ask: are ESL graduate students actually *resisting* norms established by L1 English writers? Is that what they want to accomplish? Are they unhappy with these norms? By and large, I didn't see evidence of active resistance, of rebellions on the page. No one I knew was rebelling. I knew I had to *tone it down*. And so I spent time negotiating with what I knew, the idea going through phases, from *resist* to *contest* to *struggle with* to *innovate* ... and then finally to *hybridity*, writers combining established norms with something from their own L1, and getting away with it essentially, whether it was an intentional or accidental writing choice, regardless of what was motivating it.

But *which* writers would I study? My research into genre studies had taught me well that multi-disciplinary approaches could not be sufficiently qualitative for my liking, or that the study would have to be gigantic by dissertation standards. I had read a lot of papers on engineering writers, it was a relatively popular disciplinary site of investigation, and I was at a university that boasted a world-class engineering program that counted many international students among its graduate student body. I even started to do pilot work with engineering grads, until one of my professors reminded me that like any good qualitative researcher, I had to get familiar with the discourse of the field, really learn it inside and out at the same time that I was researching texts and students.

Sigh. Doing all this just wasn't suitable, not in this time frame. What did I know? I knew ESL. I knew second language writing. I had friends in it. And I hadn't encountered any literature that looked at present or future L2 members of our field, just the students—the *clients* of our field, if you will—but not necessarily our own L2 English colleagues. That was it. The rest started to tumble in after that. Without the previous point, devoting most of the prospectus development time to your own ideas, this next moral wouldn't have been possible:

8. Don't grow attached to your initial ideas—evolution is good.

I also want to talk briefly about the *people* involved in the prospectus and the dissertation ahead, the committee. In most cases, one's advisor is an inevitable and happy choice, as Silva was for me. It wasn't too difficult to find others to serve on my committee, but during the process, it occurred to me that another issue needed to be addressed by anyone fast approaching their prospectus:

9. Decide whether you need to come up with your plan first, or your committee first.

Even though committee members are paid nothing for their extra effort (how often is *that* the case for us?) picking committee members is almost like being an employer making hiring decisions. The starting point for this question is how many faculty members are in your program and beyond who could potentially serve. With smaller programs, "shopping around" or "interviewing" candidates becomes more of a challenge. And then all the other questions. Will they fit what you need conceptually and methodologically? Who will be able to give you useful feedback on your writing? Are you connecting with their own research agendas? *Are you potentially challenging their positions?* Do they have time at present to commit to the responsibility? How good a fit are you on a personal level with them?

Silva

Because Cimasko is too nice a guy to say stuff like this, I might add: Are they flaky? Inflexible? Obnoxious? Malevolent? Crazy? And if so, how are you going to deal with this? Of course, there is not, nor has there ever been, anyone one like this in our department. I've just heard about cases in other places.

Cimasko

Only a few of these questions flashed through my head at the time; the rest came later, after the fact.

Even though I didn't pose all of these questions, everything worked out for the best, and I had a very supportive committee overall, very helpful in getting my prospectus in shape and approved. This leads to my tenth and final moral:

10. Do not wait for help to be volunteered or to be explicit.

You are trying to be a knowledge producer now. No one can be expected to provide all the information you need if you don't go looking for it. So ask questions. Email and drop by their offices often. Be a pest. I was.

Silva

Maybe. But a very a polite, considerate, and easy to work with pest.

Postscript

Cimasko

Going forward, I believe that no matter how useful—or not—this period in a doctoral student's life may be, it is one that should be made more explicit for students. Silva and I have both discussed the discursive and emotional aspects of this period, hopefully starting something that advisors will continue with their own students, *and that students should actively pursue* when it's their time. The discipline-based questions to be answered in the prelim can be a mystery until they are unveiled or fully negotiated; the prospectus and the dissertation that follow pose new inquiries and are by definition unknown. I think that's more than enough unknowns. Answer these kinds of questions, fill in some of the blanks, and give doctoral students the space to pursue the really interesting questions, instead.

Silva

Amen. On a more serious/personal note: Advising doctoral students is a mixed bag. For many faculty members, especially for those who advise large numbers of students year after year, it is hard work that is too often unrecognized and unrewarded by our departments. However, the upside—working and developing personal and professional relationships with the best and brightest students from around the world and seeing them grow and succeed in their scholarly pursuits—more than compensates for our labors.

Contributors

Tony Cimasko is head of the ESL Composition program at Miami University, Ohio. His research interests include genre analysis and genre learning, transitions between pedagogical and non-pedagogical writing, digital composition, and the complexities of plagiarism. He is a co-editor of *Foreign Language Writing Instruction: Principles and Practices* (with Melinda Reichelt, 2011).

Alister Cumming is Professor in the Centre for Educational Research on Languages and Literacies (CERLL, formerly the Modern Language Centre) at the Ontario Institute for Studies in Education, University of Toronto, where he has been employed since 1991 following briefer periods at McGill University, the University of British Columbia, Carleton University, and Concordia University. His research and teaching focus on writing in second languages, language assessment, language program evaluation and policies, and research methods. Alister's recent books are *Adolescent Literacies in a Multicultural Context* (2012), *A Synthesis of Research on Second Language Writing in English* (with Ilona Leki and Tony Silva, 2008), and *Goals for Academic Writing* (2006).

Paul Kei Matsuda is Professor of English and Director of Second Language Writing at Arizona State University, where he works closely with doctoral students specializing in second language writing. In addition, he has mentored L2 writing teachers and researchers from various parts of the world. Co-founding chair of the Symposium on Second Language Writing and editor of the Parlor Press Series on Second Language Writing, Paul has published widely on the history and definition of the field, the construction of identity in written discourse, and the negotiation of differences in writing, among other topics, and has received a number of prestigious awards.

Christina Ortmeier-Hooper is Assistant Professor of English and Director of Composition at the University of New Hampshire, where she teaches in the Composition Studies doctoral program. Her research interests include second language writing, composition theory and research, and writing teacher education. Her book, *The ELL Writer: Moving Beyond Basics in the Secondary Schools* (2013), examines the identity negotiations and writing experiences of immigrant students in U.S. high schools. She has also co-edited collections, including *The Politics of Second Language Writing: In Search of the Promised Land* (with Paul Kei Matsuda and Xiaoye You, 2006) and *Reinventing Identities in Second Language Writing* (with Michelle Cox, Jay Jordan, and Gwen Gray Schwartz, 2010). Her work has been published in *The Journal of Second Language Writing*, *TESOL Journal*, and *College Composition and Communication*.

Karen A. Power is an ESL Instructor/International Student Advisor at Urbana University in Ohio. She comes to the field of L2 writing with undergraduate training in foreign language education and graduate training in composition and rhetoric and TESOL. She has presented on L2 writing at national and international conferences and has travelled extensively abroad as an ESL teacher, most recently as an English Language Fellow in Chillán, Chile. Karen has trained foreign language teachers both in the US and abroad. She currently teaches L2 writing, focusing her research on the historical, hermeneutical disposition of L2 writing.

Tanita Saenkhum is Assistant Professor of English at The University of Tennessee, Knoxville, where she directs the ESL program and teaches graduate and undergraduate courses on second language writing, teaching English as a second language, and second language acquisition. She specializes in second language writing with a focus on writing program administration for multilingual writers. She has published in *Journal of Second Language Writing*, *WPA: Journal of the Council of Writing Program Administrators*, *Journal of English for Academic Purposes*, and *WPA-CompPile Research Bibliographies*. She received her PhD in English with a concentration in Rhetoric, Composition, and Linguistics from Arizona State University.

Iona Sarieva earned her PhD from the University of South Florida in the field of Second Language Acquisition and Instructional

Technology. She holds a Master's degree in Russian Studies and a graduate certificate in Teaching English as a Foreign Language from Sofia University, Bulgaria. She has taught English for Academic Purposes, ESOL teacher training courses, and Russian as a Foreign Language in the United States, Europe, and Latin America. Her professional experience includes instruction of face-to-face, blended, and distance learning courses as well as development of distance learning courses in the field of TESOL. Dr. Sarieva's research agenda is focused on student-centered approaches to language teaching, teacher-training, and computer-assisted learning. Currently, she is director of the EAP Bridge Program at Saint Leo University, Florida.

Tony Silva is Professor of English and Director of the Graduate Program in Second Language Studies/ESL in the Department of English at Purdue University, where he teaches graduate courses for Ph.D., M.A., and Certificate students and writing support courses for graduate and undergraduate international students. With Ilona Leki, he founded and edited the *Journal of Second Language Writing* from 1992-2007. With Paul Kei Matsuda, he founded and hosts the Symposium on Second Language Writing. He has co-edited a number of books, including *L2 Writing in Secondary Classrooms: Student Experiences, Academic Issues, and Teacher Education* (with Luciana de Oliveira, 2013) and *Practicing Theory in Second Language Writing* (with Paul Kei Matsuda, 2010). He has published articles in journals such as *College Composition and Communication, Composition Studies, ELT Journal, Modern Language Journal, TESOL Quarterly,* and *Written Communication*.

Dan J. Tannacito is Emeritus Professor of TESOL/Applied Linguistics at Indiana University of Pennsylvania. Previously, he founded and directed an intensive English program for 35 years while teaching graduate courses at IUP. At the same time, he also served as director of graduate studies at IUP several times, in addition to directing nearly 60 dissertations and the MATEFL Fulbright program in Turkey. Dan compiled the first comprehensive annotated bibliography in the field (1995) and remains active with publications in leading journals.

Luxin Yang is Professor of Applied Linguistics in the National Research Center for Foreign Language Education at Beijing Foreign Studies University, China. She holds a PhD in Second Language Education from the Ontario Institute for Studies in Education at University of Toronto. Her research interests include second language writing, foreign language learning, foreign language teacher education, and academic literacy development. She has published articles in *Journal of Second Language Writing, Language Teaching Research, Language, Culture and Curriculum, System,* and *Journal of English for Academic Purposes.* Since she returned to China in 2006, she has paid special attention to EFL education and recently completed a national project on improving the quality of EFL teaching and learning at schools in China. She is now working with Dr. Shijing Xu of University of Windsor on a large SSHRC Partnership Grant.

Wei Zhu is Associate Professor of Applied Linguistics in the Department of World Languages at the University of South Florida. She has taught a variety of graduate-level courses including Writing in the Second Language, Writing for Specific/Academic Purposes, Grammatical Structures of American English, and Language Testing. Dr. Zhu's main research areas include second language writing, writing for academic purposes, and computer-mediated communication and writing development. Her work has appeared in journals such as *TESOL Quarterly, Journal of Second Language Writing, English for Specific Purposes, Language Learning,* and *Computer Assisted Language Learning.*

About the Editors

Kyle McIntosh is Assistant Professor of English and Writing at the University of Tampa where he teaches ESL Writing, First-Year Writing, and TESOL courses. His research interests include English for Academic Purposes and English Language Teaching in China. He has published articles, chapters, and book reviews in *Asian Journal of English Language Teaching*, *Critical Inquiry in Language Study*, *Journal of English for Academic Purposes*, and *The Companion to Language Assessment*. He is a native Hoosier, a graduate of Purdue University, and a lifelong fan of Kurt Vonnegut.

Carolina Pelaez-Morales is Assistant Professor of Writing & TESOL at Columbus State University, where she teaches courses in TESOL and First-Year Composition and helps coordinate a TESOL certificate and an ESOL endorsement program. Her research interests include second language writing pedagogy, writing development in different educational contexts, and biliteracy. Her most recent research article was published by *TESOL* press, but her research has also appeared in *Critical Inquiry in Language Studies* and *INTESOL* Journal. Before relocating to the U.S, Carolina worked as an English and Spanish instructor in South America.

Tony Silva directs the Graduate Program in Second Language Studies/ESL in the Department of English at Purdue University, where he teaches graduate courses for Ph.D., M.A., and Certificate students and writing support courses for graduate and undergraduate international students. With Ilona Leki, he founded and edited the *Journal of Second Language Writing* from 1992-2007; With Paul Kei Matsuda he founded and hosted the (now annual and international) Symposium on Second Language Writing from 1998-2013. He has co-edited or co-authored a number of books, including: *L2 Writing in Secondary Classrooms: Student Experiences, Academic Issues, and Teacher*

Education (2013); *Practicing Theory in Second Language Writing* (2010); *A Synthesis of Research on Second Language Writing in English* (2008); *Research on Second Language Writing: Perspectives on the Construction of Knowledge* (2005); *Landmark Essays on ESL Writing* (2001); and *On Second Language Writing* (2001). He has published articles in a number of journals, including, *College Composition and Communication, Composition Studies, ELT Journal, Foreign Languages and their Teaching, Journal of Second Language Writing, Modern Language Journal, TESL Canada Journal, TESOL Journal, TESOL Quarterly, Writing Program Administration,* and *Written Communication.* He has served as a member of Executive Board of CCCC and is currently a member of the TESOL Board of Directors.

Index

ABD, 26, 28, 42, 185
academic: career, 1, 19, 62, 67–68, 96, 103–104, 112, 118, 122–124, 137, 140–142; community, 3–5, 23–24, 34–35, 43, 52–54, 71–73, 85–91, 104, 114, 123, 132–139, 162–164; identity, 22, 50–52, 91, 103, 112–113; literacy, 33, 145; writing, 73–75, 85–88; year, 21, 101
Academic Writing in a Second Language (Belcher & Braine), 33
acceptance letter, 72, 129
activity theory, 145–150, 153–156, 158
admission, 23, 62, 98, 174
advisor, 1–5, 8, 20–21, 25–29, 37, 117, 126, 137–142, 176, 180, 182–185
advisor-advisee relationship, 1–2, 23–25, 34, 38, 101–106, 135–138, 141–142, 145, 151, 187–188
African-American students, 18
agency, 105, 115, 150–153, 156
American Association for Applied Linguistics (AAAL), 115, 138
American Language Institute, 18, 38, 41
American Psychological Association (APA) style, 49, 67
analysis: data, 75–79, 82–83, 149–150; genre, 159, 181, 186
anecdote, 24, 111

Anglo-Indian, 22
Anglophone, 104
annotated bibliography, 8, 50, 95, 115
Annual Review of Applied Linguistics (ARAL), 47, 51–52
application: graduate school, 59–63, 94–95, 111, 173–174; grant, 85–87; job, 67–68, 97, 118–121
applied linguistics, 7–8, 49–52, 95, 99–100, 145
apprenticeship, 27, 33–35, 42–44, 48–54, 64–65, 117–118, 133
argument, 40–41, 52, 116, 121
Arizona State University (ASU), 99–100, 106, 111, 113–114, 117–118, 122
articles, 28, 35–36, 53, 67–68, 71, 74–75, 78, 83, 93, 97, 104, 106, 111, 114–115, 129, 132–133, 138
Asia, 14, 58, 104
assessment, 14–15, 18–19, 62, 108
assignments, 34, 65, 71, 84–85, 104, 107–108
assistant professor, 97, 112, 121–123, 126
Atkinson, Dwight, 17, 53, 93, 96, 128
attitude, 46, 94, 175
audience, 1, 34, 53, 88, 108, 116, 121
Australia, 58
autobiography, 33

197

autonomy, 27–28, 37, 101, 106

Baba, Kyoko, 77–78
Beckett, Gulbahar H., 73
Beijing Foreign Studies University, 58, 72, 75, 80, 88
Belcher, Diane, 14, 25, 33
Belcher, Diane and George Braine: *Academic Writing in a Second Language*, 33
belief, 104–105, 107, 131, 134, 149, 155, 160–162
Benesch, Sarah, 47
biography, 47–48
Bizzell, Patricia, 161
Blanton, Linda Lonon, 42, 126
blogs, 102, 105, 108
Boston, 44–45
Bourdieu, Pierre, 26
Boyer, Ernest L., 12, 16–17
Braine, George, 33–34
brainstorming, 40, 133, 164–165
Brautigan, Richard: "The Memoirs of Jesse James," 177
business, 27, 46, 114
Byrd, Don, 45

Calkins, Lucy M., 127
campus visit, 118–119, 121
Canada, 58, 60, 70, 72–74, 87, 90–91
Canagarajah, A. Suresh, 22, 33–34
career, 4, 19, 21, 42, 45, 60–61, 66, 69, 96, 102, 108, 112–113, 119–120, 132–133, 166, 171
Carnegie Foundation for the Advancement of Teaching (CFAT), 7, 10–11, 16
Casanave, Christine Pearson, 33, 127, 145
case study, 33, 78, 154
change, 94, 135, 148–149, 155, 160, 182; institutional, 117, 129, 138, 179; status quo, 49, 174

Chiang, Kai-shek, 46
China, 71–74, 83, 85–91; Ministry of Education, 86
Chinese (language), 76, 83–85, 87–89
Chinese students, 72–74, 76–78, 82–83
Cimasko, Tony, 5, 172–176, 179, 187–188
classroom, 17–18, 34, 36; instruction, 36, 40–43, 72–73, 96, 127–129, 142
cognitive: dissonance, 41, 108; process, 36–37
cohort, 37, 139, 163–164, 175
collaboration, 22, 30, 68, 98, 102, 104–106, 112–116, 123, 130, 134, 148, 154–156, 168
colleagues, 18–19, 64, 68, 85–91, 100, 116, 134, 137–138, 140–141
committee: advisory, 172–173, 183–185; dissertation, 20–21, 27–29, 64–66, 149–153, 165, 167, 185, 187–188; examination, 176; hiring, 62, 68
Committee on Second Language Writing, 114
communication, 34, 117, 122–123, 151–152, 160–162, 167–168, 182–183
community of practice (CoP), 2, 71, 113, 124, 137–138
Como, Frank, 12
compatibility, 17, 28
competence, 73, 77, 137
competition, 59, 62, 67, 69, 85, 93, 105
Composition and TESOL, 20, 35 (*see also* Indiana University of Pennsylvania)
composition studies, 8, 12, 18–19, 27, 33, 35–36, 49–50, 94–103,

Index   199

111–115, 126–127, 129–131, 140–141, 170–174
computer-mediated communication (CMC), 148, 151–152, 154–155
Conference on College Composition and Communication (CCCC), 15, 17, 94, 114–116, 138, 141
connection, 17–18, 36, 151, 168–169, 177; intertextual, 154–155; personal, 46, 50; professional, 114, 134
Connor, Ulla, 33–34, 97
Connors, Robert B., 98
context, 14, 18, 21, 23, 42, 66, 79, 100; academic, 7, 26, 28, 34–35, 48, 54, 62, 163, 165, 171–175, 183; computer-mediated, 155; cultural, 11, 169; disciplinary, 1, 95–96, 99, 159, 163; EFL, 14, 20; historical, 160; institutional, 68, 95, 99, 122, 145; international, 14, 20; national, 8–10, 58, 88, 101, 132; social, 34, 43, 79, 86, 91, 149, 159, 161
contextualization, 104, 182
contrastive/intercultural rhetoric, 36, 97, 100
Cooper, Marilyn M., 162
coursework, 12, 19–21, 23–24, 27, 39, 58, 113, 130, 139, 147–149, 159, 173–174, 182–184
Cox, Michelle, 98, 105, 142
critical pedagogy, 47
critical period hypothesis, 93
Crusan, Deborah, 136
culture, 15, 68–70, 72, 90, 161–162, 168
Cumming, Alister, 3, 14, 22, 28, 74–85, 100
cycle of activity, 4–5, 146–150, 153, 155–156

data, 9, 14, 65, 96; analysis, 66, 75–78, 82–84, 115, 167–168; coding, 75–77; collection, 29, 37, 48, 66, 74–75, 81–82, 115, 117, 167
Davis, Miles, 57
demands, 95, 134–135
dialogue, 24, 34, 162–163, 165
director, 27–28, 86, 106, 117, 121–122
discourse community, 2–5, 33–34, 43, 66–67, 158–169
dissertation, 7–15; advising, 8, 21, 25–28, 37, 41, 127; committee, 20–21, 27–29, 36–37, 48, 64–66, 98–99, 114, 149–153, 155–156, 165, 167, 170, 185, 187–188; defense, 29, 153, 167, 173, 185; genre, 166; process, 28, 151, 165; proposal, 37, 41, 57, 65, 151–153, 166–167, 170–171, 173, 179, 183–188; topic, 14–15, 22–23, 27–28, 85, 185; writing, 14, 17–20, 22, 26, 158, 160–162, 165–168
Dissertation Abstracts International (DAI), 9
diversity, 11, 21, 70, 99–100, 168–169
Diversity Visa Program, 160
division of labor, 146–147, 150–151, 156
doctoral candidate, 34, 61, 65–67, 153–154
doctoral (PhD) program, 7–8, 12–13, 15–21, 28, 30, 57–69, 96–100, 128–129, 132–134, 147–148, 172–178
drafting, 24–27, 48–49, 64, 73, 75, 78–79, 81, 84, 87–88, 105–106, 116, 154–155, 166–167, 183–184
dynamics, 16; classroom, 17–18, 34; departmental, 26–28, 37,

49–50, 121–123, 135–136, 174–175, 177, 183–184, 189; power, 3, 26–29, 37, 146, 177–178

ecology of writing, 22, 161
Edelsky, Carole, 127
editing, 24, 51, 78–79, 101, 145, 167
editors, 28, 89, 95, 105–106, 133, 139
email, 44–45, 51–53, 69, 75–85, 111, 119–120, 123, 151–153, 183, 188
emotion, 45, 121, 158, 164, 178, 188
empowerment, 135, 161–163
encouragement, 107–108, 116, 118, 123, 129, 131–135, 137–139, 141–142, 164
Engestrom, Yrjö, 146–147, 150
engineering, 114, 172, 186
English as a Foreign Language (EFL), 11, 14, 18, 20, 86–87, 171
English as a Second Language (ESL), 14, 42, 112; adult, 81, 154; teaching, 22–23, 45–47, 63, 72–73, 94, 116, 121–122, 127; user of, 18–20, 25, 41, 91, 93–94, 99, 104, 112, 127, 129, 134, 168, 172, 186–187 (*see also* non-native English speakers)
English department, 19, 41, 50, 73, 99, 119–122, 129, 170–175, 184
Enya, 42
Erickson, Melinda, 96, 128
ESL Magazine, 35
essay, 35, 73, 76, 79, 132, 176
ethics, 28, 81
ethnography, 43–48, 132, 135
Europe, 18, 37, 58
exchange, 2–5, 20, 34, 50–51, 76–77

expertise, 2, 5, 15, 22, 28, 34, 37–38, 64–70, 98, 100, 134–135, 153–155, 161–166, 171

faculty, 1, 4–5, 8, 11–20, 25–26, 29, 41, 55–56, 62, 67, 69, 86, 88, 97–99, 120, 122–123, 130–131, 135–136, 141–142, 148–149, 163–166, 172–180, 183, 187, 189
family, 59, 61, 85, 90, 118, 127, 129, 141, 164–165, 168
feedback, 27, 46, 50, 73–74, 77, 80, 89, 104–108, 116, 132–133, 150–151, 165–167, 187
Ferris, Dana, 39, 112, 126, 136
field building, 50, 94–96
first language (L1), 13, 22–23, 36–38, 173, 175
first-generation college student, 104, 127
first-generation L2 writing scholar, 40–43, 51
first-year composition, 18–19, 99–100, 106, 111–114, 117, 122
foreign language education, 86–87, 159–160
framework, 5, 14, 19–20, 79, 158, 184–185
French, 70
full-time position, 23–24, 45, 72, 96, 119, 129, 168
funding, 59, 62, 86, 164

Gannett, Cinthia L., 98
Generation (Gen) 1.5, 49, 127
genre, 2, 25, 66–67, 121, 159, 166, 175, 180–181, 186
Genre Analysis (Swales), 159
goals, 30, 34–35, 43, 59, 62, 95–96, 103, 107, 112, 123, 136, 147–149, 154, 159–160, 165–166, 173
Goldstein, Lynn M., 17

Index

Guide to Writing in English as a Second or Foreign Language: An Annotated Bibliography of Research and Pedagogy (Tannacito), 50
Grabe, William, 38, 44, 155
Grabe, William, and Robert Kaplan: *Theory and Practice of Writing*, 155
graduate program, 7, 10–11, 16–19, 25, 69–71, 103–104, 142, 172–175
Graduate Record Examination (GRE), 111, 174, 178
graduate school, 58, 126–127, 131, 134–135, 145
graduate student, 1–5, 38, 65–66, 71–75, 77, 90, 103, 124, 126, 138, 160–161; ESL, 186; supervision of, 84–85, 100–101, 103–107, 166, 179
grammar, 15, 50, 74, 76, 167
grant writing, 85–88, 90–91, 115
Graves, Donald H., 97
Great Vowel Shift, 177
growth, 16; in L2 writing research 1, 8–11, 29, 50, 100; professional, 75, 134–135, 158, 163–164, 189; program, 11, 29, 98, 108–109, 171, 175
Guo, Yan, 73

haigui (海归), 85
Hall, Chris, 23, 36, 48, 53
Hartwell, Patrick, 12
Hedgcock, John S., 39
higher education, 26, 95, 99, 118, 127, 130, 140
hiring committee, 62, 68
history, 37, 43, 51; of graduate programs, 8, 12–13, 60, 174–175; of L2 writing, 3, 19, 23–24, 38–39, 42–47, 49–51, 53, 81, 94–96
Hudelson, Sarah, 127, 129, 136

Hunter College, 45
hybridity, 186
Hyland, Ken, 52, 97

identity, 2–4, 22, 30, 50, 52, 71, 91, 95, 103, 111–113, 131–135, 153–154; crisis, 51–52
ideology, 14–15
immigrant, 49, 129–130, 132, 140
independence, 52, 81, 115, 135, 166
independent study, 23, 63, 97, 100, 130–131, 175
Indiana University of Pennsylvania (IUP), 7, 10–15, 17–23, 26, 28–29, 35, 37–38, 41
initiation, 3–4, 33–34, 47, 50–51, 159–161
innovation, 154, 186; curricular, 63, 100; program, 2, 20–21, 28–29
institution, 9–10, 18, 97; constraints upon, 12, 131; culture of, 68–69, 94, 96, 99, 122–123, 135–137; procedures of, 28, 37, 131–132; reputation of, 13, 30, 60–62; survey of, 115
institutionalized roles, 151–153
instructional technology, 147–148, 154–156
integration, 19, 29; of research, 20, 41, 100, 154; of technology, 148
intensive English program, 18–19, 165
interdisciplinarity, 12–13, 19–20, 103, 154
International Association of Applied Linguistics (AILA), 77, 80
international students, 12–13, 20, 25, 130, 168, 171–172, 186
internationalism, 15–16, 20
Internet, 59, 69
interpersonal communication, 34, 168

intertextuality, 154–155
interview, 23–25, 43–45, 48, 75–78, 81–82, 115; job, 121; journalistic, 113–114
investment, 22, 61–63, 111, 118, 123, 137–139, 167
isolation, 26, 28–29

James, Mark A., 100, 114
Japan, 93
Japanese students, 77
job market, 45–46, 67–68, 97, 102, 118–121, 124, 135–137
Journal of Second Language Writing (JSLW), 8, 13–14, 50, 94–96, 115, 173
journalism, 94, 112

Kaplan, Robert B., 46–47, 51, 53, 155
karaoke, 93
knowledge, 2, 5, 37, 49–50, 54, 66, 94–95, 102, 132; development, 16–17, 61–64, 74–77, 147–149, 155, 158–160, 164, 171, 181–182, 188; dissemination, 51, 67; metadisciplinary, 105; transfer, 100, 113–114, 133
Korea, South, 47, 171, 174
Kramer-Simpson, Elisabeth, 98
Kroll, Barbara, 39, 45, 129
Kutztown State College, 170

labor-management agreement, 12
LaGuardia Community College, 45–46
Language Teaching Research, 89–90
Lapkin, Sharon, 78
Lauer, Janice, 101
Lave, Jean, 113, 133
learners, 38, 76, 79, 163
Lee, Alison, 7
Leki, Ilona, 8, 14, 34, 41, 50, 52, 94, 112, 121, 129

limitations, 5, 16, 51, 98–99, 159–162, 166, 185
linguistic pride, 45, 47
linguistics, 97–100, 111–113, 130, 140, 160, 172–174, 177
listserv, 68, 74, 118
literacy, 22, 37, 78–79, 99, 140; academic, 33, 91, 145; immigrant, 129–130; second language, 12–13, 134
literature, 12–13, 45, 72
literature review, 87–88, 95, 184
longitudinal studies, 167–168

mainstream composition, 95, 117, 173
Manen, Max van, 24
manuscript, 24–25, 48–49, 67, 89, 107–108
master's degree, 18, 62–64, 72, 94, 112
MATESOL, 98, 100, 112, 170
Matsuda, Aya, 130
Matsuda, Paul Kei, 4, 8, 19, 22, 24, 30, 50, 53, 112–121, 124, 127–128, 130–136, 141–142
Maui, 44
mediating tool, 146–151, 154–156
mediation, 17, 25–27, 34, 146, 150–153
membership, 2–5, 33–34, 43–44, 47–48, 50–51, 53–54, 66, 71, 90–91, 103, 108, 137, 149, 159–168
"Memoirs of Jesse James, The" (Brautigan), 177
mentoring, 1–5, 18–19, 21, 25–26, 28, 37–39, 50–52, 68, 98–99, 101–108, 112–113, 122–124, 136–138, 164
metadisciplinary knowledge, 105
metaphor, 23, 42, 61
methodology, 13–14, 28, 35, 64, 66, 70, 72, 98, 139, 147, 148,

Index 203

156; historical, 19, 23, 37, 38, 95; interpretive, 14, 66; qualitative, 14, 77, 78, 143, 148, 154, 167, 168, 173, 179, 186; quantitative, 14, 88, 148, 173, 179
Miami University of Ohio, 97, 130, 171
Middle East, 14
Modern Language Centre (MLC), 79–80
motivation, 18, 21–22, 63, 158, 160–161, 166, 182
multilingual writers, 115, 117–120
Murray, Donald, 97, 127, 143

narrative, 23, 47–48, 104, 126, 131, 158
National Council of Teachers of English (NCTE), 49, 138, 141
National Science Foundation (NSF), 9, 20
navigation, 2, 28, 122, 132–137
New York City, 45, 127
New York Times, 93
Newkirk, Thomas, 97
next generation scholars, 30, 96, 104
non-native English speakers (NNES), 20, 22, 26, 33–36, 94, 104, 117
North America, 7, 9–11, 29, 37, 58, 70, 95
novice, 3–5, 21, 26, 34, 42, 75–77, 87, 90–91, 133, 153, 161–166

Obama, Barack, 93
objectives, 53, 166, 168, 185
objects, 7–8, 145–150, 154–156
obstacles, 33, 103, 131, 154, 167–168
"On the Future of Second Language Writing" (Santos et al.), 96, 128

Ontario Institute for Studies in Education (OISE), 58, 69, 75, 79–80 (*see also* University of Toronto)
options, 15, 28, 129, 175–176, 179–180; flexible residency, 20–21, 61; placement, 117
oral defense, 167, 185
Ortmeier-Hooper, Christina, 4, 97–99, 105, 124
outcomes, 27–28, 34, 137, 146–148, 150, 155–156, 160, 163, 167, 185
outlining, 40–42

participation, 20, 37, 45, 65–66, 69, 71–72, 74, 76–77, 80, 90, 92, 97, 102, 113–114, 118, 120, 124, 130, 131, 134–135, 143, 146, 155, 159, 161–163, 168
partnership, 27, 29, 137–138
part-time doctoral studies, 61
pedagogy, 8, 13, 47, 94, 186
peer, 64, 66–69, 138–139, 161, 163–167
peer feedback, 116,
periphery, 2, 71
perseverance, 44, 63, 68, 111, 123, 126, 131, 137
personal life 102–103, 129, 136, 141–142
PhD process, 25–26, 57, 145–146, 158
PhD student, 18–20, 28–29, 42, 58–59, 63–65, 68–69, 71–73, 98–100, 131–133, 136–141, 145, 149, 153, 158, 164, 171–173, 178, 183, 188–189 (*see also* doctoral candidate)
philosophical disagreement, 39–40, 42–43
placement, 106, 113, 115, 117, 121–122
potluck dinner, 101, 108, 138

power, 26–29, 37, 45–46, 146, 162, 177–178
Power, Karen, 3, 8, 23–25
Practicing Theory in Second Language Writing (Silva & Matsuda), 17
preliminary examination, 171, 173, 176–185, 188
pre-writing, 40, 148, 154
primary and secondary (K-12) education, 23, 35–36, 50, 87, 127, 133–134, 140
problem space, 146–149, 154
process writing, 13, 23–24, 35–36, 154, 160–162, 180
professional community, 5, 65, 126, 160, 161
professional development, 1, 3, 5, 7, 17, 19, 63, 90, 96, 99, 101–102, 104–106, 108, 113, 124, 134, 135, 160–162
professional organizations, 98, 113–115
proficiency, 36, 93, 154
program development, 2, 8, 12–13, 15, 19, 30, 119, 175
progress: individual, 25, 27, 135, 142, 162–164; monitoring, 51, 105–106, research, 122, 152, 166
promotion, 21, 26, 102, 107, 123
prospectus/dissertation proposal, 38, 65–66, 81–83, 171, 173, 179, 183–188
publication, 18, 25–26, 28, 37, 39, 65–69, 74–75, 78, 83, 85, 87–90, 92, 95, 96, 104, 106, 108, 115, 120, 129, 131–133, 136, 141, 163–164, 170; in Chinese, 88–89; in English, 67, 85, 89–90
Purdue University, 11, 28, 94, 101, 128–129, 170–180

qualifications, 11, 12, 21, 44, 62, 67, 80, 88, 97, 120
questionnaire, 17, 66, 115

Raimes, Ann, 45–47
reading, 39–43, 48, 64, 76–77, 87–88, 94, 104, 166, 177–179, 182
reflection, 8, 45–53, 57, 86, 90–91, 126, 140–142, 145, 148–149, 153, 154, 158, 186
Reid, Joy M., 40, 41, 42, 44, 55, 56, 129, 143
rejection, 89–90, 102, 132–133
requirements: course, 73; dissertation, 52–53, 154, 166–168; job, 119, 121; program, 21, 24, 58, 63, 69, 100, 112, 173–176, 178–179, 183; publication, 28, 68; writing, 73
research, 3–4, 8, 16, 24, 40, 43, 50, 60–63, 71–72, 75–80, 95–97, 99–100, 102, 112, 115, 119–120, 145–148, 155–156, 163–164, 181; agenda, 5, 68, 185–187; article, 53, 68, 74–75, 83; dissertation/thesis, 7–11, 18, 20–22, 25–29, 34, 39, 43–44, 64–67, 74–75, 80–84, 127, 148–152, 154–155, 165–168; grant, 85–87; instrument, 65–66, 71, 149; paper, 36, 75, 77; participant, 17, 18, 20, 45, 50, 74, 75, 115, 161, 168; proposal, 65–66, 81–82, 87; question, 22, 26–27, 65–66; topic, 33, 36–38, 52–53, 85, 101, 153; tradition, 8, 16; university, 7, 10–11, 16, 59, 126
resistance, 87–88, 174–175, 186
respect, 24, 38, 53, 68–69, 81, 89, 102, 141
reviewer, 67, 87, 90
revision, 26–29, 36, 78, 87, 89, 105, 108, 115–116, 150–151

Rhetoric, Composition and Linguistics, 99–100, 111, 113 (*see also* Arizona State University)
rhetorical situation, 159, 161
rite of passage, 34
rules, 52, 91, 103, 146, 150, 156, 183–184
Rutgers University, 171

Saenkhum, Tanita, 4, 99–101, 106, 142
Santos, Terry, 96, 128
Sarieva, Iona, 4–5, 145–156
second language acquisition (SLA), 12–13, 147–148, 160, 163
Second Language Acquisition and Instructional Technology (SLA/IT), 147–148, 153–154, 159, 162–164
second language education, 46, 69–70, 75, 81
second language studies, 1, 12, 19, 95–96
Second Language Studies/ESL, 170, 172–176 (*see also* Purdue)
second language (L2) writers, 11, 13–14, 19, 22, 36, 38, 49, 94, 96–97, 99, 111, 130, 152, 175 (*see also* multilingual writers)
Second Language Writing Interest Section, 114, 134, 138
second language (L2) writing specialist, 4, 33, 94–96, 100, 103–106, 111–113, 113–121, 140
service, 16–17, 68, 122
Shaughnessy, Mina, 11
Shi, Ling, 74–75
shopping, 59–61, 187
shutting, 3, 91
Silva, Tony, 5, 8, 14, 23, 28, 39, 41, 50, 52–53, 94–96, 101, 112, 114, 128–129, 171, 173–176, 180–183, 187–188

Silva, Tony, and Paul Kei Matsuda: *Practicing Theory in Second Language Writing*, 17
Simpson, Steve, 98
situated learning, 101–103, 131
social turn, 37, 161–162
socialization, 3, 25–26, 33–34, 72–85, 90, 106, 108
socioacademic relationship, 34,
Southern Illinois University Carbondale (SIUC), 11, 112–113
Spack, Ruth, 40–42, 44
Spanish, 23, 35, 99, 170
statement of purpose, 62, 116
Sternglass, Marilyn S., 12
Stoller, Frederika, 44
stories, 23–24, 45–47, 54, 74, 90, 102–104, 107, 136–137
Strevens, Peter, 42
style, 48, 50, 67, 71, 87, 102; APA, 49, 67; interactional, 28, 102, learning, 35, 75; teaching, 35, 72; writing, 40, 48, 87–88
Sullivan, Patricia A., 98
support network, 27–29, 64–65, 68–69, 87–91, 101, 123, 134
Survey of Earned Doctorates, 9, 13
surveys, 17–20, 22, 46, 115, 117, 130
Swain, Merrill, 78
Swales, John M., 26; *Genre Analysis*, 159
Symposium on Second Language Writing, 1, 22, 95, 106, 114, 115, 138
synthesis, 52–53, 65, 67, 151

Taiwan, 46–48; Ministry of Education, 46
Tannacito, Dan J., 2–3, 37–39, 41–43, 48–50, 53

Tannacito, Dan: *A Guide to Writing in English as a Second or Foreign Language: An Annotated Bibliography of Research and Pedagogy*, 50
Tardy, Christine M., 126
teaching, 16–22, 35, 98, 112, 127–129, 142; assistant, 18–19, 59, 98–99, 160, 174; load, 12, 16, 120–122; method, 79, 160; philosophy, 119–120; practicum, 95, 100
tenure, 67–68, 99
tenure track, 97–98, 112, 119–123, 126, 131–132, 135–141
TESOL, 35–36, 42, 46, 130, 134; conference, 42, 44, 77–78, 94, 96, 114, 116, 127–128, 130, 134, 138, 141; program, 20, 35, 72–75, 119
TESOL Journal, 129
TESOL Quarterly, 36, 40, 89, 95, 109
testing, 117, 177–178
Thailand, 112, 118
theory, 13, 16–20, 23, 38–39, 66, 79, 81–82, 101, 131, 133, 137–139, 145–149, 153, 158, 163
Theory and Practice of Writing (Grabe & Kaplan), 155
time frame, 39–40, 81, 152–153, 183–185, 187
topic, 14–15, 33, 42, 60, 64–65, 99–100, 148; development, 23–25, 37–38, 52–53, 85–86, 106, 148–150, 153, 180–182, 185–186; selection, 18–19, 22, 27, 35–37, 65–66, 73–74, 87, 101, 104–105
transcription, 75–77, 83–84
transformation, 4–5, 145–150, 155–156, 158
translation, 73, 83–84, 87–88

trust, 27–29, 37, 102, 105–106, 137, 168, 183

undergraduate students, 14, 98, 113
unified theory of L2 writing, 38
United States, 97, 112, 118, 160
University of British Columbia (UBC), 72–74
University of Illinois at Urbana-Champaign, 11, 170
University of Massachusetts, 44–45, 135, 171
University of New Hampshire (UNH), 97–100, 129–131, 134–135, 138
University of South Florida, 159
University of Tennessee Knoxville (UTK), 112, 119–122
University of Toronto, 11, 28, 58, 60

validity, 66, 178
Vandrick, Stephanie, 126
Vietnam War, 47
vocabulary, 74, 159
voice, 34, 52, 133, 153–154, 161–163

Wenger, Étienne C., 133, 137
workplace, 63, 131–132
workshops, 101, 103–105, 129–130
world Englishes, 130
Wright State University, 23, 35
writing center, 18–19, 32, 130, 134
writing companion, 123
writing in the disciplines (WID), 113–114
writing practice, 18–19
writing process, 15, 38, 40, 97, 116, 148, 154, 160, 180

writing program administration (WPA), 106, 113, 115, 117–119, 122

Yang, C.M., 46

Yang, Luxin, 3, 77–79, 82–84, 89

Zamel, Vivian, 44

Zhu, Wei, 4–5, 17, 25–26, 151, 158, 165

www.ingramcontent.com/pod-product-compliance
Lightning Source LLC
Chambersburg PA
CBHW032214230426
43672CB00011B/2551